Book of Ruins

Book of Ruins

JOHN DIXON HUNT
and
DAVID LEATHERBARROW

First published in 2022 by Lund Humphries

Lund Humphries
Huckletree Shoreditch
Alphabeta Building
18 Finsbury Square
London, EC2A 1AH
UK

www.lundhumphries.com

Book of Ruins © John Dixon Hunt and David Leatherbarrow, 2022
All rights reserved

ISBN: 978-1-84822-555-8

A Cataloguing-in-Publication record for this
book is available from the British Library

All rights reserved. No part of this publication may be reproduced, stored in a retrieval system or transmitted in any form or by any means, electrical, mechanical or otherwise, without first seeking the permission of the copyright owners and publishers. Every effort has been made to seek permission to reproduce the images in this book. Any omissions are entirely unintentional, and details should be addressed to the publishers.

John Dixon Hunt and David Leatherbarrow have asserted their right under the Copyright, Designs and Patent Act, 1988, to be identified as the Authors of this Work.

Copy edited by Chris Schüler
Designed by Oliver Keen
Cover design by Mark Thomson
Printed in Estonia

Contents

	Introduction	9

Part I: Ancient & Medieval

1	Scipio, 146 BC	21
2	Pausanias, second century AD	24
3	Pliny the Younger, 79 AD	26
4	Old English Poems 'The Ruin' and 'The Wanderer', eighth or ninth century	33
5	Old English Advent Lyric, tenth century	37
6	Ruins in Medieval Words and Images	39
7	Theoderich on Jerusalem, 1173	42
8	Petrarch on Rome, 1341	47
9	*Hypnerotomachia Poliphili*, 1499	54

Part II: The Renaissance

10	Flavio Biondo, 1446	58
11	Raphael Sanzio, 1519	64
12	'Rometta', Villa D'Este, c.1568	69
13	Sebastian Serlio, c.1540	71
14	Ludovico Ariosto, 1516	74
15	Joachim du Bellay, 1558	77
16	Edmund Spenser, 1591 and 1596	82
17	Giacomo Lauro, 1612	87
18	John Webster, 1613-14	88
19	Inigo Jones, 1655	90
20	Gianlorenzo Bernini, 1665	92

PART III: THE LONG 18TH CENTURY

21	Thomas Burnet, 1681	96
22	John Vanbrugh, 1709	101
23	Antiquarianism and Samuel Buck, 1718	103
24	Travelers in Great Britain; Daniel Defoe and Others, 1734	106
25	Alexander Pope, c.1724	108
26	William Kent, 1730s–1740s	111
27	John Dyer, 1740	113
28	Giovanni Battista Piranesi, 1743	118
29	Fountains Abbey and Studley Royal, 1744	122
30	William Shenstone, 1764	124
31	Denis Diderot, 1767	126
32	John Cunningham, 1766	129
33	Thomas Whately, 1770	133
34	William Gilpin, 1772	136
35	Georges Louis Le Rouge, 1775–89	141
36	J. W. von Goethe, 1786	143
37	C. C. L. Hirschfeld, 1779–89	148
38	Bernardin de Saint-Pierre, 1784–97	153
39	Constantin-François de Chasseboeuf, Comte de Volney, 1789	156
40	Uvedale Price and Richard Payne Knight, 1794	162
41	Humphry Repton, 1795–6	167
42	Periodical Verses on Ruins, 1776–1832	169
43	Alexandre de Laborde, 1808	176
44	John Soane, 1815	179

Part IV: The 19th Century

45	William Wordsworth, 1835	187
46	François-René de Chateaubriand, 1802	191
47	Lord Byron, 1818	196
48	Percy Bysshe Shelley, 1818	199
49	Victor Hugo and Charles Marville, 1832	200
50	Arthur Hugh Clough, 1858	205
51	John Ruskin, 1843–60	206
52	Eugène-Emmanuel Viollet le Duc, 1868	209
53	William Morris, 1877, 1893, and 1895	212
54	Thomas Hardy, 1870 and 1922	215

Part V: Modern and Contemporary

55	Alois Riegl, 1903	221
56	Le Corbusier, 1911	227
57	Georg Simmel, 1911	231
58	John Piper, 1947	237
59	Dimitris Pikionis, 1957	241
60	Robert Smithson, 1967	245
61	Louis I. Kahn, 1969	246
62	Carlo Scarpa, 1978	249
63	Aldo Rossi, 1981	252
64	Issues of Conservation/Preservation, 1998 and 2002	255
65	Cinematic Ruins, 1979, 1987 and 2010	259
66	Drosscape and After: 1, Duisburg-Nord, 1991	263
67	9/11, 2001	266
68	David Chipperfield, 2009	268
69	Drosscape and After: 2, The High Line, 2009	271

Notes	275
Further Reading	277
Acknowledgments	279
Image credits	281
Index	283

INTRODUCTION

> To delight in the aspects of sentient ruin might appear a heartless pastime, and the pleasure, I confess, shows a note of perversity.
> Henry James, *Italian Hours*

Book of Ruins is neither perverse nor sentimental, as James implies, although some of the materials here reveal that their original writers may have thought it so. Instead, we offer a survey – not encyclopedic, but substantial – of leading moments when the fact and idea of ruins were taken up by writers, travelers, and artists – painters, film makers, landscape architects, and architects. It provides a perspective upon what the past has meant to different cultures at different times. As we are both historians and at the same time teaching and writing about the modern world, the book gains in scope and depth as we proceed to the point where we can begin to think about how we might deal with ruins today. The book is divided into five sections, sequenced historically, beginning in the ancient world.

When the Roman general Scipio Aemilianus oversaw the final defeat and destruction of Carthage in 146 BC, he lamented whether his Rome might one day suffer the same fate as Troy. His friend Polybius narrates that moment of uncertainty and insight, and provides one of the early ways in which the perception of ruins prompted reflection on past cultures. For ruins gave rise to thought.

An early eye-witness account of the destruction of Pompeii was famously chronicled by Pliny the Younger in AD 79, but the remains there and at nearby Herculaneum ('discovered' in 1738) were explored and documented only from the 18th century. In Pliny's case, the concern for ruins was anticipatory, hardly dispassionate, for the voices he heard 'bewailed their fate' and feared they had been abandoned by their gods. It was that Roman culture that Pausanias, a Greek traveler roaming throughout Greece in the third quarter of the second century, sought to explore in what remained, and how the myths associated with place, continued to shape Roman culture.

By the eighth and ninth century, Anglo-Saxon writers discovered the ruins of Bath and other sites of Roman origin, and their work was collected in the Exeter Book during the tenth century. That book also includes an Old English Advent lyric where a world of 'rubble and wreckage' became a metaphor and analogy for the advent of

Ruins and reconstructed garden at Pompeii.

Christ who will 'redeem the ruin'. In the 12th century, both Gerald of Wales and William of Malmesbury wrote factual descriptions of Roman ruins. During the late medieval period and the Renaissance, classical ruins became a favored setting for images of Christ's birth and adoration by the Magi.

But at the same time, more detailed and confident analyses and descriptions of ancient cultures appeared: Jerusalem featured in a book of Holy Places in 1172, while Petrarch in 1341 wrote of 'remarkable places in the city of Rome'. Ruins had become the goal of pilgrimage, objects of veneration and worship, even if there was no real correlation between the holy events said to have occurred there and the actual sites.

The slippage of ideas and attitudes from medieval to Renaissance culture is wonderfully captured in the 1499 *Hypnerotomachia Poliphili*. Structured as a medieval dream narrative, it salutes some remarkable ruins, with obelisks and inscriptions, as the protagonist and his lover discover them towards the end of the narrative.

Poliphilo was interested in understanding what inscriptions told him of the ruins he had discovered. A similar, if much larger ambition was to establish what ancient ruins would have been like, hence drawing plans and perspectives of ancient Rome based on surviving remains and earlier descriptions. Gradually, there developed

Pseudo-Blesius, *Adoration of the Magi*, c.1510, oil on panel. Museum of Fine Arts, Warsaw.

Hypnerotomachia Poliphili, 1499, engraving. University of Pennsylvania Libraries.

two different approaches: factual, approximately scientific, even if mistaken – like Inigo Jones's account of what Stonehenge had originally been – or nostalgic, affected responses. This latter response was prompted and promoted by people with less interest in factual discovery than keen attention to a ruin's nuances, its affective meanings. Writers clearly contributed to this emphasis, and by the 19th century it was as much about what was *not* in a ruin. Subject matter other than its physical structure spurred interest – echoes not materials, sentiments not shapes and sizes. By the later 20th century this changed once again and the instinct to leave visible remains while making them 'new' or refurbished seems to have consolidated a dual emphasis on both the physical essence, its original being, and its associations and current appeals.

INTRODUCTION

The Renaissance was clearly concerned with enquiries into early ruins and the use that could be made of them, devising different descriptions and interpretations, and sometimes adding to them. The remains of ancient Rome were explored and explained, by archaeologists such as Flavio Biondo, or the painter Raphael, and architects like Serlio, whose Third Book on architecture discusses ruins, first in Italy but later, while he was working in France, Egyptian 'marvels'. Serlio's attempt to name every fragment he encountered indicates that ruins at this time were meant to be seen, documented, and compared to written accounts, which were often as ambiguous as the ruined fragments. Pirro Ligorio was an antiquarian as well as architect, and his contributions to the making of Villa d'Este at Tivoli included a physical recollection of the Eternal City, obviously reduced in size, rather like a model or a child's toy landscape. Later writers thought to reimagine exactly, but also speculatively, how ancient Rome might have looked, sometimes with elaborate graphic reconstructions of its former cityscape.

But the profusion of knowledge and imagination about ruins found its way into a variety of literary works. Ariosto and the young Edmund Spenser both found ruins a powerful topic and metaphor, and in *The Faerie Queene* the latter narrates the destruction of the Bower of Bliss and the House of Cupid. Joachim du Bellay in France devoted a sonnet sequence to *Les Antiquitez de Rome*, while what ruins suggested, what actual echoes they produced, was a theme increasingly taken up by scientists who studied their incidence and acoustical properties. Inigo Jones, as we have already observed, mistakenly thought Stonehenge was Roman and proposed, luckily unsuccessfully, that it be restored as a model for contemporary architecture.

What has been termed the 'long 18th century' saw a considerable increase in the scope and investigation of ruins. Antiquarian research, both professional and amateur, increased, and the Society of Antiquarians was established in 1707 and received its Royal Charter in 1751 to promote and further the study of antiquities in various counties. Its members, such as Robert Plot, surveyed the histories of Oxfordshire (1677) and Staffordshire (1686), and the exploration of English and Scottish places became an absorbing area of study, where ruins of all sorts were prominent, as they seemed to mark key moments of local history. As continental wars prevented excursions on the Grand Tour, more and more people, often those who might not have attempted the Grand Tour anyway, traveled through the counties of Great Britain. Abbeys, deserted after the Dissolution of the monasteries between 1536 and 1541, and castles, equally rendered redundant with the use of gunpowder, were among the topics canvassed in guide books. The rise and sophistication of aesthetic discussions of the picturesque found rough texture and associative prominence in how ruins could feature in the larger vocabulary of 'variety' in landscapes. Where genuine ruins were unavailable, new 'fakes' were devised and built, prominent among them being the works of Sanderson Miller.

A growing tension between documentation and speculation can be seen in the work of continental ruinists, most famously perhaps Giovanni Battista Piranesi, but also painters like Hubert Robert. For the Italian, ruins required both exact description and imaginative reconstruction; his audience included contemporary architects, of course, but also travelers on the Grand Tour, who desired some memento of what they'd seen – a memory of a memory, desirable even if doubly incomplete. Hubert Robert looked back to even more remote antiquity, from Rome to Egypt, but also into the future, depicting, through a series of paintings, the fate of the great monuments of modern Paris at the hands of revolutionaries, as in the case of his painting of the destruction of the Bastille, but also thanks to the forces of nature. A specific sense of time comes into focus here, not *time as the mother of truth*, as Leonardo once said, but *time with teeth*.

Many of these enthusiasms and preoccupations persisted into the 19th century. Wordsworth *Guide to the Lakes*, among many other local travel guides, Byron's (or Childe Harold's) response to the ruins of Italy, and the continuing work and publications of William Gilpin or Humphry Repton maintained much of the previous century's fascination with ruin. And as with Victor Hugo in France, British writers such as John Ruskin and William Morris found excitement in what ancient structures could teach their contemporaries. Thomas Hardy, trained as an architect, would in his poetry, especially, respond to the nostalgias, the elegiac losses, of ancient castles and abbeys.

So a slightly new emphasis emerged – less the description of ruins themselves than the nuances and emptiness that ruins readily announced. Echoes had been a topic that scientists of the Royal Society had explored to understand their acoustical properties; Plot listed many examples in his county histories, but Tennyson added to *The Princess* (1847) a lyric on the dying echoes of a bugle mingling with the sunset on castle walls, inspired by echoes at Killarney in 1848 (it has been magically set to music by Benjamin Britten in *Serenade for Tenor, Horn and Strings*). So physical ruins produced wonderful echoes, as writers sought to fill their vacancies with their own narratives.

Modern and contemporary attention to ruins has been of considerable moment in large part because they offered opportunities for architects and landscape architects to remake their fragments, not to eliminate them but to enrich with new ideas memories of original, if ruined, structures. War, earthquakes, and, more recently, the appalling frequency of terrorist attacks on buildings have drawn renewed potency from ruins – John Piper sought out bombed sites and ancient castles for some of his more powerful paintings. And land artists discovered that there was poetry in the debris, the casual leftovers of human activity, and then – beyond that – the determination to reuse and reanimate derelict factories and railway lines rather than to destroy them. Some of the

INTRODUCTION

most powerful films of the post-war decades, such as those of Andrei Tarkovsky and Wim Wenders, explore the same theme and amplify the same sentiments.

Ruins are everywhere if you want to notice them. Google will even provide you with instances of 'ruins near you'. It lists the 'Ice House Ruins' at Long Pond in the Pocono Mountains of Pennsylvania ('good for kids'), but misses other examples that an old-fashioned lover of ruins may like. Also, in the Poconos, an enormous hotel founded in 1901 as part of a Quaker retreat fell vacant and derelict by the early 21st century (lost to the profusion of cheaper lodgings and B&Bs). So, it was demolished over three years, leaving on the crest of the wonderfully empty hill a fireplace from the original hallway.

For those who came there over the previous century it will remind them that it was the place where Quaker meetings took place on Sundays. But that memory will fade and leave the fireplace, should it survive, for others to understand. Less comforting, perhaps, but no less part of the story is the encounter with destroyed and deserted fabric of cities like Detroit, narrated in the elegiac mode in the film *Requiem for Detroit*,

Sanderson Miller, Folly in the grounds of Wimpole Hall, Staffordshire, late 18th century.

A sculpture of rocks at an old slate mine, Honister Pass, Cumberland.
Photograph: John Dixon Hunt.

though residents there today continually speak of the new city to come, potentially better than the ruined one in which they live.

We have structured this collection by selecting texts that are extracted from larger works, along with images; these are sometimes directedly related to the text, or sometimes plausible adjuncts. Some texts are brief, others lengthy when the topic invites a more substantial narrative. Each item is prefaced with short introductory remarks,

INTRODUCTION

or headpieces, that point a reader to the interest in each selected item. Some smaller quotations or remarks on ruins culture are invoked within the headpiece. A reading list at the end is an indication both of further readings and of those books on which we have relied in our research.

I

Ancient & Medieval

Jacobus Buys, *Scipio and Polybius after the Defeat of Carthage*, 1797, engraving.

1

Scipio

146 BC

One of the functions of the ruin in ancient culture was to serve as an instrument or tool for reflection on the fate of individual men, their cultures, and entire empires. A ruin was something to think with – and the thoughts were rather dark. The burning fabric or broken body of a defeated city was an unambiguous sign of human finality. The victorious Roman general Scipio Aemilianus was prompted to follow this line of thought at the very moment when great celebrations were in order. With wet cheeks – the famous Tears of Scipio – he wondered if Rome's hope of *aeternitas* was any more likely than that of Troy's. Wouldn't the pattern repeat itself? Rome rising out of the ruins of Carthage, so that it could serve some future empires in the same way?

In the spring of 146 the Roman Senate had ordered that Carthage be destroyed. That meant its walls would be razed to the ground and the ruins that remained plowed over. Before that, in the final agony of the battle and unending days of street-fighting, Scipio, surveying the scene from a nearby hill, succumbed to doubt about the long-term consequences of success. With embers hardly cooled, but the division between victor and vanquished finally settled, he couldn't suppress a profound doubt about human greatness. With Troy, Media, Persia, Assyria, Macedon, and now Carthage too in mind, he asked in terms that had ample precedent in Greek culture: wouldn't his city and empire come to a comparable end? Who could say for sure? Fortuna is blindfolded when she pilots her ship.

Scipio's tears were not caused by the suffering and misery of the Carthaginians, but by his realization of the transitory character of all human achievement, his own, his army's, and his city's. All of it would decline and fall, inevitably, *by nature*. His friend and confidant Polybius expressed this last explanation elsewhere in his *Histories*: 'Every organism, every form of government, and every action undergoes a natural cycle of growth, reaches its acme, and finally decays.'

POLYBIUS

Histories, book 38 from Plutarch, *Apophthegmata*, translated by Bernadette Perrin, Loeb Edition (Cambridge, MA., 1922)

Scipio had reached the wall, the Carthaginians still defending themselves from the citadel, and as he found that the depth of the sea between them was not very great, Polybius advised him to set it with iron caltrops or to throw into it planks furnished with spikes to prevent the enemy from crossing and attacking the mole. 'But it is absurd,' said Scipio, 'now we have taken the wall and are inside the town to take steps to prevent our fighting the enemy.'

When Hasdrubal, the Carthaginian commander, threw himself as a suppliant at Scipio's knees, the general turning to those around him said, 'Look, my friends, how well Fortune knows to make an example of inconsiderate men. This is that very Hasdrubal who lately rejected the many kind offers I made him and said that his native city and her flames were the most splendid obsequies for him; and here he is with suppliant boughs begging for his life from me and reposing all his hopes on me. Who that witnesses this with his eyes can fail to understand that a mere man should never either act or speak presumptuously?' Some of the deserters now came forward to the edge of the roof and begged the front ranks of the assailants to hold back for a moment, and when Scipio gave this order they began to abuse Hasdrubal, some of them for having violated his oath, saying that he had often sworn solemnly that he would not desert them, and others for his cowardice and general baseness of spirit. And this they did with jeers and in the most insulting, coarse, and hostile language.

At this moment his wife, seeing Hasdrubal seated with Scipio in front of the enemy, came out from the crowd of deserters, herself dressed like a great lady, but holding her children, who wore nothing but their smocks, by each hand and wrapping them in her cloak. At first, she called on Hasdrubal by his name, but when he maintained silence and bent his eyes to the ground, she began by calling on the gods and expressing her deepest thanks to Scipio for sparing as far as he was concerned not only herself but her children. Then, after a short silence, she asked Hasdrubal how without saying a word to her he had deserted them all and betaken himself to the Roman general to secure his own safety; how he had thus shamelessly abandoned the state and the citizens who trusted in him, and gone over secretly to the enemy; and how he had the face to sit now beside the enemy with suppliant boughs in his hands, that enemy to whom he had often boasted that the day would never dawn on which the sun would look on Hasdrubal alive and his city in flames.

Turning around to me at once and grasping my hand Scipio said, 'A glorious moment, Polybius; but I have a dread foreboding that someday the same doom will be pronounced on my own country.' It would be difficult to mention an utterance more statesmanlike and more profound. For at the moment of our greatest triumph and of disaster to our enemies to reflect on our own situation and on the possible reversal of circumstances, and generally to bear in mind at the season of success the mutability of Fortune, is like a great and perfect man, a man in short worthy to be remembered.

APPIAN
Punica from Plutarch, *Apophthegmata*, translated by Bernadette Perrin, Loeb Edition (Cambridge, MA., 1922)

Scipio, when he looked upon the city as it was utterly perishing and in the last throes of its complete destruction, is said to have shed tears and wept openly for his enemies. After being wrapped in thought for long, and realizing that all cities, nations, and authorities must, like men, meet their doom; that this happened to Ilium, once a prosperous city, to the empires of Assyria, Media, and Persia, the greatest of their time, and to Macedonia itself, the brilliance of which was so recent, either deliberately or the verses escaping him, he said:

> A day will come when sacred Troy shall perish,
> And Priam and his people shall be slain.
> *Iliad VI. 448–9*

And when Polybius speaking with freedom to him, for he was his teacher, asked him what he meant by the words, they say that without any attempt at concealment he named his own country, for which he feared when he reflected on the fate of all things human. Polybius actually heard him and recalls it in his history.

2

PAUSANIAS

SECOND CENTURY AD

Pausanias, who flourished around AD 143–176, was a Greek traveler and geographer, whose *Periegesis Hellados* (*Description of Greece*) is an invaluable guide to ancient ruins. While he witnessed ruins as he travelled through mainland Greece, his main concern was meticulously to survey the remains so as to aid his readers in understanding the impact on Rome of Greek culture, and to tell the stories or myths associated with what he found; so it is clear, as he narrates his excursions, what was in good shape at that time, or by then somewhat ruined. Yet his account is nonetheless an early view of how ancient Athens would be understood. That task was at the center of Jane E. Harrison's substantial 1890 book, *Mythology and Monuments of Ancient Athens*, in which she listed and commented upon Pausanias's itineraries in the city and reproduced 19th-century photographs and earlier engravings of the items discussed. She included bits of Pausanias translated by Margaret de G. Verrall; we have been occasionally been directed by her writings (our own salute to ruined fragments).

Description of Greece, translated by W. H. S. Jones,
Loeb Edition (London: Heinemann, 1926)

[The Kerameikos] Within the precinct there are statues of Athena Paionia, Zeus, Mnemosyne [goddess of memory] and the Muses, an Apollo, the work and offering of Eubulides and Akratos, one of the divinities who accompany Dionysos this last is only a face built into the wall…

[The Odeion] In the entrance of the Odeion at Athens, among other things, is a Dionysos worth seeing. Near to it is a spring which they call Enneakrounos (nine columns). Peisistratos gave it this convenient arrangement, because, although there are wells through all the city, this is the only spring…

[The sanctuary of Aphrodite] The image [of Aegeus] still existing in my time is of Parian marble, and the work of Pheidias…

[The Stoa Poikile] In the Colloade are some bronze shields. Some of these are inscribed as having been taken from the inhabitants of Skione, but those are smeared with resin, to escape injury from rust in the course of time…

The Acropolis, Athens, 2010. Photograph: David Leatherbarrow.

[The Erechtheion] The paintings on the walls represent the race of the Butadae. And the building being divided into two compartments, within there is a well containing seawater. This itself is not wonderful, for there are salt wells even far inland... But the remarkable point is also the imprint of a trident in the rock. These things are said to have been produced by Poseidon in support of his claim to the country...

[On the Street of Tombs, outside the city] Close to the city is the Academy, once belonging to a private individual but in my time a gymnasium. On the way to the Academy is the precinct of Artemis, with wooden images of Ariste and Calliste. In my own belief, confirmed by the poems of Sappho, these are the epithets of Artemis...

3

Pliny the Younger

79 AD

Pliny the Younger's two letters on the destruction of Pompeii reveal less about his perception of ruins than their formation. The sequence of events he describes remains as compelling today as it must have been to the historian Tacitus, to whom the letters were sent: convulsive motions of the earth, buildings tottering, houses shaking all the way down to their foundations, ash falling, fires burning under steadily darkening skies, leading to 'shrieks of women, screams of children, and shouts of men... bewailing their fate' and imagining they had been abandoned by their gods.

As for the landscape before Pliny, every object seemed completely changed or changing, as ruination proceeded before his eyes. Roofs, walls, streets, and gardens were being 'covered deep' with ashes, we suppose rather like black snow.

Later writers report that Pompeii was re-inhabited soon after the eruption, but no numismatic evidence from later than the reign of Titus confirms that. Where Bosco Reale and Torre del Greco stand today there seem to have been post-eruption settlements, but much later. Subsequent eruptions – a bad one in the fifth century – covered the landscape more widely, piling ash more deeply. Domenico Fontana cut a canal through the site at the end of the 16th century. Excavations were undertaken in earnest in the coming decades. Francesco Piranesi's study of Magna Graecia, *Les Antiquités de la Grande Grèce*, a plate of which we reproduce here, was published in the early years of the 19th century. But long before that, in the years immediately after 79 AD, Pompeii was already used as a quarry, with *spolia* finding their way into cities throughout the Campania.

To Tacitus, translated by Betty Radice,
Loeb Edition (Cambridge, MA., 1915)

Your request that I would send you an account of my uncle's death, in order to transmit a more exact relation of it to posterity, deserves my acknowledgments; for, if this accident shall be celebrated by your pen, the glory of it, I am well assured, will be rendered forever illustrious. And notwithstanding he perished

Francesco Piranesi, *The Gate of the Ancient City of Pompeii*, in *Les antiquitiés de la Grande Grèce*, 1804–7, engraving. Fisher Fine Arts Library, University of Pennsylvania.

by a misfortune, which, as it involved at the same time a most beautiful country in ruins, and destroyed so many populous cities, seems to promise him an everlasting remembrance; notwithstanding he has himself composed many and lasting works; yet I am persuaded, the mentioning of him in your immortal writings, will greatly contribute to render his name immortal. Happy I esteem those to be to whom by provision of the gods has been granted the ability either to do such actions as are worthy of being related or to relate them in a manner worthy of being read; but peculiarly happy are they who are blessed with both these uncommon talents: in the number of which my uncle, as his own writings and your history will evidently prove, may justly be ranked. It is with extreme willingness, therefore, that I execute your commands; and should indeed have claimed the task if you had not enjoined it. He was at that time with the fleet under his command at Misenum.

On the 24th of August, about one in the afternoon, my mother desired him to observe a cloud which appeared of a very unusual size and shape. He had just taken a turn in the sun and, after bathing himself in cold water, and making a light luncheon, gone back to his books: he immediately arose and went out upon a rising ground from whence he might get a better sight of this very uncommon appearance. A cloud, from which mountain was uncertain, at this distance (but it was found afterwards to come from Mount Vesuvius), was ascending, the appearance of which I cannot give you a more exact description of than by likening it to that of a pine tree, for it shot up to a great height in the form of a very tall trunk, which spread itself out at the top into a sort of branches; occasioned, I imagine, either by a sudden gust of air that impelled it, the force of which decreased as it advanced upwards, or the cloud itself being pressed back again by its own weight, expanded in the manner I have mentioned; it appeared sometimes bright and sometimes dark and spotted, according as it was either more or less impregnated with earth and cinders. This phenomenon seemed to a man of such learning and research as my uncle extraordinary and worth further looking into. He ordered a light vessel to be got ready, and gave me leave, if I liked, to accompany him. I said I had rather go on with my work; and it so happened, he had himself given me something to write out. As he was coming out of the house, he received a note from Rectina, the wife of Bassus, who was in the utmost alarm at the imminent danger which threatened her; for her villa lying at the foot of Mount Vesuvius, there was no way of escape but by sea; she earnestly entreated him therefore to come to her assistance. He accordingly changed his first intention, and what he had begun from a philosophical, he now carries out in a noble and generous spirit.

He ordered the galleys to be put to sea and went himself on board with an intention of assisting not only Rectina, but the several other towns which lay thickly strewn along that beautiful coast. Hastening then to the place from whence others fled with the utmost terror, he steered his course direct to the point of danger, and with so much calmness and presence of mind as to be able to make and dictate his observations upon the motion and all the phenomena of that dreadful scene. He was now so close to the mountain that the cinders, which grew thicker and hotter the nearer he approached, fell into the ships, together with pumice-stones, and black pieces of burning rock: they were in danger too not only of being aground by the sudden retreat of the sea, but also from the vast fragments which rolled down from the mountain, and obstructed all the shore. Here he stopped to consider whether he should turn back again; to which the pilot advising him, 'Fortune,' said he, 'favours the brave; steer to where Pomponianus is.' Pomponianus was then at Stabiae, separated by a bay, which the sea, after several insensible windings, forms with the shore. He had already sent his baggage on board; for though he was not at that time in actual danger, yet being within sight of it, and indeed extremely near, if it should in the least increase, he was determined to put to sea as soon as the wind, which was blowing dead in-shore, should go down. It was favourable, however, for carrying my uncle to Pomponianus, whom he found in the greatest consternation: he embraced him tenderly, encouraging and urging him to keep up his spirits, and, the more effectually to soothe his fears by seeming unconcerned himself, ordered a bath to be got ready, and then, after having bathed, sat down to supper with great cheerfulness, or at least (what is just as heroic) with every appearance of it.

Meanwhile broad flames shone out in several places from Mount Vesuvius, which the darkness of the night contributed to render still brighter and clearer. But my uncle, in order to soothe the apprehensions of his friend, assured him it was only the burning of the villages, which the country people had abandoned to the flames: after this he retired to rest, and it is most certain he was so little disquieted as to fall into a sound sleep: for his breathing, which, on account of his corpulence, was rather heavy and sonorous, was heard by the attendants outside. The court which led to his apartment being now almost filled with stones and ashes, if he had continued there any time longer, it would have been impossible for him to have made his way out. So he was awoke and got up, and went to Pomponianus and the rest of his company, who were feeling too anxious to think of going to bed. They consulted together whether it would be most prudent to trust to the houses, which now rocked from side to side with frequent and violent concussions as though shaken from their very foundations; or fly to the open fields, where the calcined stones and cinders, though light indeed, yet fell in large showers, and threatened destruction. In this choice of dangers they resolved for the fields: a resolution which, while the rest of the company were hurried into by their fears, my uncle embraced upon cool and deliberate consideration. They went out then, having pillows tied upon their heads with napkins; and this was their whole defense against the storm of stones that fell round them.

It was now day everywhere else, but there a deeper darkness prevailed than in the thickest night; which however was in some degree alleviated by torches and other lights of various kinds. They thought proper to go farther down upon the shore to see if they might safely put out to sea, but found the waves still running extremely high, and boisterous. There my uncle, laying himself down upon a sail cloth, which was spread for him, called twice for some cold water, which he drank, when immediately the flames, preceded by a strong whiff of sulphur, dispersed the rest of the party, and obliged him to rise. He raised himself up with the assistance of two of his servants, and instantly fell down dead; suffocated, as I conjecture, by some gross and noxious vapour, having always had a weak throat, which was often inflamed. As soon as it was light again, which was not till the third day after this melancholy accident, his body was found entire, and without any marks of violence upon it, in the dress in which he fell, and looking more like a man asleep than dead. During all this time my mother and I, who were at Misenum – but this has no connection with your history, and you did not desire any particulars besides those of my uncle's death; so I will end here, only adding that I have faithfully related to you what I was either an eye-witness of myself or received immediately after the accident happened, and before there was time to vary the truth. You will pick out of this narrative whatever is most important: for a letter is one thing, a history another; it is one thing writing to a friend, another thing writing to the public.

Farewell

Pliny to Tacitus, II

The letter which, in compliance with your request, I wrote to you concerning the death of my uncle has raised, it seems, your curiosity to know what terrors and dangers attended me while I continued at Misenum; for there, I think, my account broke off:

Though my shocked soul recoils, my tongue shall tell. My uncle having left us, I spent such time as was left on my studies (it was on their account indeed that I had stopped behind), till it was time for my bath. After which I went to supper, and then fell into a short and uneasy sleep. There had been noticed for many days before a trembling of the earth, which did not alarm us much, as this is quite an ordinary occurrence in Campania; but it was so particularly violent that night that it not only shook but actually overturned, as it would seem, everything about us. My mother rushed into my chamber, where she found me rising, in order to awaken her. We sat down in the open court of the house, which occupied a small space between the buildings and the sea. As I was at that time but eighteen years of age, I know not whether I should call my behaviour, in this dangerous juncture, courage or folly; but I took up Livy, and amused myself with turning over that author, and even making extracts from him, as if I had been perfectly at my leisure. Just then, a friend of my uncle's, who had lately come to him from Spain, joined us, and observing me sitting by my mother with a book in my hand, reproved her for her calmness, and me at the same time for my careless security: nevertheless, I went on with my author. Though it was now morning, the light was still exceedingly faint and doubtful; the buildings all around us tottered, and though we stood upon open ground, yet as the place was narrow and confined, there was no remaining without imminent danger: we therefore resolved to quit the town. A panic-stricken crowd followed us, and (as to a mind distracted with terror every suggestion seems more prudent than its own) pressed on us in dense array to drive us forward as we came out. Being at a convenient distance from the houses, we stood still, in the midst of a most dangerous and dreadful scene. The chariots, which we had ordered to be drawn out, were so agitated backwards and forwards, though upon the most level ground, that we could not keep them steady, even by supporting them with large stones. The sea seemed to roll back upon itself, and to be driven from its banks by the convulsive motion of the earth; it is certain at least the shore was considerably enlarged, and several sea animals were left upon it. On the other side, a black and dreadful cloud, broken with rapid, zigzag flashes, revealed behind it variously shaped masses of flame: these last were like sheet-lightning, but much larger. Upon this our Spanish friend, whom I mentioned above, addressing himself to my mother and me with great energy and urgency: 'If your brother,' he said, 'if your uncle be safe, he certainly wishes you may be so too; but if he perished, it was his desire, no doubt, that you might both survive him: why therefore do you delay your escape a moment?' We could never think of our own safety, we said, while we were uncertain of his. Upon this our friend left us, and withdrew from the danger with the utmost precipitation. Soon afterwards, the cloud began to descend, and cover the sea. It had already surrounded and concealed the island of Capri and the promontory of Misenum. My mother now besought, urged, even commanded me to make my escape at any rate, which, as I was young, I might easily do; as for herself, she said, her age and corpulency rendered all attempts of that sort impossible; however, she would willingly meet death if she could have the satisfaction of seeing that she was not the occasion of mine. But I absolutely refused to leave her, and, taking her by the hand, compelled her to go with me. She complied with great reluctance, and not without many reproaches to herself for retarding my flight. The ashes now began to fall upon us, though in no great quantity. I looked back; a dense dark mist seemed to be following us, spreading itself over the country like a cloud. 'Let us turn out of the high-road,' I said, 'while we can still see, for fear that, should we fall in the road, we should be pressed to death in the dark, by the crowds that are following us.' We had scarcely sat down when night came upon us, not such as we have when the sky is cloudy, or when there is no moon, but that of a room when it is shut up, and all the lights put out. You might hear the shrieks of women, the screams of children, and the shouts of men; some calling for their children, others for their parents, others for their husbands, and seeking to recognize each other by the voices that replied; one lamenting his own fate, another that of his family; some wishing to die, from the very fear of dying; some lifting their hands to the gods; but the greater part convinced that there were now no gods at all, and that the final endless night of which we have heard had come upon the world.

Among these there were some who augmented the real terrors by others imaginary or willfully invented. I remember some who declared that one part of Misenum had fallen, that another was on fire; it was false, but they found people to believe them. It now grew rather lighter, which we imagined to be rather the forerunner of an approaching burst of flames (as in truth it was) than the return of day: however, the fire fell at a distance from us: then again we were immersed in thick darkness, and a heavy shower of ashes rained upon us, which we were obliged every now and then to stand up to shake off, otherwise we should have been crushed and buried in the heap. I might boast that, during all this scene of horror, not a sigh, or expression of fear, escaped me, had not my support been grounded in that miserable, though mighty, consolation, that all mankind were involved in the same calamity, and that I was perishing with the world itself. At last this dreadful darkness was dissipated by degrees, like a cloud or smoke; the real day returned, and even the sun shone out, though with a lurid light, like when an eclipse is coming on. Every object that presented itself to our eyes (which were extremely weakened) seemed changed, being covered deep with ashes as if with snow. We returned to Misenum, where we refreshed ourselves as well as we could, and passed an anxious night between hope and fear; though, indeed, with a much larger share of the latter: for the earthquake still continued, while many frenzied persons ran up and down heightening their own and their friends' calamities by terrible predictions. However, my mother and I, notwithstanding the danger we had passed, and that which still threatened us, had no thoughts of leaving the place, till we could receive some news of my uncle.

And now, you will read this narrative without any view of inserting it in your history, of which it is not in the least worthy; and indeed you must put it down to your own request if it should appear not worth even the trouble of a letter.

Farewell.

4

Old English Poems
'The Ruin' and 'The Wanderer'

eighth or ninth century

These lines were recorded in the tenth century in the Exeter Book, a collection of poems from the preceding centuries. There is uncertainty about whether 'The Ruin' refers to a specific city – Bath was suggested by Heinrich Leo in 1865, which references in the poem to hot springs and bathing halls support. Other Roman remains such as Chester and Hadrian's Wall, and even Babylon or the Apocalypse, have also been proposed, but the thrust of this wonderful poem is less about any specific structure than a metaphor for human fragility, which the first line's emphasis on fate supports. The poem hovers between a sentimental perspective and visual images of how a civilization, like Rome's, can be reduced to rubble, yet the emphasis on a 'hundred generations' seems to point to a longer time span than the loss of the material structures of Roman civilization. The last lines, with their several gaps – an indication of the fragmentary status of the text – are a tangible image of a ruinous erosion. 'The Wanderer' is both less particular and more thoughtful, more elegiac, even accepting of ruin.

'The Ruin' in Benjamin Thorpe, *Codex Exoniensis: A Collection of Anglo-Saxon Poetry* (London: William Pickering, 1842)

Wondrous is this stone-wall, wrecked by fate;
the city-buildings crumble, the words of the giants decay,
Roofs have caved in, towers collapsed,
Barred gates are broken, hoar frost clings to mortar,
houses are gaping, tottering and fallen,
undermined by age. The earth's embrace,
its fierce grip, holds the mighty craftsmen;
they are perished and gone. A hundred generations
have passed away since then. This wall, grey with lichen
and red of hue, outlives kingdom after kingdom,

BOOK OF RUINS

withstands tempests; its tall gate succumbed.
The city still moulders, gashed by storms ...
. . . .
A man's mind quickened with a plan;
subtle and strong willed, he bound
the foundations with metal rods – a marvel.
Bright were the city halls, many the bath-houses,
lofty all the gables, great the martial clamour,
many a mead-hall was full of delights
until fate the mighty altered it. Slaughtered men
fell far and wide, the plague-days came,
death removed every brave man.
Their ramparts became abandoned places,
the city decayed; warriors and builders
fell to the earth. Thus these courts crumble,
and this redstone arch sheds tiles.
The place falls to ruin, shattered
into mounds of stone, where once many a man
joyous and gold-bright, dressed in splendour,
proud and flushed with wine, gleamed in his armour;
he gazed on his treasure – silver, precious stones,
jewellery and wealth, all that he owned –
and on this bright city in the broad kingdom,
Stone houses stood here; a hot spring
gushed in a wide stream; a stone wall
enclosed the bright interior; the baths
were there, the heated water; that was convenient.
They allowed the scalding water to pour
Over the grey stone into the circular pool. Hot ...
. . . . where the baths were
. . . . that is a noble thing,
How the . . . . the city.

OLD ENGLISH POEMS 'THE RUIN' AND 'THE WANDERER'

'The Wanderer' translated by Kevin Crossley-Holland,
in *The Anglo-Saxon World: An Anthology* (Oxford University Press, 1982)

A wise man will perceive how mysterious will be the time when the wealth of all this age will lie waste, just as now in diverse places throughout the earth walls are standing beaten by the wind and covered with rime. The bulwarks are dismantled, the banqueting halls are ruinous... He then who in a spirit of meditation has pondered over this ruin, and who with an understanding heart probes the mystery of our life down to its depth, will call to mind many slaughters of long ago, and give voice to such words as these: What has become of the steed? What has become of the squire?... What has become of the banqueting houses? Where are the joys of the hall? O shining goblet! O mailed warrior! O glory of the prince! How has that time passed away, grown shadowy under the canopy of night as though it had never been!

Francesco di Giorgio Martini, *Adoration of the Child*, oil on panel, 1485. Basilica of San Domenico, Siena.

5

OLD ENGLISH ADVENT LYRIC

TENTH CENTURY

The Gospel of St Matthew says that when Joseph and Mary did not secure a room in the inn for the birth of their son, they were forced to do so in a stable, though the text is translated simply as a 'house' (i.e. a building). Subsequent narratives of the birth and the greeting of Jesus by shepherds and the Magi have been offered in both word and image. The late Middle Ages and Renaissance produced at least a dozen well-known images of the Adoration, each of which used a ruined building as background and setting.

The ruins were not just a backdrop for narrative images: their implication – verbal as well as visual – was that the advent of Christ heralded the renovation and repair of ancient cultures. That relation is explicit in the Old English Advent lyric from the Exeter Book, which describes the advent of Christ as the rebuilding of a ruined house, based upon Psalm 118: 'The stone that the builders rejected has become the chief cornerstone,' which Jesus himself quotes in Matthew 21.

With the Renaissance, in paintings by Leonardo, Botticelli, Dürer and Di Giorgio, the style of the ruins became distinctly Roman, with less emphasis on the animals. Here, into the collapsed Roman archway, Di Giorgio has inserted a simple wooden roof to shelter the cattle.[1]

> Advent lyric: Christ 1 in *The Christ of Cynewulf, A Poem in Three Parts: The Advent, the Ascension, and the Last Judgment* (Boston: Ginn, 1900)
>
> > To the king.
> > You are the wall-stone the workers rejected,
> > The rock of strength they once cast away.
> > Now you are the fitting and firm foundation,
> > Cornerstone of the great and glorious hall,
> > Unbroken flint securely joined,
> > So that those with eyes to see your glory
> > Throughout the cities may marvel forever
> > And know the miracle of your mighty work.

BOOK OF RUINS

Lord of victory and truth triumphant,
Let everyone gaze on the beautiful form,
The breadth and binding, of your great work,
The brawn of standing wall against wall,
Strength and support, buttress and beauty.
But we live in a world of rubble and wreckage.
Now we need our Creator, our Craftsman and King,
To reshape the structure and restore the hall,
Rebuild the ruin and reclaim the rooms
Beneath the roof. He built the first man,
Created the body, the limbs of clay.
Now may the Lord of life rescue the weary,
Release the multitude from life's misery,
Free the wretched from torment and woe,
Redeem the ruin as he has so often done.

6

Ruins in Medieval Words and Images

In 12th-century Britain, Gerald of Wales's description of the Roman ruins at Caerleon and William of Malmesbury's account of those at Carlisle emphasize the skill and workmanship of their construction, and their evidence of running water and central heating – advanced technologies long since lost.

GERALD OF WALES
The Journey through Wales, translated by Lewis Thorpe
(New York: Penguin Books, 1978)

Caerleon is of unquestioned antiquity. It was constructed with great care by the Romans, the walls being built of brick. You can still see many vestiges of its one-time splendour. There are immense palaces, which, with the gilded gables of their roofs, once rivalled the magnificence of ancient Rome. They were set up in the first place by some of the most eminent men of the Roman state, and they were therefore embellished with every architectural conceit. There is a lofty tower, and beside it remarkable hot baths, the remains of temples and an amphitheatre. All this is enclosed within impressive walls, parts of which still remain standing. Wherever you look, both within and without the circuit of these walls, you can see constructions dug deep into the earth, conduits for water, underground passages and air-vents. Most remarkable of all to my mind are the stoves, which once transmitted heat through narrow pipes inserted in the side-walls and which are built with extraordinary skill.

WILLIAM OF MALMESBURY
Gesta Pontificum Anglorum, in *William of Malmesbury's Chronicle of the Kings of England. From the Earliest Period to the Reign of King Stephen*
(London: G. Bell and Sons, 1883)

In some of the ruined buildings, though, whose walls were not completely destroyed, you may see remarkable Roman work: for example, at Carlisle

Giovan Pietro Birago, *Adoration of the Magi*, from the Sforza Hours, ink and gilding on parchment, *c.*1490. British Library.

a *triclinium* vaulted in stone that no violence of the elements, or even the intentional setting alight of timbers piled up against it, has succeeded in destroying. The district is called Cumberland, and its inhabitants Cumbrians. On the front of the structure one can read the inscription 'To the victory of Marius'. I am doubtful what this means; it may be that some of the Cimbri settled of old in these parts after being driven from Italy by Marius.

7

Theoderich on Jerusalem

1173

Apart from his role of the author of this text, Theoderich is completely unknown, though some historians have identified him with an early 13th-century Bishop of Würzburg. His book shows that he was well travelled, because of his first-hand account of sites and cities in Palestine but also locations elsewhere, mentioned *en passant* or for purposes of comparison. His *Libellus de locis sanctis* ('Little Book of Holy Places') is rather like the guide written by a predecessor he mentions, John of Würzburg, though Theoderich's report is more ample in detail and more legibly written. He describes what he saw, but also relies on what he read in other accounts. The narration comes to life when he notes events he witnessed (the stacking of pilgrims' crosses on the top of the rock of Calvary, for example, or the bonfire made of them on Easter Eve). His journey took place during the Crusades, while the city was under the control of the French King Amalric. Some interpreters have suggested Theoderich may have been an architect, given his rather elaborate descriptions of buildings and their parts. As a whole, it can certainly be read as a travelogue or guidebook, but he explains his purpose was to help bring Christ to mind for those who could not visit the Holy Land themselves.

Ruins are invoked at the beginning and end of the parts excerpted here. In the first instance, Theoderich is concerned to note that the ruined condition of many sites in the Holy Land resulted from different kinds and phases of destruction: first the violence of the Jews themselves against Christ and early Christians, which was followed by the campaigns of the Romans against the Jews. His account implies just retribution in this latter phase of destruction, as if ruins, sad though they are, communicate a positive, even salvational message. His report on the House of Pilate, which ends our selection, notes that much in this part of the city is lost, compelling him to work with mere traces. Yet overall it seems like King David and Jesus Christ walked these streets days before Theoderich arrived there, for his text largely overlooks both loss and historical distance, rendering the sites with a kind of immediacy and concreteness that suggests ruins, when used in religious practices, could make something absent seemingly present. These types of practices, which figure more prominently here than in other such reports, no doubt aided his ahistorical sense of ruins, for the events he

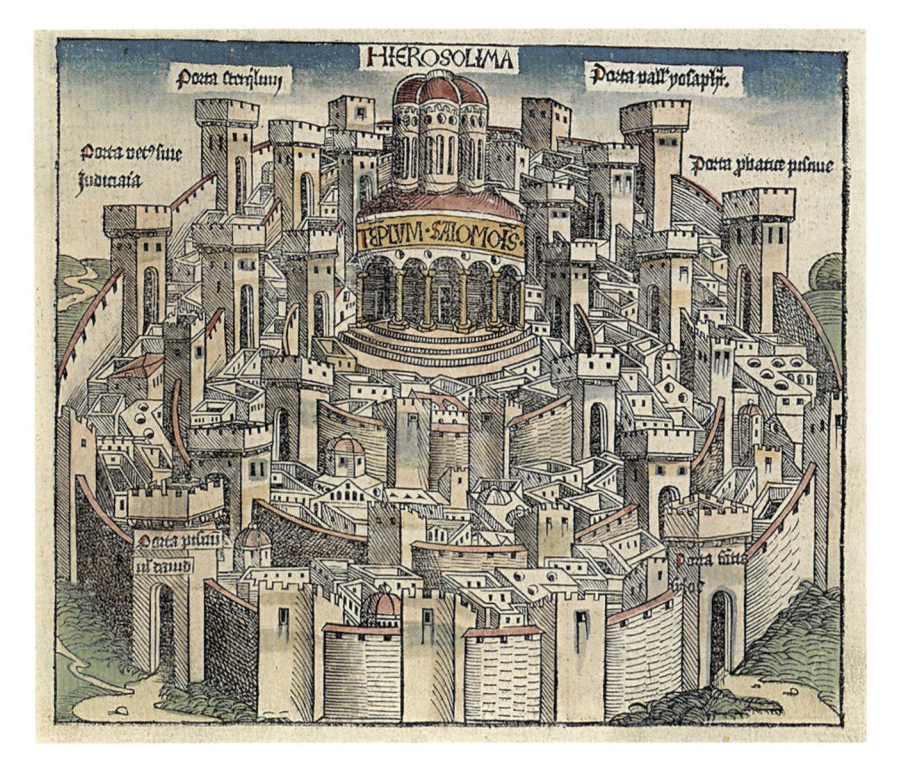

Michael Wohlgemut, *Jerusalem*, in Hartmann Schedel's *Liber Chronicarum* (Nuremberg Chronicle), wood engraving, 1493.

witnessed were taken to be the same as those that inaugurated the traditions, having survived into the present, seemingly intact, as if time hadn't passed, despite what the ruins themselves made obvious.

Theoderich's Description of the Holy Places, translated by Aubrey Stewart (London: Palestine Pilgrims' Society, 1896)

i. The Ruin of the Land and the Changing of Its Names

It is evident to all who read the pages of the Old and New Testament that the land of Canaan was, by divine ordinance, given as a possession to the twelve tribes of the people of Israel. This land, divided into the three provinces of Judaea, Samaria, and Galilee, was in antiquity enriched by many cities, towns, and castles. The names and situations of all these cities were in former days well known to everyone; but the moderns, being strangers in the land, and not its original inhabitants, know only the names of a few places that we shall describe in their proper place. For since our dearest Lord Jesus Christ required vengeance for his blood – which was shed on the cross by the cruel hands of the impious Jews – the Roman princes, Vespasian and Titus, entered Judaea with an army, leveled the Temple and city to the ground, destroyed all the cities and villages throughout Judaea, and drove the murderers themselves out of their own country and forced them to depart and live among foreigners. In consequence of this all works and constructions of that people, and of the entire province, have been destroyed, so that although some traces of certain places still remain, nearly all their names have been altered.

ii. Judaea

First, then, we must speak of Judaea, which is known to have been the chief province of the Jewish kingdom, which we have been able to examine with our own eyes and ears. There, as an eye in the head, is placed the Holy City of Jerusalem, from which, through our mediator with God, our Lord Jesus Christ, grace and salvation and life have flowed to all nations. Judaea is bounded on the west by the Great Sea. On the south it is separated by the desert from the mountains of Arabia and Egypt. On the east it is limited by the River Jordan, and on the north it is skirted by Samaria and Idumaea.

Now Judaea is for the most part mountainous, and round about the Holy City rises into very lofty ranges, sloping on all sides down to its aforesaid boundaries, just as, on the other hand, one ascends to it from them. These mountains are in some places rough with masses of the hardest rock, in other places they are adorned with stone excellently suited to be cut into ashlar, and in others they are beautified by white, red, and variegated marble. But wherever any patches of earth are found among these masses of rock the land is seen to be fit for the production of every kind of fruit. We have seen the hills and mountains covered with such vineyards and plantations of olive trees and fig trees, and the valleys abounding with corn and garden produce.

iii. Jerusalem, the Valleys of Josaphat and Gehinnom, Mount of Rejoicing (Mons Gaudii), Position of the Holy City, Its Fortifications, Gates, Streets, Houses, Cisterns, Wood

Now, on the very topmost peak of these mountains, as is affirmed by both Josephus and Jerome, is placed the city of Jerusalem, which is held to be holier and more notable than all the other cities and places throughout the world, not because it is holy in itself, or by itself, but because it has been glorified by the presence of God himself, and of our Lord Jesus Christ and his holy mother, and by the dwelling there, the doctrine, the preaching, and the martyrdom of patriarchs, prophets, Apostles, and other holy people. Although it has mountain ridges higher than itself all around it, it is itself hilly, being built on a mountain. Hence it follows that it attracts the eyes of viewers away from all the mountains by which it is surrounded.

Now, between the Hill of Moriah, on which stands the Temple of the Lord, and the Mount of Olives, which raises its head higher than any of the other mountains, lies the Cedron Brook and the Valley of Josaphat. This valley starts from the Mount of Rejoicing (Mons Gaudii), from which one enters the city on the northern side, passes by the Church of St Mary, which is so called after her, passes the Tomb of Josaphat, king of Judaea, from whose death it itself has received this name, and passes close to the bathing Pool of Siloe, where another valley meets it. This valley bends its course from the right-hand corner of the city past the new cisterns between Mount Sion and the Field of Acheldemach, thus embracing two sides of the city with a very deep ravine. The Tomb of Josaphat stands in the midst of this valley, built of squared stone in the form of a pyramid. Round about it there are a great number of dwellings of servants of God, or hermits, all of which are placed under the care of the abbot of St Mary's.

Now, the longest part of the city reaches from north to south, and the width of it is from west to east, and it is most strongly fortified by walls and bastions on the top of the mountain above the aforesaid valleys. There is also a barrier, or fosse, placed outside the wall and furnished with battlements and loopholes, which they call the Barbican. The city has seven gates, of which they firmly lock six every night until after sunrise; the seventh is closed by a wall and is only opened on Palm Sunday and on the day of the Exaltation of the Cross.

Since it has an oblong form, the city has five angles, one of which is transverse. Almost all its streets are paved with great stones below, and above many of them are covered with a stone vault, pierced with many windows for the transmission of light. The houses, which are lofty piles of carefully wrought stonework, are not finished with high-pitched roofs after our style but are level and flat. The people catch the rainwater that falls on them and store it up in cisterns for their own use – they use no other water, because they have none. Wood, suitable for building or for fires, is expensive there, because Mount Libanus – the only mountain that abounds in cedar, cypress, and pine wood – is a long way off from them, and they cannot approach it for fear of the attacks of the infidels.

iv. The Tower of David, Mounts Sion and Moriah, the field of Aceldama, Mount Gion, the House of Pilate, Antonia

The Tower of David is the property of the King of Jerusalem and is incomparably strong, being built of squared stones of immense size. It stands near the western gate, from which the road leads toward Bethlehem, together with the newly built solar chamber and palace that adjoins it, and it is strongly fortified with ditches and barbicans. It is situated on Mount Sion, of which we read in the Book of Kings (2 Sam. 5:7), 'Now David took Sion.' It is also situated over against the Temple of the Lord in the part of the city that extends sideways, with Mount Sion on the south and the Mount of Olives on the east. Mount Sion reaches from the tower as far as the Church of St Mary outside the Walls and from the church nearly as far as the Palace of Solomon and as far as the way that leads from the Beautiful Gate to the tower, being wider but lower than the Mount of Olives. Although Mount Moriah, which overhangs the Valley of Josaphat and on which stands the Temple of the Lord and the Palace of Solomon, may be thought to be a great hill, Mount Sion surpasses it by as much as the latter seems to surpass the Valley of Josaphat. In the Field of Acheldemach, which is only separated from it by the above-mentioned valley, is the pilgrims' burying ground, in which stands the Church of St Mary, the Virgin Mother of God, in which also on the holy day of Palm Sunday we buried one of our brethren, named Adolf, a native of Cologne. This field is overhung by Mount Gion, on which Solomon was crowned, as may be read in the Book of Kings.

Of the other buildings, whether public or private, we have scarcely been able to find any traces, or at least very few, with the exception of the House of Pilate, near the Church of St Anne, the mother of our Lady, which stands near the Sheep Pool. Of all the work that Josephus tells us was built by Herod and is now utterly ruined, nothing remains save one side, which is still standing, of the palace that was called Antonia, with a gate placed outside, near the court of the Temple...

8

PETRARCH ON ROME

1341

Petrarch's famous letter to Cardinal Giovanna Colonna di San Vito is among the very first antiquarian documents of humanism. It is one of a number of letters to Colonna, among the 350 that comprise the *Rerum familiarum libri*, written between 1325 and 1366. The report seems to have been drafted after his second visit to Rome, in 1341, the year he was crowned poet laureate on the Capitol. With Cicero and Seneca as his models, Petrarch combined the separate letters into a single text that could serve his readers as a book of instruction for daily living. Unlike devotional texts and manuals for spiritual exercise (in ancient, medieval, or Renaissance cultures), the concerns of the book were prosaic: matters of prudence, political action, and public discourse, for example, but also emotional life, diet, and coping with the passing of time. The last of these topics formed the personal and intellectual horizons for Petrarch's concerns with the ruins of Rome.

Of course, history was also at issue, both secular and sacred. His survey begins with the pagan sites and ends with an invocation of Christ. But the account Petrarch left is not one that was composed on the spot; instead, it was reworked from memory. No one doubts that he did, indeed, visit the places he names, but neither does anyone turn to his list of famous spots for archaeological detail. Later antiquarians, with an odd sense of superiority, have condescendingly pointed out his mistaken attributions – republican instead of imperial walls, for example. If the letter is to be taken as an early instance of antiquarianism, it must be of a special sort, where meanings and memories were not to be found in *things* but in the verbal and mental *images* with which they could be associated. Just as toponyms subordinated the palpable remains of Rome's former glory, readings supplied what the settings no longer possessed: vividness, particularity, and narrative layout or organization. 'At each step,' as he so frequently says, pages turn and centuries pass. Paces connected places that had been imagined before being seen. The pleasures to which the 'here is' and 'there is' of fragments gave rise were those of a journey through Virgil, Livy, Ovid, and Lucan, as well as (more swiftly) the Gospels. A sense of profound loss is expressed in the text, but also an almost youthful excitement, as when physical evidence suggests that something one wants to believe might actually have happened, right here, over there.

Letters on Familiar Affairs (Rerum familiarium libri),
in James Harvey Robinson, *Petrarch: The First Modern Scholar
and Man of Letters* (New York: Putnam, 1907)

To Giovanni Colonna of the Order of Preachers, that one must love not sects but the truth, and concerning the remarkable places in the city of Rome.

We used to walk widely by ourselves throughout Rome, and you are indeed acquainted with my peripatetic habit. I enjoy it very much and find it most appropriate to my nature and personal habits. Of the opinions of the Peripatetics certain ones please me, others hardly at all, for I do not love sects but the truth. Therefore, I am at one time a Peripatetic, and at another a Stoic and sometimes an Academic. Often however I am none of these, especially at those times when something suspect appears in their writings which is opposed to our true and blessed faith. For we are permitted to love and approve philosophical schools if they are not opposed to the truth, and if they do not turn us from our primary purpose. When by chance they attempt this, whether it be Plato or Aristotle or Varro or Cicero, they are all to be disdained and trampled upon freely and steadily. Let no sharpness of

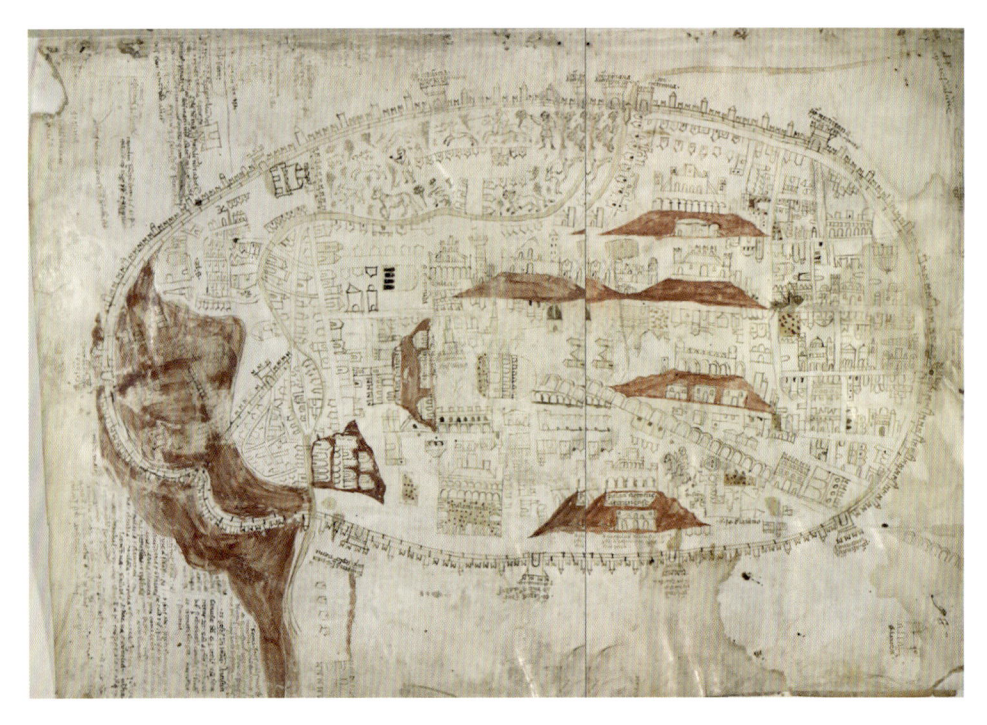

Fra Paolino da Venezia, detail from map of Rome, ink on parchment, 1323.
Biblioteca Nazionale Marciana, Venice.

disputation, no mildness of words, no authority of names affect us. They were men, and to the extent that they could accomplish this through human curiosity, they had both knowledge of things and clarity of expression and were fortunate in natural genius. But they were wretched in their lack of the knowledge of the highest and ineffable good, and like those who trust their own strength and do not desire the true light, they often stumbled over an immovable stone in the manner of the blind. Therefore let us admire their genius in such a way that we venerate the author of such genius; let us have compassion for their errors as we rejoice in our grace; and let us realize that without any merit we have been honored and have been raised above the greatest thinkers by Him who deemed worthy of revealing to children what he had hidden from the wise. In short let us philosophize in a manner which the very name of philosophy suggests, for the love of wisdom. Indeed, the true wisdom of God is Christ so that in order to philosophize rightly we must first love and cherish Him. Let us be such in all things that above all things we may be Christians. Let us thus read philosophical, poetic, or historical writings so that the Gospel of Christ resounds always in the ear of our heart. In this alone are we sufficiently happy and learned; without it no matter how much we learn we become more ignorant and more wretched. To it all things must be referred as if to the loftiest stronghold of the truth; on it as if on a single immovable foundation of literary truths, human labor can safely build. And we must not restrain ourselves from diligently cultivating other teachings which are not contrary to it, for although the returns may be limited in so far as any real accomplishment is concerned, we shall appear to have added a considerable measure to the enjoyment of the mind and the cultivation of life. I have said these things at random as far as they seem to befit a letter of this type. Now I shall proceed.

We used to wander together in that great city which, though it appeared empty because of its vast size, had a huge population. And we would wander not only in the city itself but around it, and at each step there was present something which would excite our tongue and mind: here was the palace of Evander, there the shrine of Carmentis, here the cave of Cacus, there the famous she-wolf and the fig-tree of Rumina with the more apt surname of Romulus, there the overpass of Remus, here the circus games and the rape of the Sabines: there the marsh of Capri and the place where Romulus vanished, here the conversations of Numa and Egeria, there the battle line of the trigemini. Here the conqueror of enemies who was in turn conquered by a thunderbolt, and the builder of the militia; there the architect king Ancus Marnus; here the organizer of social classes, Priscus Tarquinius, lived; there the head of Servius glowed; there sitting in her carriage cruel Tullia crossed and made the street infamous because of her crime. Here however is Via Sacra while over there are the Esquiline Hill, the Viminal, the Quirinal; here the Campus Celius, there the Campus Martius and the poppies cut down by the hand of the proud one. Here one can still see the wretched Lucretia lying upon her sword and the adulterer fleeing his death, as well as Brutus the defender of the violated chastity. There is threatening Porcina and the Etruscan Army, and Mutius beset by his erring right hand, and the son of the tyrant competing with liberty, and the Consul pursuing (to hell itself) the enemy expelled from the city; and the Sublician bridge broken behind the brave man, and Horatius swimming and Cloelia returning on the Tiber. There may be seen the house of Publicola which was fruitlessly suspected; here Quintius used to plow until through his merit the plowman was made dictator; from here Serranus was led away to become Consul. This is the Janiculum, this is the Aventine, that is Monte Sacra, on which the angered plebeians withdrew from the rulers; here the lustful tribunal of Appius stood, and Virginia was rescued from violence by the sword of her father and there occurred a worthy end to the dissipation of the Decemvirs. From here Coriolanus, who was perhaps about to triumph with his arms, departed after having been conquered by the devotion of his supporters. This is the rock that Manlius defended and then fell from; here Camillus repelled the Gauls as they gaped at the unexpected gold and taught the despairing citizens how to recover a lost fatherland with a sword and not with gold. Here armed Curtius descended; there was found underground the head of a man with an immovable face which was viewed as a prediction of the highest and firmest form of empire. There a deceitful Virgin fell under arms after having been deceived by her own deceits; here is the Tarpeian fortress, and the wealth of the Roman people collected throughout the world; here is the silver goose; there is Janus the guardian of arms; here is the temple of Jupiter Feretrius; this was the temple of Jupiter, this was the home of all the triumphs; here Perses was brought, from here Hannibal was driven away, here Jugurtha was destroyed as some believe, others indeed believe that he was slain in prison. Here Caesar triumphed, here he perished. In this temple Augustus viewed the prostrate kings and the whole world at his feet; here is the arch of Pompey, here is the portico, here is the Cimbrian arch of Marius. There is Trajan's Column where he alone of all the emperors, according to Eusebius, is buried inside the city; here is his bridge which eventually assumed the name of St Peter, and Hadrian's fortress, under which he also lies buried and which they call Castel Sant'Angelo. This is that massive rock surmounted by two bronze lions which was sacred to the deified emperors, and on whose summit, rumor has it, rest the bones of Julius Caesar. This is the shrine to the goddess Tellure, this is the temple of Fortune, this is the temple of Peace, which was rightly destroyed at the arrival of the King of Peace; this is the work of Agrippa taken from the false gods to be dedicated to the mother of the true God. Here is where it snowed on the fifth of August; from here a stream of oil flowed into the Tiber; from here, according to tradition, the old Augustus, following the Sibyl's advice, saw the Christ child. This is the insolence of Nero and his raging extravagance in the buildings he raised; there is the house of Augustus, on Via Flaminia, where some maintain is the tomb of the Emperor himself; this is the Column of Antoninus; this is the palace of Appius; this is the Septizonium of Severus Afrus which you call the temple of the sun but whose name I find in the form I use written in history. On these stones still survives after so many centuries the great rivalry in talent and skill between Praxiteles and Phidias; here Christ appeared to his fleeing Vicar; here Peter was crucified; there Paul was beheaded; here Lawrence was burned, who after being buried here, was succeeded by Stephan. Here John scorned the burning oil; there Agnes after her death came back to life and forbade her kin to weep; here Sylvester hid; there Constantine got rid of his leprosy; there Calixtus mounted his glorious bier. But where shall I end? Can I really describe everything in this short letter? Indeed, if I could, it would not be proper; you know all these things not because you are a Roman citizen but because since your youth you have been intensely curious especially about such information. For today who are more ignorant about Roman affairs than the Roman citizens? Sadly do I say that nowhere is Rome less known than in Rome. I do not deplore only the ignorance involved (although what is worse than ignorance?) but the disappearance and exile of many virtues. For who can doubt that Rome would rise again instantly if she began to know herself? But this is a complaint to be dealt with at another time.

We used to stop often at the baths of Diocletian after the weariness which ceaseless walking about that city had produced in us, and indeed we would often ascend to the roof of that building, once a home, because only here could we enjoy the healthy air, the unimpeded view, silence, and desired solitude. There we did not discuss business, household problems, or public affairs of which we had previously sufficiently unburdened ourselves. And as in our travels through the remains of a broken city, there too, as we sat, the remnants of the ruins lay before our eyes. What else may be said? Our conversation was concerned largely with history which we seemed to have divided among us, I being more expert, it seemed, in the ancient, by which we meant the time before the Roman rulers celebrated and venerated the name of Christ, and you in recent times, by which we meant the time from then to the present. We also spoke much about that part of philosophy which deals with morals, whence it gets its name; and sometimes indeed we discussed the arts and their authors and rules...

Thus, once when we had entered into this latter subject you asked me to explain clearly where I thought the liberal arts and the mechanical arts had their beginning because you had from time to time heard me talk on the subject. I responded quite simply because the hour, the absence of trivial cares, and the very place encouraged me to go into the subject at some length, and because your attentiveness suggested that the subject was indeed pleasing to you. I assured you, however, that I would say nothing new, nothing that was really mine, and yet nothing that was basically borrowed, for from whatever source we learn anything it is ours unless by chance forgetfulness takes it from us. You request now that what I said that day I repeat and commit to a letter. I confess that I did say many things which I can only repeat with different words. Give me back that place, that idle mood, that day, that attention of yours, that particular vein of my talent and I could do what I did then. But all things are changed: the place is not present, the day has passed, the idle mood is gone, and instead of your face I look upon silent words, my spirit is impeded by the din of the business matters I have left behind, matters which until recently roared in my ears, although I fled as soon as I could in order to answer you more freely. I shall, however, obey as best I can. I could send you to some ancient and modern writers from whom you can learn what you seek; but you made provisions for me not to do so when you asked that I say whatever I have to say on the subject in my own words because, as you observed, everything I say appears most pleasing and clear to you. I thank you for this opinion whether it is really true or whether you do it by way of stimulating my mind. Here is then what I said at that time, perhaps with the words of others but certainly the same thoughts. But really, what are we doing? The subject is clearly not a small one, this letter is already too long, and we have not yet started, though the end of this day is at hand. Would it not be a good idea for me to give some rest to my fingers and to your eyes? Let us put off what remains until another day; let us divide the labor and the letter and let us not cover two very different matters in the same letter. But what do I have in mind? What am I promising you when I say another letter tomorrow? This is neither the work of a single day nor a task for letters, it requires a book which I shall undertake (if I am not impeded and frustrated by major cares) when fortune returns me to my solitude. Only there and not elsewhere am I myself; there lies my pen which at present rebels everywhere I go and refuses my orders because I am preoccupied with burdensome matters. Thus, while it is constantly busy when I have plenty of leisure, it prefers to have leisure when I have much to do, and almost like a wicked and insolent servant, it seems to convert the fervor of the master into its own desire for rest...

However, as soon as I get back home I shall compel it to take on its duties and I shall... write about what you seek in a separate book, indicating what has been written by others and what are my own ideas. Indeed, just as I am accustomed to writing these friendly letters almost as amusement in the very midst of conversations and bustle, in the same way I have need of solitary quiet and pleasant leisure and great and uninterrupted silence in order to write books.

Farewell.

9

Hypnerotomachia Poliphili

1499

The authorship of this text is disputed, but the prime candidate is a Venetian friar, Francesco Colonna; the engravings, which include several images of ruined fragments, are even more uncertain, and many artists have been proposed for what is, indeed, a remarkable visual imagination, among them Andrea Mantegna, Gentile Bellini, and the young Raphael. The printing by Aldus Manutius (c.1450–1515) is one of the treasures of early Renaissance book production.

Its basic literary form is the story of how Polifilo, in a double dream, pursues and finally meets up with his beloved Polia, in the process finding himself first asleep in a dark wood, reminiscent of Dante's *selva oscura* in the *Divine Comedy*, and then in a dream within that dream he is led through an astonishing landscape of buildings, gardens, and ruined structures and artifacts covered with inscriptions. In that section he and Polia encounter a ruined temple filled with fragments of sarcophagi, columns, and other architectural elements.

The language is Italian, yet its author has played with neologisms derived from Greek and Latin, which makes it extremely hard to translate. The first English version, less than half of the whole original, was *The Strife of Love in a Dream*, published in London in 1592: a useful introduction to this is provided by Lucy Gent in the Scholars' Facsimiles & Reprints (New York, 1973); there was a French version by Jean Marin in 1546, and a modern version by Joscelyn Godwin was published by Thames & Hudson, in 1999. Another version of the whole text by Ian White has not appeared in print, but was cited by contributors to an issue in *Word & Image* (2015), in which he also wrote. The major critical edition by Giovanni Pozzi and Lucia A. Ciapponu, in two volumes, was published in Padua by Editrice Antenore, 1980.

Published in Venice in 1499, this wonderful and curious incunabulum marks, among many other things, the emergence of the Renaissance from a medieval literary and narrative world. This suggests its place here, at the intersection of the medieval with the new world of the European Renaissance. Polifilo's love of antiquity and his delight in deciphering inscriptions is best revealed in the long section where he and Polia arrive a ruined temple, a part of which is provided here.

FRANCESCO COLONNA
Hypnerotomachia Poliphili (Venice: Aldus Mantius, 1499)[2]

...absorbed and without any other thought, from Polia, between these unfrequented mounds of heaped and waste accumulation and ruin, for the most part taken over by ground-ivy and the earth-rambler terrambula and entwined with thorns, driven by excitement I concluded that this had been a magnificent and marvellous temple of rare and superb construction... Here then it was apparent that, in the circuit of the round temple, tribunes had been arranged, because some parts were still left half-entire or half-ruined, and great fragments of pillars, with curved pieces of architrave and horns (or haunches) of vaulting, and of

Harbour and Temple in Ruins, from the second (1545) edition of *Hypnerotomachia Poliphili*, wood engraving. This and the following images are identical to those in the first edition of 1499. University of Pennsylvania Libraries.

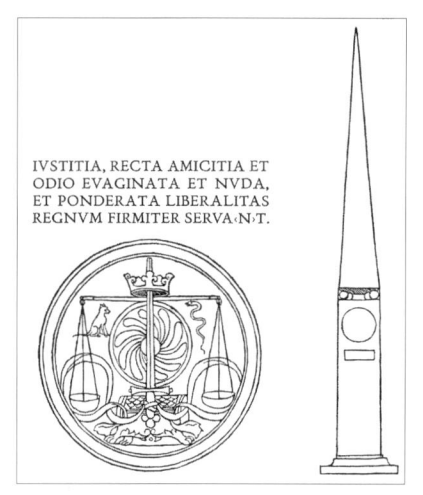

IVSTITIA, RECTA AMICITIA ET
ODIO EVAGINATA ET NVDA,
ET PONDERATA LIBERALITAS
REGNVM FIRMITER SERVA‹N›T.

lofty columns of various kinds of stone, some Numidian and some Hymettian and Laconian, among those named above, and other sorts, very beautiful, clear and disengaged in lineament (or profile); from the arrangement of these tribunes in this laid open way, I judged that it was in these had been located the sepulchres.

In this place, before everything else, at the rear side of that archaic and arch-curial temple, I admired a great lofty obelisk of red-colored stone. And on the squared base set underneath I saw in one face hieroglyphs engraved like this: first, in a circular figure, a balance or pair of scales in the middle of which was a plate; in the triangular areas between the scales and the circle of the plate, on one side was a dog and on the other a snake; below it lay an antique casket, and from this rising straight up was an unsheathed sword, with the point going further above the scales' balance beam; and here was introduced a royal crown. These (hieroglyphs) I interpreted (or translated) thus: JUSTICE UPRIGHT, FROM FRIENDSHIP AND ENMITY UNSHEATHED, AND BARE, AND WELLWEIGHED LIBERALITY, FIRMLY PRESERVE THE KINGDOM.

Then returning into the front part, I found the propylaeum all broken up, and lying at the entrance of the destroyed doorway I saw a piece of architrave, zophorus, and part of the cornice in a solid block: on that zophorus I saw inscribed in an elegant inscription of majuscules this motto: D.M.S. (CONSECRATED TO THE DIVINE SHADES). FOR THE CORPSES OF THOSE FROM LOVE RAVING MAD, WHICH ARE PITIFUL, POLYANDRION. This notable and valuable fragment still in one solid piece also retained a small portion of its pediment gable, or frontispiece, excellently featured, in whose triangular flat face I saw two images carved on it, but not entire: a bird without its head, I decided it was an owl, and an old lamp; all in perfect alabastrite. I interpreted (or translated) them thus: TO LIFE A DEATH-BEARING MESSENGER...

.D. .M. .S.
CADAVERIB. AMORE FVRENTIVM
MISERABVNDIS POLYANDRION

II

The Renaissance

10

Flavio Biondo

1446

When Flavio Biondo, often called one of Europe's first archaeologists, climbed the Capitol in Rome he saw largely deserted fields, interrupted here and there by fragments of ancient buildings, none prominent enough to prevent animals from grazing, hence the vernacular name Campo Vaccino. Sharing the sentiments of his contemporaries Poggio Bracciolini and Leon Battista Alberti, Flavio was inspired by the sad state of the built legacy of Rome's greatness to undertake an ambitious project of surveying, documenting, and interpreting, published in the three volumes of his *Roma Instaurata* between 1444 and 1446.

Though modern commentators have praised the work as the first systematic account of ancient Roman ruins, the text is hardly well organized. Unlike Alberti's *Descriptio Urbis Romae* (c.1444), Flavio's survey was visual and verbal only; he does not seem to have measured and mapped what he saw. Nor are its many short chapters similarly structured: some attest to on-site perception, others include references to numismatic materials and lengthy quotations from ancient written sources (approximately 25), and still others offer lengthy explanations and derivations of names that are alternately learned and speculative. The same variation can be seen in subject matter: some chapters study single buildings, others building types, and still others distinct areas of the ancient city. Many of the closest descriptions are, unsurprisingly, of sites near his home. Sites that later descriptions determined to be legendary were also given specific locations.

Chapter to chapter, the mood varies from pride to lament, sensations of glory to those of loss. Still, his energy and dedication are impressive. He confessed that his affection for Rome was second only to his love for God, as if topographical description were only slightly subordinate to religious practice. His justification: the ruins of Rome attested to the city's immortality. Because the evidence was so very partial, the conviction was a matter of faith, 'the substance of things hoped for, the evidence of things unseen'. While undertaking his work, Flavio remained in regular contact with Pope Eugene IV. Recognition of the curia's support for his project is plain in the book's Preface. Like his benefactor, Flavio believed that recognition and restoration of Rome's ancient legacy would strengthen the modern city's cultural standing and significance.

FLAVIO BIONDO

To illustrate Flavio's approach to ruins, we have selected three excerpts from his massive study: the Preface, the account of the Porta Triumphalis, and his description of aqueducts, with inferences about the various causes of ruination.

'Roma Instaurata, 1444-6' in
'*Viget Certe Viget Adhuc*: The Invention of the Eternal City
in Flavio Biondo's Roma Instaurata', translated by Ryan Warwick,
Senior Projects Spring 2016, Bard Digital Commons

Preface

Many things which are now seen in the city of Rome, the mistress more of ruins than of edifices, persuade me to create this publication on behalf of your power, most sacred Pope Eugene, but this one thing compelled me the most: there has been so much ignorance of the study of the humanities in previous generations that, since few of the structures of this very city which once existed are understood in their single parts not only by the inexperienced multitude but also by those who are more learned with respect to doctrine, we then see many, nearly all things fouled, or rather defamed, by false and barbarous names. Therefore, in short, it seems that Rome, the parent of our genius, the nursling of our bravery, display of praise, height of glory, the garden of all good things that the world has, obscured by its structures, will suffer a bigger loss of celebrity and fame than we see has happened in the case of earlier wealth and power. The return of your pontificate onto its seat confirmed our resolution to write, a return so useful and necessary for its conservation that it is evident that the papacy already destroyed by calamity and decline, would be completely lost if you had been absent another ten years. Not only do you nurture Romans by your presence in the curia, a thing which mostly benefits the opulence of the city, but also in many locations you restore and remake fallen, misshapen buildings at the greatest cost. This is certainly honorable, a deed most fitting for a magnanimous *princeps* and one which surpasses in praise and glory all the foundations that were built and the structures of buildings that were made when Rome once blossomed by the degree to which the poverty of our age has a need for the immense wealth of our forebears. I owe everything I have to your holiness and for this reason I will not assert that you proceed to renew Rome with the remnant in letters of my small genius as much as you do by the labor of cement workers or carpenters. This renewed account of my works adds to the restoration of our city, which might please in particular the sanctity of your dignity and add to your glory, that of the Roman Popes who came before you. While describing the old parts of the city and their new names, I will explain through

Leonardo da Besozzo, *Rome*, watercolour, *c.*1440, reproduced in Ferdinand Gregorovius, *Una Pianta Di Roma Delineata Da Leonardo Da Besozzo, milanese*, Rome, 1883.

which Pope or other Christians the basilicas, temples, and other sacred places which we call *ecclesia* were founded, begun, or renewed. While describing the magnificence of our city, inasmuch as I will not defraud eminent Romans of praise, even if they are idolaters and gentiles, I have a mind to highlight the glory of our martyrs, namely whenever someone conquered by endurance or triumphed by succumbing to the pleasure, the insanity, of tyrants. I will thus approach your glory for this duty which I have taken up, having trusted that it will be that our descendants will decide at some later time whether or not at this time of such great loss I was able to imitate with my undignified pen the architecture that has been built: the basilica of the prince of the apostles, remade and renovated in great part, as well as the walls of the Lateran palace, or the large bronze doors added to the most famous temple of St Peter, or the restoration of the suburban walls of the Vatican palace and the paved roads of the city. Our descendants will decide whether a restoration remains stronger and lasts longer when made with lime or brick or stone or bronze or, perhaps, with words. But now, let me turn back to my great work.

FLAVIO BIONDO

41. Porta Triumphalis

This gate is the *Triumphalis*. Through it and none other are triumphs led. And so I can recover this thing lost entirely in the shadows by a more exact method, a work which, if the works of men hold firm at all, must flash with eternal clarity, I will first tell you its location. Then I will put forward the evidence on which my assertion stands. The bridge, the foundations of the pillars of which are now seen in the Tiber near the Hospital of *Sanctus Spiritus*, as well as the gate on the deepest bank of the Tiber, the mound of the foundations of which still stand, and the road from the bridge to the obelisk of Caesar and the altar that lies in front of the Basilica of St Peter, following the foot of the Vatican hill, all are named Triumphalis. This road, I might contend, was extended no further than the Basilica of St Peter. Now, it stands to reason that this road was not longer than this because it was adjacent to something, either a basilica dedicated to the sun or an obelisk and a temple of Apollo called *Triumphale*. Josephus in the seventh book of *De Captivitate Iudaica* has clearly and abundantly examined the thing I said about the gate, describing the triumph of the emperors Titus and Vespasian. He said that the emperors who had been sleeping not in a major temple but the temple of Isis that night went through 'Octavian's paths' where the senate and the honored knights waited. And when favor decorated them with military honors, praise, and prayers celebrated according to tradition, they returned to the gate which from this received its name: the fact that the procession of *triumphators* has always been led through it. The end of the procession was the temple of Jupiter Capitolinus. There is not infrequent testimony about the territory called *Triumphalis* in the life of St Peter, prince of the apostles by St Hieronymus, the *Presbyter*, as he preferred that title, or, as some desire, the writings by Pope Damasus where it is said that St Peter was buried in the church of his name which was next to a temple of Apollo built in the Triumphal territory. And our age keeps this reputation to this day as the bridge from which we said that it was for nobles and the people who till the land never cross it. They have incidental evidence of this change that was made on the Kalends of the month of August or Sextilis by the memory of the victory of Octavius Caesar Augustus over Antony and Cleopatra for the liberation of St Peter from prison and the chains of Herod from where the festal day of St Peter in chains is celebrated, the ashes of Gaius Caesar were placed in a special obelisk which can be seen in the Triumphal Territory. I also contend that the temple of Isis was for Minerva in Sextus Ruffus' description of the city of Rome, whose name still endures, then called Chalcidica and Via Lata. Suetonius Tranquillius explains 'Octavian's paths' in these words: 'They buried their remains in the Mausoleum. He built this work along the via Flaminia and the bank of the Tiber, in his sixth consulship, and he made the surrounding forests and paths public for the use of the people.' A little bit before this Suetonius recalls the *Porta Triumphalis* where he says that certain senators decided to lead Augustus' funeral through it. Thus, Vespasian and Titus, once they had spent the night at Isis on the Via Lata, they descended towards the paths of Augustus, which is now called 'Augusta'. And from there, once the Tiber had been crossed, through the closest bridge, the foundations of which are seen they returned towards the *via* and *porta Triumphalis* where Hospital de Sancti Spiritus in Sassia now stands.

101. Aqueducts

... the only hands that must be accused and renounced [for the destruction of aqueducts] are those shameless hands that belong to those who, in order to build private and certainly ugly structures, did not fear to take stones either to be cooked down into lime or taken into the walls of their homes from the majesty of the walls. So that I defer in some small part to time, I will say that it destroyed the forms of the aqueducts only in so much as, while Rome was growing old in all parts of its governance, care for its service structures also ceased. Frontinus also had these words about the care that was once brought to the aqueducts: 'I find that a watch was accustomed to be assigned to each fountain and a certain number was placed as a necessity around each of the ducts outside the walls, it was decided that craftsmen were to be had from the city and indeed so much so that the names of those who were going to be given this position, were distributed through each of the region on signs. Great care was taken in testing these engineers throughout the *censors* at one point and then the *aediles* while the province fell to the consuls as it appears from the thing which was done while Gaius Luctatio and Ceson were consuls. How much care there was that someone not violate the aqueducts and not dare to divert it, could become evident from many things, but this is one of those: the fact that the Circus Maximus did not have water even during the days of the games unless the *aediles* or the *censors* approved. We read in Athenius Capito that this practice endured even after the government passed into the hands of the emperors under Augustus. Even the fields that were irrigated with public water against the law were distributed to the public.' And further: 'For this reason the *aediles* were ordered to choose in each district two men who either lived there, or had business there, at whose order the public water would leap forth. First Marcus Agrippa, after he performed this consular *aedileship*, was the seemingly perpetual curator of his own works and wealth who wrote down what should be given to the public waterworks, what to the lakes, and what to private use, at least while the treasury permitted. He also had his own establishment of the waterworks, which protected the ducts and the reservoirs and the lakes. Augustus made this service, left by him as a hereditary duty, a public office.' And further Frontinus says these words about the decision of the senate: 'The senate decided that when those who are in charge of public water are outside the city for the sake of this office, two lictors, three public servants, architects and scribes and secretaries, bailiffs and secretaries were assigned, as many as were had to distribute the grain to the people.'

11

RAPHAEL SANZIO

1519

Addressed to Pope Leo X, this document, generally referred to as a letter or memorandum, has been attributed to a number of early Renaissance architects, artists, and humanists, including Raphael, Baldassare Castiglione, Antonio da Sangallo the Younger, Baldassare Peruzzi, Donato Bramante, and a number of scholars in the papal court. Today, there is general consensus on Raphael's authorship of the earliest of the several surviving manuscripts, with the assistance of Castiglione and possibly Sangallo the Younger.

The letter describes the aims and methods of an important and ambitious project concerning the city of Rome: a survey of all its ancient monuments, no matter how ruined and incomplete, as individual works located in specific topographical positions. The survey was to be verbal and visual, and as exacting as possible in both measurement and meaning. First, there were to be accurate survey and reconstruction drawings, zone by zone, building by building – Bramante had discovered the true size of the ancient foot two decades earlier – and second, explanatory articles taking full advantage of ancient texts, assembled and translated by a collaborating group of scholars. Though the letter can be read as a preface to the map, it was also to be used a guideline for surveying procedures: plotting positions, mapping locations, and drawing buildings (field sketches would first be done on site, then reconstruction drawings made in a studio). To some degree, Alberti's *Descriptio Urbis Romae* served as a model for this project, though it did not propose the study of individual ruins, only plotting their positions within the city. One of the most remarkable aspects of the letter is its specification of the types of drawings that could serve as reliable documentation, which is to say plans, sections, and elevations, orthogonal 'cuts', not three-dimensional projections in perspective. The latter, Alberti had cautioned, were more suited to the aims of a painter than an architect, though Raphael admitted that they could convey a sense of the whole. Like many medieval and Renaissance guides to the city, the letter opens with a lament about the destruction of Rome's cultural patrimony, followed by an appeal to safeguard and preserve the remnants of a past that would inspire and instruct the present. Two concerns dominate Raphael's recommendations: exactitude of both representation and reconstruction, and attention

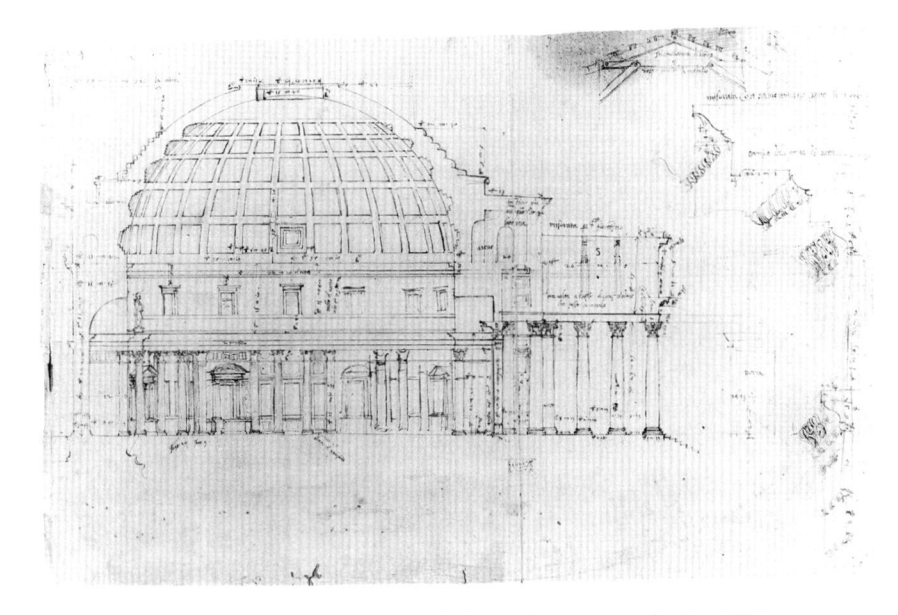

Baldassare Peruzzi, section through the Pantheon, pen and ink, c. 1531.
Bibliotecca Communale, Ferrara.

to the aesthetic quality of the works, not as ruins *per se* but as concrete evidence of ancient building practices (materials, details, ornaments, and elements), which could serve as models for future building.

> Letter to Pope Leo X, 1519 in Vaughan Hart and Peter Hicks,
> *Palladio's Rome* (New Haven: Yale University Press, 2006)

Most Holy Father, there are many who, on bringing their feeble judgment to bear on what is written concerning the great achievements of the Romans – the feats of arms, the city of Rome, and the wondrous skill shown in the opulence, ornamentation, and grandeur of their buildings – have come to the conclusion that these achievements are more likely to be fables than facts. I, however, have always seen – and still do see – things differently. For, bearing in mind the divine quality of the ancients' minds as revealed in the remains still to be seen among the ruins of Rome, I do not find it unreasonable to believe that much of what we consider impossible seemed, to them, exceedingly simple. With this in mind, since I have been so completely taken up by these antiquities – not only in making every effort to consider them in great detail and measure them carefully but also in assiduously reading the best authors and comparing their writings with the built works – I think that I have managed to acquire a certain understanding of ancient architecture. This is something that gives me, at once, enormous pleasure – from the intellectual appreciation of so excellent a matter – and enormous grief – at the sight of what you could almost call the corpse of this great, noble city, once queen of the world, so cruelly butchered. Hence, given that all men owe respect to their parents and their homeland, I feel obliged to muster what little ability I have so that, as far as possible, an image may survive – barely more than a shadow – of what is, in fact, the universal homeland of all Christians and which, at one time, was so noble and powerful that men began to believe that she alone, of all earthly things, was above fate and, contrary to the natural course of things, not subject to death and destined to last forever. Wherefore it appeared that time, as if envious of the glory of mortals and yet not fully confident in its own strength alone, worked in concert with fate and the wicked, infidel barbarians who, in addition to time's gouging file and poisonous bite, brought the fierce onslaught of fire and steel. Thus, those celebrated works that would today have been in the full flower of their beauty were burnt and destroyed by the evil wrath and ruthless violence of wicked men, beasts indeed. The destruction, however, is not entire – the framework survives almost intact, but without ornaments; you could almost describe this as the bones of a body without the flesh. And yet, why are we complaining about the Goths, Vandals, and other perfidious enemies of the Latin name when the very men who, as fathers and guardians, should have defended Rome's wretched remains did in fact spend a great deal of time and energy trying to destroy those relics and to expunge their memory? How many Pontiffs, Holy Father – men who held the same office as Your Holiness but who had neither your wisdom nor your qualities or magnanimity – how many of these Pontiffs, I say again, allowed ancient temples, statues, arches, and other buildings – the glory of their founders – to fall prey to ruin and spoliation? How many of them allowed the excavation of the foundations to get at some pozzolana, such that in a very short time those buildings collapsed? How much mortar was made from the statues and other ornaments of the ancients? I would go so far as to say that all this new Rome that can be seen today – however grand, beautiful, and marvelously ornamented with palaces, churches, and other buildings – is built using mortar made from ancient marbles. Not without great sorrow can I reflect upon the fact that since I have been in Rome – which is more or less twelve years now – many fine things have been ruined: for example, the Meta that was in the Via Alexandrina, the arch that was at the entrance to the Baths of Diocletian, the Temple of Ceres in the Via Sacra, and a part of the Forum Transitorium, which only a few days ago was burnt and destroyed, the marbles being made into mortar; the greater part of the basilica in the forum ruined [blank space] and in addition to this the multitude of columns being damaged or broken in two and the many architraves and fine friezes reduced to fragments. It was an outrage similarly for our times to have tolerated such a thing. Indeed, you could say that such actions make Hannibal, to name but one, look God-fearing. Therefore, Holy Father, let it not be the lowest of Your Holiness's priorities to ensure that – out of respect to those divine spirits, the remembrance of whom encourages and incites to virtue the intellects among us today – what little remains of this ancient mother of the glory and renown of Italy is not to be completely destroyed and ruined by the wicked and the ignorant. Unfortunately, even here these people have perpetrated evil deeds against those souls who, with their blood, brought so much glory to the world, to this state and to us. Rather, by preserving the example of the ancients, may Your Holiness seek to equal and better them, as indeed you have done through your magnificent buildings, by supporting and favoring the virtues, reawakening genius, rewarding virtuous endeavors, and by sowing that most holy seed of peace among Christian princes...

However, to return to the matter I mentioned briefly earlier, I record that Your Holiness commanded me to make a drawing of ancient Rome – at least as far as can be understood from that which can be seen today – with those buildings that are sufficiently well preserved such that they can be drawn out exactly as they were, without error, using true principles, and making those members that are entirely ruined and can no longer be seen correspond with those that are still standing and can be seen...

And since telling the difference between ancient and modern buildings, or between those more ancient and less ancient, might seem to some to be difficult, and so as not to leave any doubt whatsoever in the mind of someone who wishes to acquire this ability to discriminate, I say that this can be done with little effort. The fact is, there are only three styles [*maniere*] of buildings in Rome: the first is that built by the worthy ancients, who lasted from the first emperors up until the time when Rome was destroyed and ruined by the Goths and other barbarians; the second lasted for the period that Rome was dominated by the Goths and one hundred years thereafter; the third, from that time up until our time...

Thus having been sufficiently clear concerning which ancient buildings in Rome we wish to demonstrate, and also how easy it is to distinguish them from the rest, all that remains is to tell you of the way in which we decided to survey and draw them, so that whoever wishes to work in architecture may know how to do both one and the other without making mistakes and be aware that, in our drawing up of this work, we were not guided by chance or practice alone but relied on true theory. As for the method we used – surveying with a magnetic compass – since I have never seen it mentioned nor learnt of its use by any of the ancients, I think that it was invented by the moderns. However, it seems to me to be worthwhile to give careful instruction in it to those who know nothing about it. You should therefore make yourself an instrument that is round and flat, like an astrolabe, and has a diameter of two palms – it may be more or less, following the judgment of the person who wants to use it...

And since the way of drawing specific to the architect is different from that of the painter, I shall say what I think opportune so that all the measurements can be understood and all the members of the buildings can be determined without error. The way the architect draws buildings, then, is divided into three parts. The first part is the plan – what they mean is the flat drawing. The second is the exterior wall, with its ornaments. The third is the interior wall, also with its ornaments...

Besides the three styles [*modi*] of architecture proposed and mentioned above, and in order to satisfy even more completely the desire of those who like to see and understand well all the things that are to be drawn, we have in addition drawn in perspective some buildings we thought lent themselves to it. We did this so as to enable the eye to see and judge the grace of their likeness, which is demonstrated by the beautiful proportion and symmetry of these buildings, and which does not appear in the drawing of buildings that are measured architecturally... And even though this type of drawing in perspective is the preserve of the painter, it is nevertheless also useful for the architect. Just as the painter must have knowledge of the architecture in order to be able to render the ornaments to their correct measurements and proportions, so the architect needs to know perspective because through this exercise he can better imagine the whole building furnished with its ornaments. Of these ornaments, there is no need to say more than that they all derive from the five orders [*ordini*] used by the ancients, namely Doric, Ionic, Corinthian, Tuscan, and Attic...

As and when necessary, we shall describe the orders of all of them, taking as a presupposition the things in Vitruvius. There are two further works [*opere*] in addition to the three mentioned: namely Attic and Tuscan, which were not, however, much used by the ancients... And there will also be many buildings composed of multiple styles [*maniere*], such as Ionic and Corinthian, Doric and Corinthian, Tuscan and Doric, depending upon what seemed best to their maker [*arthefice*] when matching these buildings appropriately to their intention, especially in the case of temples.

12

'ROMETTA', VILLA D'ESTE

c.1568

When visitors originally entered the gardens of the Villa d'Este, built for Cardinal Ippolito d'Este at Tivoli between 1563 and 1568, it was from the bottom, and they made their way across the initial level spaces before climbing towards the villa itself. When they reached the Walk of a Hundred Fountains (with its terracotta reliefs of events from Ovid's *Metamorphoses*), they could turn right and arrive at the Fountain of Rome, which was in itself a metamorphic attempt to recreate the now ruined temples and moments of the eternal city. Like a stage set, or architectural *fons scenae*, the *Rometta* (little Rome) was represented by a range of temples, reconstituted on a reduced scale, as a backdrop; these are placed in seven groups to symbolize the Seven Hills of Rome.

Three sculptures or 'performers' are in front, and on a lower level is represented the island of San Bartolomeo, which in antiquity was shaped as a boat, with an obelisk at its center. The statues on the 'stage' were of a wolf feeding Romulus and Remus, a

Giovanni Francesco Venturini, Pirro Ligorio's *Rometta* (Little Rome) at the Villa D'Este, from *Le Fontane di Roma*, 1691. University of Pennsylvania.

statue of Roma Victrix showing the triumph of virtue, and a copy of a famous Roman sculpture of a Lion Attacking a Horse (an allegory of Rome conquering Tivoli).

It recalls Joachim du Bellay's poem sequence *Les Antiquitez de Rome* (*see* Extract 15) in which the 'corpse' of ancient Rome or its 'dust of ruins' could be resuscitated. But the Tivoli scene is based upon the extensive explorations of Roman antiquities in the 16th century by Pirro Ligorio, who excavated the site of Hadrian's villa, adjacent to his reformulation of the monastery and garden that became the Villa d'Este. He also drew an elaborate reconstruction of the ancient city in his *Libri dell'antichita* and *Antiquae Urbis Imago* (both 1561), a cartographic reconstruction of fourth-century AD Rome. This endless project to re-envisage ancient Rome was taken further by Giovanni Francesco Venturini in the late 17th century.

13

SEBASTIAN SERLIO

c.1540

As we read Serlio's account of ancient Roman ruins in Book Three of his treatise *On Architecture* (written around 1540 but not published until 1584), and think about his labors, we should imagine him equipped with not only a pencil and paper for drawing and writing, but also instruments of measure: rulers of various lengths, measuring tapes, fixed and adjustable angles, and plumb bobs. Types of stone and of shape obviously mattered in his surveys, but also – and maybe more so – dimensions. He was also concerned with names, or more exactly naming the bits and pieces he unearthed or observed. In several instances, material things clarified verbal representations. Ruins, then, prompted different kinds of descriptive and interpretative work: sizing them up, rendering what he had measured in both orthogonal and perspective views, and then naming all their parts with the right designation, checked against, and sometimes challenging, his written sources. About their significance, and by implication Rome's greatness, he had no doubt, hence the inscription that caps the frontispiece's broken arcade: ROMA QUANTA FUIT IPSA RUINA DOCET (Rome's very ruins teach how great she was).

One imagines he had a shovel, too, for many of the ruins were partially buried. The Arch of Constantine, near the Colosseum, for example, was buried under fragments and soil up to its arches. Had the accumulation not been cleared away, his survey and close description would have been limited to the upper decorative parts. The Arch of Septimius was similarly difficult: 'This arch is at present buried up to the top of the pedestals, but it was partly excavated to measure it. However, it was impossible to measure the base of the pedestal because it was buried amongst many ruins which were difficult to move.'

Rome was the focus of his study, but Serlio also went in search of ruins elsewhere, in Italy of course, but also in France, for that is where he sought both recognition and employment. Architectures and ruins still farther afield interested him too, in Greece, of course, but also Egypt, to whose buildings he devoted a short 'Treatise on Some of the Marvels of Egypt', appended to his book on antiquities. Though he hadn't seen what he describes, the treatise's opening sentences, which we have included here, after our excerpt from the book's dedicatory preface, show that while ruins of all sorts

Frontispiece to Book Three of Sebastian Serlio's *On Architecture*, 1584.
Fisher Fine Arts Library, University of Pennsylvania.

compelled him to use his instruments of measurement and knowledge of texts, they also inspired a dreamy sort of wonder.

>Book Three, *Sebastian Serlio On Architecture*, translated by
>Vaughan Hart and Peter Hicks (New Haven: Yale University Press, 2001)

To the Most Christian King, François, Sebastiano Serlio,
I have often thought about the grandeur of the ancient Romans and their fine judgment in building, which can still be seen in the ruins of the very many buildings of great variety in ancient Rome and in many parts of Italy as well as abroad. Therefore, in addition to my other labors on architecture, I decided to put in one volume, if not all, then at least a majority of those antiquities so that any person who enjoyed architecture could, wherever they find themselves, take this book to hand and see all the marvelous ruins of those Roman buildings. If these were not still standing, the writings which recount the many marvels of their constructions would perhaps not have been believed. Since the beautiful and useful art of architecture has in these times returned to the heights it reached in the happy era of the Roman and Greek inventors of the beautiful arts, and since your Majesty is not only gifted in the theory and practice of the many other branches of learning, but also a knowledgeable lover of architecture - as the large number of very beautiful and marvelous buildings commissioned by you in many parts of your great kingdom bear witness - I wanted to set this volume of mine, into which I have put all my skill, under the very broad branches of your Majesty's intelligence in the hope that it, with its shade, may be able to make this small thing large.

Treatise on Some of the Marvels of Egypt

It is true that to our eyes the things of the ancient Romans are wonderful. However, anyone who could have seen the buildings of the Greeks - which have by now all disappeared and many of whose spoils adorn Rome and Venice - would perhaps say that they surpassed those of the Romans. But what should we ourselves say to the absolutely extraordinary remains of Egypt, which seem more like dreams and visions than real objects? Nevertheless, the fact that Diodorus Siculus professes to have seen the remains of some of them makes me believe that they really existed. Amongst other things, he describes in wonderment a tomb belonging to an Egyptian King called Ozymandias...

14

LUDOVICO ARIOSTO

1516

The Italian poet Ariosto's epic poem *Orlando Furioso* tells how Orlando is driven mad by jealousy but eventually his friend, the English knight Duke Astolfo, travels to the Moon to recover Orlando's lost wits. The extract reproduced here is from John Harington's English translation of 1591.

Orlando Furioso, translated by John Harington (London: J. Parker, 1634), book 34, stanzas 78-82

78

He saw great Cities seated in faire places,
That ouerthrowne quite topsie turvie stood,
He askt and learnd, the cause of their defaces
Was treason, that doth neuer turne to good:
He saw fowle serpents, with faire womens faces,
Of coyners and of thieues the cursed brood,
He saw fine glasses, all in peeces broken,
Of seruice lost in court, a wofull token.

79

Of mingled broth he saw a mightie masse,
That to no use, all spilt on ground did lye,
He askt his teacher, and he heard it was,
The frutlesse almes that men giue when they dye:
Then by a faire greene mountaine he did passe,
That once smelt sweet, but now it stinks perdye,
This was that gift (be't said without offence)
That *Constantin* gaue *Silvester* long since.

Frontispiece to John Harington's English translation of Ariosto's *Orlando Furioso*, 1591.

80

Of birdlymd rodds, he saw no little store,
And these (O Ladyes sayre) your bewties be,
I do omit ten thousand things and more
Like vnto these, that there the Duke did see:
For all that here is lost, there euermore
Is kept, and thither in a trise doth flee,
Howbeit more nor lesse there was no folly,
For still that here with vs remaineth wholly.

81

He saw some of his owne lost time and deeds,
But yet he knew them not to be his owne,
They seemd to him disguisd in so strange weeds,
Till his instructer made them better knowne:
But last, the thing which no man thinks he needs,
Yet each man needeth most, to him was showne,
By name mans wit, which here we leese so fast,
As that one substance, all the other past.

82

It seemd to be a body moyst and soft,
And apt to mount by eu'ry exhalation,
And when it hither mounted was aloft,
It there was kept in pots of such a fashion,
As we call Iarrs, where oyle is kept in oft:
The Duke beheld with no small admiration,
The Iarrs of wit, amongst which one had writ,
Vpon the side thereof, *Orlandos* wit.

15

Joachim du Bellay

1558

Du Bellay (1522-60) was one of the great early modern French poets, much influenced by Petrarch and by his friend, Pierre de Ronsard. From his four and a half years in Rome, he composed two sonnet sequences: *Les Regrets*, and *Les Antiquitez de Rome* (1558). In the second he is 'intent on the sheer fact of ruin', writes Richard Helgerson (Penn Press, 2006); Helgerson also notes that good translations are best read *en face* with the original. So in this instance the first and the last of the selected sonnets (numbered according to the original sequence) are provided with parts of the French text. The sequence was translated in 1591 by Edmund Spenser as *The Ruins of Rome*, which is used here. Helgerson's prose versions are good modern renditions.

Les Antiquitez de Rome, 1558, in Edmund Spenser,
The Ruins of Rome in Poetical Works of Edmund Spenser
(Boston: Little and Brown, 1842)

Nouveau venu que cherchez Rome en Rome,
Et rien de Rome en Rome n'apperçois,
Ces vieux palais, ces vieux arcz que tu vois,
Et ces vieux murs, c'est ce que Rome en nomme.

Voy quel orgueil, quelle ruine: et comme
Celle qui mist le monde sous ses loix
Pour donner tout, se donta quelquefois,
Et devint proye au temps, qui tout consomme...

Thou stranger which for Rome in Rome here seekest,
And nought of Rome in Rome perceiv'st at all,
These same old walls, old arches, which thou seest,
Old Palaces, is that which Rome men call.
Behold what wreak, what ruin, and what waste,
And how that she, which with her mighty power

BOOK OF RUINS

Tam'd all the world, hath tam'd herself at last,
The prey of time, which all things doth devour.
Rome now of Rome is th' only <u>funeral</u>,
And only Rome of Rome hath victory;
Ne ought save Tyber hastening to his fall
Remains of all: O world's inconstancy.
That which is firm doth flit and fall <u>away</u>,
And that is flitting, doth abide and stay.

Who lists to see, what ever nature, art,
And heaven could do, O Rome, thee let him see,
In case thy greatness he can guess in <u>heart</u>,
By that which but the picture is of thee.
Rome is no more: but if the shade of Rome
May of the body yield a seeming sight,
It's like a corse drawn forth out of the tomb
By Magick skill out of eternal <u>night</u>:
The corpse of Rome in ashes is entombed,
And her great sprite rejoinèd to the sprite
Of this great mass, is in the same enwombed;
But her brave writings, which her famous merit
In spite of time, out of the dust doth rear,
Do make her idol through the world appear…

Ye sacred ruins, and ye tragic sights,
Which only do the name of Rome retain,
Old monuments, which of so famous sprites
The honour yet in ashes do maintain:
Triumphant arcs, spires neighbors to the sky,
That you to see doth th' heaven itself appall,
Alas, by little ye to nothing fly,
The people's fable, and the spoil of all:
And though your frames do for a time make war
'Gainst time, yet time in time shall ruinate
Your works and names, and your last relics mar.
My <u>sad</u> desires, rest therefore moderate:
For if that time make ends of things so sure,
It also will end the <u>pain</u>, which I endure…

JOACHIM DU BELLAY

Hieronymus Cock, after Maerten van Heemskerck, *St Jerome in a Landscape with Ruins*, etching on paper, 1570. National Gallery of Art, Washington, D.C.

These heapes of stones, these old wals which ye see,
Were first enclosures but of salvage soyle;
And these brave pallaces, which maystred bee
Of Time, were shepheards cottages some-while.
Then tooke the shepheards kingly ornaments,
And the stout hynde arm'd his right hand with steele:
Eftsoones their rule of yearely presidents
Grew great, and sixe months greater a great deele;
Which, made perpetuall, rose to so great might,
That thence th' imperiall eagle rooting tooke,
Till th' heaven it selfe, opposing gainst her might,
Her power to Peters successor betooke;
Who, shepheard like, (as Fates the same foreseeing)
Doth shew that all things turne to their first being...

When that brave honour of the Latine name,
Which mear'd her rule with Africa and Byze,
With Thames inhabitants of noble fame,
And they which see the dawning day arize,
Her nourslings did with mutinous uprore
Harten against her selfe, her conquer'd spoile,

Which she had wonne from all the world afore,
Of all the world was spoyl'd within a while.
So, when the compast course of the universe
In six and thirtie thousand yeares is ronne,
The bands of th' elements shall backe reverse
To their first discord, and be quite undonne:
The seedes, of which all things at first were bred,
Shall in great Chaos wombe againe be hid…

Who list the Romane greatnes forth to figure,
Him needeth not to seeke for usage right
Of line, or lead, or rule, or squaire, to measure
Her length, her breadth, her deepnes, or her hight;
But him behooves to vew in compasse round
All that the ocean graspes in his long armes;
Be it where the yerely starre doth scortch the ground,
Or where colde Boreas blowes his bitter stormes.
Rome was th' whole world, and al the world was Rome,
And if things nam'd their names doo equalize,
When land and sea ye name, then name ye Rome,
And naming Rome, ye land and sea comprize:
For th' aunciency plot of Rome, displayed plaine,
The map of all the wide world doth containe…

Hope ye, my verses, that posteritie
Of age ensuing shall you ever read?
Hope ye that ever immortalitie
So meane harpes worke may chalenge for her meed?
If under heaven anie endurance were,
These moniments, which not in paper writ,
But in porphyre and marble doo appeare,
Might well have hop'd to have obtained it.
Nath'les, my lute, whom Phoebus deigned to give,
Cease not to sound these olde antiquities:
For if that Time doo let thy glorie live,
Well maist thou boast, how ever base thou bee,
That thou art first which of thy nation song
Th' olde honour of the people gowned long

JOACHIM DU BELLAY

Esperez vous que la posterité
Doive (mes vers) pour tout jamais vous lire?
Esperez vous que l'oeuvre d'une lyr
Puisse acquerir telle immortalité?

Si sous le ciel fust quelque eternité
Les monuments que je vous ay faire dire,
Non en papier, mais en marbre et porphyre...
Eussnet gardé leur vive antiquité...

16

Edmund Spenser

1591 and 1596

Spenser was much concerned with mutability, on which he wrote two cantos that would presumably have gone into his uncompleted poem *The Faerie Queene* (1596), and were first published in the folio of 1609. His *Ruines of Time* is narrated by the ghost of Verulamium (Roman St Albans) and specifically addresses actual ruins, both real and imaginary, while the mutability cantos touch upon the frailty of almost everything. In *The Faerie Queene*, two passages in particular describe the destruction of the Bower of Bliss, and Britomart, personifying Chastity, departing the decayed and vanished glories of the House of Cupid.

The Ruines of Time, in *Poetical Works of Edmund Spenser*
(Boston: Little and Brown, 1842)

O Rome! thy Ruin I lament and rue,
And in thy Fall, my fatal Overthrow,
That whilom was, whilst Heavens with equal View
Deign'd to behold me, and their Gifts bestow,
The Picture of thy Pride in pompous Show:
And of the whole World as thou wast the Empress,
So I of this small Northern World was Princess.

To tell the Beauty of my Buildings fair,
Adorn'd with purest Gold, and precious Stone;
To tell my Riches, and Endowments rare,
That by my Foes are now all spent and gone:
To tell my Forces, matchable to none,
Were but lost Labour, that few would believe,
And with rehearsing, would me more agrieve.
High Towers, fair Temples, goodly Theaters,
Strong Walls, rich porches, princely palaces,
Large Streets, brave Houses, sacred Sepulchers,

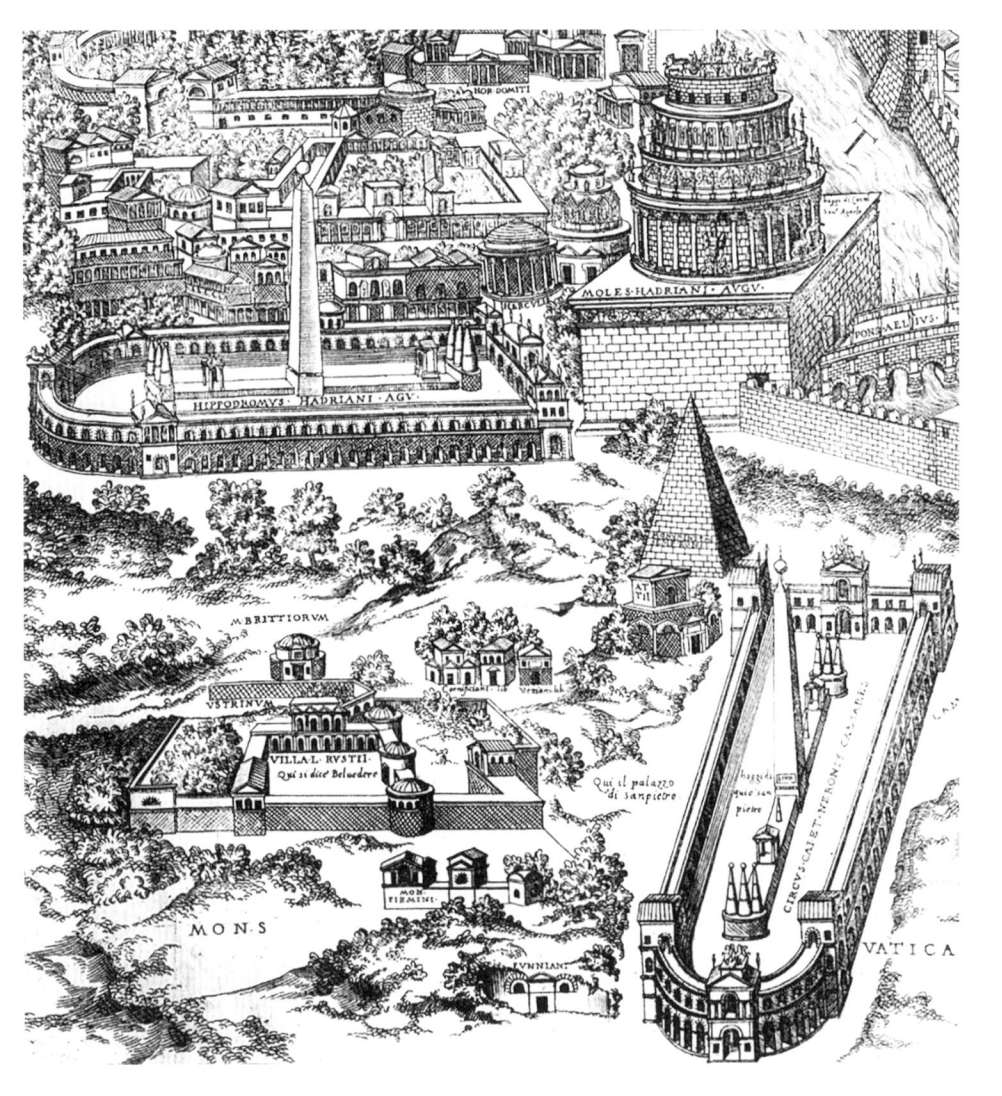

Pirro Ligorio, Rome (detail), from *Antiquae Urbis Imago*, copper engraving, 1561.
Fisher Fine Arts Library, University of Pennsylvania.

> Sure Gates, sweet Gardens, stately Galleries,
> Wrought with fair Pillors, and fine Imageries:
> All those (O pity!) now are turn'd to Dust,
> And overgrown with black Oblivion's Rust.
>
> Thereto for warlike Power, and Peoples Store,
> In Britanny was none to match with me,
> That many often did aby full sore:

Ne Troynovant, though elder Sister she,
With my great Forces may compared be;
That stout Pendragon to his Peril felt,
Who in a Siege seven Years about me dwelt.

But long e'er this, Bunduca, Britonness,
Her mighty Hoast against my Bulwarks brought;
Bunduca, that victorious Conqueress,
That lifting up her brave heroick Thought
'Bove Womens Weakness, with the Romans fought,
Fought, and in Field against them thrice prevailed;
Yet was she foil'd, whenas she me assailed.

And though at last by Force I conquer'd were
Of hardy Saxons, and became their Thrall;
Yet was I with much Bloodshed bought full dear,
And priz'd with Slaughter of their General:
The Monument of whose sad Funeral,
For Wonder of the World, long in me lasted,
But now to nought through Spoil of Time is wasted.

Wasted it is, as if it never were;
And all the rest that me so honour'd made,
And of the World admired every where,
Is turn'd to Smoak, that doth to nothing fade:
And of that Brightness now appears no Shade,
But griesly Shades, such as do haunt in Hell,
With fearful Fiends, that in deep Darkness dwell.

The destruction of the Bower of Bliss,
from *The Faerie Queene*, Book II, canto 12, in
Poetical Works of Edmund Spenser (Boston: Little and Brown, 1842)

But all those pleasant bowres and Pallace braue,
Guyon broke downe, with rigour pittilesse;
Ne ought their goodly workmanship might saue
Them from the tempest of his wrathfulnesse,
But that their blisse he turn'd to balefulnesse:
Their groues he feld, their gardins did deface,

Their arbers spoyle, their Cabinets suppresse,
Their banket houses burne, their buildings race,
And of the fairest late, now made the fowlest place.
Then led they her away, and eke that knight
They with them led, both sorrowfull and sad:
The way they came, the same retourn'd they right,
Till they arriued, where they lately had
Charm'd those wild-beasts, that rag'd with furie mad.
Which now awaking, fierce at them gan fly,
As in their mistresse reskew, whom they lad;
But them the Palmer soone did pacify.
Then *Guyon* askt, what meant those beastes, which there did ly.

Said he, These seeming beasts are men indeed,
Whom this Enchauntresse hath transformed thus,
Whylome her louers, which her lusts did feed,
Now turned into figures hideous,
According to their mindes like monstruous.
Sad end (quoth he) of life intemperate,
And mournefull meed of ioyes delicious:
But Palmer, if it mote thee so aggrate,
Let them returned be vnto their former state.
Streight way he with his vertuous staffe them strooke,
And streight of beasts they comely men became;
Yet being men they did vnmanly looke,
And stared ghastly, some for inward shame,
And some for wrath, to see their captiue Dame.
But one aboue the rest in speciall,
That had an hog beene late, hight *Grille* by name,
Repined greatly, and did him miscall,
That had from hoggish forme him brought to naturall.

Said *Guyon*, See the mind of beastly man,
That hath so soone forgot the excellence
Of his creation, when he life began,
That now he chooseth, with vile difference,
To be a beast, and lacke intelligence.
To whom the Palmer thus, The donghill kind
Delights in filth and foule incontinence:
Let *Grill* be *Grill*, and haue his hoggish mind,
But let vs hence depart, whilest wether serues and wind.

BOOK OF RUINS

    Britomart departs the House of Cupid,
        from *The Faerie Queene*,
           Book III, canto 12

Returning backe, those goodly roomes, which erst
She saw so rich and royally arayd,
Now vanisht vtterly, and cleane subuerst
She found, and all their glory quite decayd,
That sight of such a chaunge her much dismayd.
Thence forth descending to that perlous Porch,
Those dreadfull flames she also found delayd,
And quenched quite, like a consumed torch,
That erst all entrers wont so cruelly to scorch.
More easie issew now, then entrance late
She found: for now that fained dreadfull flame,
Which chokt the porch of that enchaunted gate,
And passage bard to all, that thither came,
Was vanisht quite, as it were not the same,
And gaue her leaue at pleasure forth to passe.
Th'Enchaunter selfe, which all that fraud did frame,
To haue efforst the loue of that faire lasse,
Seeing his worke now wasted deepe engrieued was.

17

Giacomo Lauro

1612

Giocomo Lauro (active 1583-1645) first published his *Antiquae Orbis Splendor*, or *The Splendors of Ancient Rome*, in two editions in 1612. Subsequent editions of what was obviously a much used survey, were enlarged around 1630, appeared between 1637 and 1641. An exhibition of this collection was presented at the Getty Museum by Penny Buckley in 1974.

Lauro's central ambition was to draw how he envisaged the original buildings of Rome – its amphitheatres, circuses, temples, tombs – rather than to represent, as others would so, their current state in the early 17th century, overgrown with ivy and partly ruined. He drew upon miscellaneous literary descriptions as he sought to envisage the original appearance of Rome's splendors. His specific images, over 160 eventually, take us to the Capitoline, the Campus Martius, the Baths of Agrippa, the Naumachia of Nero, and dozens of other monuments. But the overall vision of the original city makes wonderfully clear his imaginative grasp of the task he set himself.

Giacomo Lauro, *The Naumachia of Nero, Rome*, from *Antiquae Urbis Splendor*, engraving, 1612. Fisher Fine Arts Library, University of Pennsylvania.

18

JOHN WEBSTER

1613–14

In Act V, Scene III of Webster's macabre Jacobean tragedy *The Duchess of Malfi*, the characters Delio and Antonio admire the melancholy of ruins and the echoes that they themselves contrive. Cities and churches, says Antonio, 'Must have like death that we have,' emphasizing the way that ruins act a reminder of our own mortality.

The Duchess of Malfi (London: J. M. Dent, 1940)

Delio This fortification
Grew from the ruins of an ancient Abbey:
And to yond side o' the river lies a wall
(Piece of a cloister) which in my opinion
Gives the best echo that you ever heard;
So hollow and so dismal, and withal
So plain in the distinction of our words
That many have supposed it is a spirit
That answers.

Antonio I do love these ancient ruins:
We never tread upon them, but we set
Our foot upon some reverend history…
But all things have their end:
Churches and Cities (which have diseases like to men)
Must have like death that we have.
    Echo – like death that we have

Delio Now the Echo hath caught you.

Antonio It groan'd (me thought) and gave
A very deadly accent?
    Echo – Deadly accent

JOHN WEBSTER

Delio I told you 'twas a pretty one; you may make it
A huntsman, or a falconer, a musician,
Or a thing of sorrow.
      Echo – A thing of sorrow.

19

INIGO JONES

1655

The famous ruins on Salisbury Plain prompted the architect Inigo Jones to go beyond mere admiration and propose a 'restoration', a reconstruction of ancient architectural work, untainted by 'modern conceits' (medieval chronicles) or more recent 'popish' affectations. The enigmatic site had recently attracted the interest of others, including John Aubrey, who was simply curious about it, Francis Bacon, for whom it demanded respect, and King James, whose interest seems to have been a matter of national pride. Unlike later interpreters, Jones mistakenly viewed the ruins as the remnants of a Roman building, and his drawings and text sought to 'restore' it to the lineage of Roman architectural history, roughly parallel to the Roman Verulamium to which Spenser referred in *The Ruines of Time*.

Understood as an example of an architecture that had achieved 'rare perfection', it was to serve as a model for contemporary and future building. Interpreting the disproportionately wide monoliths as classical columns required a considerable leap of imagination, and a rather free interpretation of the simplest of the architectural orders, the Tuscan, whose 'rude, plain, and simple' form and construction Alberti

Hassal, *Stone-Heng Restored*, engraving, 1725. Fisher Fine Arts Library, University of Pennsylvania.

and Palladio also understood as radically primitive, and therefore germinal. Walpole's later quip, 'It is remarkable that whoever has treated of that monument, has bestowed it on whatever class of antiquity he was particularly fond of,' likewise attests to the hermeneutic challenge of the 'first face of *Antiquity*' on British soil.

20

Gianlorenzo Bernini

1665

The idea that all things fall to ruin in time was addressed in a number of Bernini's works, both architectural and sculptural. According to Fréart de Chantelou, the master explained to Louis XIV that the figure of *Father Time*, half of the sculpture he dedicated to the famous commonplace *Truth Discovered by Time*, would rise above 'columns, obelisks, and mausoleums, and these, ruined and destroyed by *Time*, would serve to support him in the air'. Although the other half of the planned work, *Truth*, was finished and can be seen today in the Galleria Borghese in Rome, the block of stone from which *Time* was to be carved remained untouched on the day Bernini died, standing in the forecourt of his house, straight from the quarry. The only indication of his intention for the ruin-seated figure that survives is a crude sketch.

Bernini was hardly alone among Baroque artists in his use of uncarved rock and ruined architecture as the base for sculptural groups. Most famous among the works that utilize this conceit is perhaps Nicola Salvi's Trevi Fountain, carved decades later. But no less interesting is the Four Rivers Fountain in Piazza Navona, 1651, by Bernini himself. Possibly the most curious indication of his attitude toward ruins is the so-called ruined bridge that connected the Palazzo Barberini in Rome to its extensive gardens, illustrated here.

Though built in 1689, the bridge seems to have been conceived in 1678; the idea may have come from Bernini himself, his patron Cardinal Francesco Barberini, or someone from the latter's circle of scholars, artists, and antiquarians. The cardinal's dedication to erudition was unmatched at the time. No less impressive was his support of leading intellectuals, including the great Jesuit polymath Athanasius Kircher, whom Barberini supported for 30 years, the Frenchman Francoise Peiresc, one of Europe's leading antiquarians, Girolamo Aleandro, a leading archaeologist, and a surprising range of painters and poets: Peter Paul Rubens, Nicolas Poussin, and John Milton. As part of his ambitious cultural program he built up a library second only to the Vatican collection, a museum of antiquities, and in the Palazzo's gardens a zoo, while also serving as a great patron of musical, operatic, and theatrical productions – Italy's first opera house was attached to his palazzo.

Gian Lorenzo Bernini, ruined bridge at Palazzao Barberini, 1689.

Also attached to the palazzo were gardens at the level of the *piano nobile*. They could be reached by the ruined bridge, which extended one of the building's main axes to a corresponding line in the garden, terminating in an obelisk (the hieroglyphs of which were 'deciphered' by Kircher). The ruined arch also combined contemporary and ancient emblems, from Barberini bees to Egyptian symbols. As for the bridge itself, Time's corrosive effects are evident in the combination of *spolia*: column capitals of different dimensions, broken, displaced, or absent arch segments, sub-surface materials exposed next to dressed surfaces, and an apparently improvised deck.

PAUL FRÉART DE CHANTELOU
Diary of Cavaliere Bernini's Visit to France, 1665, translated from M. de Chantelou,
Journal du Voyage du Cavalier Bernini en France
(Paris: Gazette des Beaux-Arts, 1885)

August 13
[discussing with Bernini and King Louis XIV the difficulty of making a figure carved in marble appear to be lightweight] M. de Créqui mentioned the statue of Truth which is in the Cavaliere's [Bernini's] house in Rome: it was the perfection of beauty. The Cavaliere said he had done this statue for his house, but

that the figure of Time, which supports the figure of Truth and points to its meaning, was not yet finished: his idea is to represent Time bearing Truth aloft, and to show by the same means the effects of time which in the end ruin or consumes everything; for in the model he had made columns, obelisks, and tombs which appear to be overturned and destroyed by time, though they were nevertheless the things that support him in the air; without them he could not remain there, 'although he has winds', he added with a smile. He said it was a saying current in Rome that Truth was only to be found in Bernini's house.

Then he began to describe to the King something from one of his plays where a character is reciting the tale of his misfortunes and speaks of the unjust persecution of which he is the victim. In order to console him, one of his friends begs him to take courage, saying that the reign of calumny will not endure forever, and that time will at last reveal the Truth: to which the unhappy creature replied, 'It is true that Time reveals Truth, but he often doesn't reveal it in time.' The King let it be seen that the idea much amused.

III

THE LONG 18TH CENTURY

21

THOMAS BURNET

1681

One of the central works on the ruins of the 'natural' world was Thomas Burnet's *Telluris Theoria Sacra* (1681, with an English translation, *The Sacred Theory of the Earth*, appearing in 1684-89). This important book and the responses to it were discussed in the fifth chapter of Marjorie Hope Nicolson's *Mountain Gloom and Mountain Glory* (1959). Burnet's thesis was that the world was originally a perfect globe, 'so marvellous, that it ought to be considered as a particular Effect of Divine Art... A Piece without Foundation or Corner-Stone... A Piece of Divine Geometry or Architecture'. But that was destroyed at the Great Deluge, unleashed by God to punish humans. This huge history he learnt while traveling in the Alps. Such an idea was both embraced and almost as quickly celebrated for the excitements of such a ruined universe and seems to have authorized humans to find instances of ruins with which to decorate designed landscapes. Passages from Burnet here are followed by two selections from Charles Cotton (1639-87) who, in *The Wonders of the Peak* (1681), asserted that the gardens of Chatsworth House in Derbyshire 'show... what Art could, in spite of Nature, do'; in other words, human ingenuity could reform the ruins of nature in specific places and make a paradise after the deluge. In contrast, he vilified the surrounding Derbyshire countryside, which 'teems with warts and torrents, the Pudenda, of nature', one of which he named the 'The Devil's Arse'.

The Sacred Theory of the Earth (London: John Hooke, 1719)

But when we speak of a *Rising World*, and the Contemplation of it, we do not mean this of the *Great Universe*; for who can describe the Original of that vast Frame? But we speak of the *Sublunary World*, this Earth and its dependencies, which rose out of a Chaos about six thousand years ago; And seeing it hath faln to our lot to act upon this Stage, to have our present home and residence here, its seems most reasonable, and the place design'd by Providence, where we should first imploy our thoughts to understand the works of God and Nature. We have accordingly therefore design'd in this Work to give an account of the

Frontispiece and title page of Thomas Burnet's
The Sacred Theory of the Earth (1681),
an English translation 1684-89.

Original of the Earth, and of all the great and General Changes that it hath already undergone, or is hence forwards to undergo, till the Consummation of all Things. For if from those Principles we have here taken, and that Theory we have begun in these Two First Books, we can deduce with success and clearness the Origin of the Earth, and those States of it that are already past; Following the same Thred, and by the conduct of the same Theory, we will pursue its Fate and History through future Ages, and mark all the great Changes and Conversions that attend it *while Day and Night shall last*; that is, so long as it continues an Earth.

BOOK OF RUINS

CHARLES COTTON
The Wonders of the Peake (London: Joanna Brome, 1681)

The sixth WONDER, Peak's Arse, commonly call'd the DEVIL'S ARSE.
Hence an uneven mile below, in sight
Of this strange Cliffe, and almost opposite,
Lies *Castleton*, a place of noted fame,
Which from the *Castle* there derives its name.
Ent'ring the *Village* presently y'are met
With a clear, swift, and murm'ring *Rivolet*,
Towards whose *source*, if up the stream you look
On your right hand close by, your Eye is strook
With a stupendous Rock, raising to high
His craggy *Temples* t'wards the Azure Sky,
That if we this should with the rest compare,
They *Hillocks*, *Mole-hills*, *Warts* and *Pebbles* are.
This, as if *King* of all the *Mountains* round,
Is on the top with an old *Tower* crown'd,
An *Antick* thing, fit to make people stare;
But of no use, either in Peace; or War.
Under this *Castle* yawns a dreadful *Cave*,
Whose sight may well astonish the most brave,
And make his pause, ere further he proceed
T'explore what is those gloomy vaults lie hid.
The *Brook*, which from one mighty *Spring* does flow,
Thro' a deep stony Channel runs below,
Whilst ore a Path level, and broad enough
For human *Feet*; or for the armed *Hoof*,
Above you, and below all precipice,
You still advance towards the Court of *Dis*...

Now to the *Cave* we come, wherein is found
A new strange thing, a *Village* under ground;
Houses and *Barns* for Men, and *Beasts behoof*,
With distinct *Walls*, under one solid *Roof*.
Stacks both of *Hay*, and *Turf*, which yields a scent
Can only fume some *Satan's* fundament;
For this black *Cave* lives in the voice of *fame*
To the same sence by yet a coarser *Name*.

THOMAS BURNET

The *Subterranean People* ready stand,
A Candle each, most two in either hand
To guide, who are to penetrate inclin'd
The *intestinum rectum* of the *Fiend*.
Thus, by a blinking and promiscuous light
We now begin to travel into *Night*,
Hoping indeed to see the *Sun* agen;
Tho' none of us can tell, or how, or when.
Now in your way a soft descent you meet,
Where the sand takes th'impression of your feet.
And which, ere many yards you measur'd have,
Brings you into the *level* of the *Cave*.

The 'Devil's Arse', Derbyshire, from a 1741
edition of Charles Cotton's *The Wonders of the Peak* (1681).

BOOK OF RUINS

Some paces hence the roof comes down so low,
The humblest statures are compell'd to bow,
First low, then lower; till at last we go
On four feet now who walkt but now on two;
Then straight it lets you upright rise, and then
It forces you to stoop, and creep agen;
Till to a silent *Brook* at last you come,
Whose lympid waves dart rays about the room:
But there the Rock its bosom bows so low,
That few *Adventurers* further press to go;
Yet we must through; or else how can we give
Of this strange place a perfect Narrative?

The seventh WONDER, Chatsworth, the seat of his Grace the Duke of Devonshire
Southward from hence ten miles, where Derwent laves
His broken Shoars with never clearing waves,
There stands a stately, and stupendious *Pile*
Like the proud *Regent* of the *Brittish* Isle,
Shedding her beams over the barren Vale,
Which else bleak *winds*, and nipping *Frosts* assail
With such perpetual *War*, there would appear
Nothing but *Winter* ten months of the year.
This *Palace*, with wild prospects girded round,
Stands in the middle of a falling ground,
At a black *Mountains* foot, whose craggy brow
Secures from *Eastern-Tempests* all below,
Under whose shelter *Trees* and *Flowers* grow,
With early *Blossom*, maugre native snow;
Which elsewhere round a *Tyranny* maintains,
And binds crampt *Nature* long in *Crystal-Chains*.
The *Fabrick*'s noble Front faces the *West*,
Turning her fair broad shoulders to the *East*,
On the *South*-side the stately *Gardens* lye,
Where the scorn'd *Peak* rivals proud *Italy*.
And on the *North* sev'ral inferior *plots*
For servile use do scatter'd lye in spots.

22

John Vanbrugh

1709

In 1709 John Vanbrugh, when he was in the process of designing Blenheim, proposed without success that the Duchess of Marlborough retain the ruins of Woodstock Manor. He was familiar enough with castles, invented or rebuilt, as he had worked in 1702 at Castle Howard and had designed and occupied a 'castle' – a miniature Scottish tower house – on Maze Hill near Greenwich.

In a letter of 11 June, he offered three main reasons for retaining the remains; all three were fundamental arguments in defense of ruins. He was concerned with how their associations shaped visitors' appreciation of his new landscape. His emphasis on its value in adding 'variety' to the new parkland was premised on the aesthetic assumption that variety was an essential aspect of design. His argument that his proposal would share the qualities of the best landscape painters also aligned him with

Woodstock Manor, anonymous drawing, 1714. British Library.

the crucial impact of picturesque assumptions through the 18th century. He must himself have attached a sketch of what he imagined, but that has unfortunately not survived (but see engraving p.101). His letter, however, did survive and was annotated by the Duchess that it was 'something ridiculous', and yet 'I think there is something material in it concerning the occasion of building Blenheim.'

23

ANTIQUARIANISM AND SAMUEL BUCK

1718

Interest in antiquarianism during the 18th century was sharpened by the activities of the Society of Antiquaries, formally established in 1718 with articles that defined its mission as making knowledge of British antiquities more universal. An earlier Elizabethan College of Antiquaries, which included scholars such as William Camden, Sir Robert Cotton, and John Stow, was disbanded in the reign of James I, but the establishment of the Society at the Restoration reaffirmed and gave new focus for such activity by exploring writings, buildings, topography, and genealogy. By 1751, when the Society was granted a royal charter by King George II, it had a membership of about 150.

Ruins were central to the enquiries of many antiquarians. They were largely the result of two crucial moments in modern history: the Reformation, and the success of gunpowder. The former saw places of Catholic faith abandoned, while the latter eliminated the security of castles they were left to fall into decay. Among early antiquarians, John Warburton, as an officer of the Excise, traveled frequently throughout England, and at his death in 1759 left a large archive of MSS, mostly now in the British Library. Among them is his account of several visits across Yorkshire, of which he published a map in 1720–21. In the hope of making money with a history of his native county, he employed a young artist, Samuel Buck, to draw the places he wrote about. Warburton's text never achieved publication, but Buck, with his brother Nathanial, went on to issue several portfolios of engravings known as *Buck's Antiquities*.

Buck's drawings for Warburton are in the British Library (Lansdowne MS 914), and were published in facsimile by the Wakefield Historical Publications in 1979. His sketchbook of over 100 sheets shows dozens of sites; many of the images are brief, hurried sketches made at the scene, and the ink (and sometimes pencil) is often faint. Some are 'prospects', large and extensive topographical views, but there are also plans and close-ups of garden layouts, largely old-fashioned garden layouts, perhaps indicative of a taste slowly being displaced. Most are at full page, but on occasion the page is divided into 15 squares in which mainly specific houses are drawn in.

Samuel Buck, *Ruins of Whorlton Castle*, drawing, c.1718. British Library.
Samuel Buck, *Ruins of Ethelstone, alias Eglestone Abbey, near Barnard Castle*,
drawing, c.1718. British Library.

There are at least a dozen drawings of the ruins of former abbeys and castles, sometimes sketched by themselves, and sometimes juxtaposed with an adjacent, more modern manor, presumably built of materials taken from its dilapidated predecessor.

The corpus of Buck's drawing, however fragmentary, is more eloquent of antiquarian activity than Warburton's brisk text.

24

Travelers in Great Britain: Daniel Defoe and Others

1734

Early explorations of English ruins by authors such as John Aubrey, Francis Bacon, and Inigo Jones (*see* Extract 19) largely focused on the monuments themselves. From the 17th century onwards, however, travelers through what Daniel Defoe called 'the Whole Island of Great Britain' indulged a wider curiosity and saw the remains of antiquity as part of a larger cultural understanding of place. Defoe himself drew on earlier books such as William Camden's *Britannia* (1586) and more recent work such as John Macky's *Journey Through England* (1714-23). His title page listed, among other topics, his interest in the situation of principal towns and cities, and 'Publick Edificies, Seats, and Palaces of the Nobility and Gentry', which inevitably included ruins.

Antiquarians were foremost in visiting, drawing, and writing about ruins. While many English travelers took a grand tour throughout Europe in the 17th and early 18th centuries, wars on the continent deterred many from going, so they, along with others who would not have afforded or wished for a grand tour, took to visiting the countries of England, Wales, and Scotland. Defoe's book, published in 1724, was widely read both for itself and as a guide for travelers.

Defoe's interest was remarkably personal and lively. He saw evidence of castles at Cambridge, Carnarvon, Chepstow, Colchester, Corfe, Dunbar, Rochester; abbeys at Bury St Edmunds, Glastonbury, and Melrose; city gates, or ancient, sometimes re-inhabited, ruins of mansions at Holdenby. He also found pleasure in ancient trees on Box Hill, Surrey, the 'great woods' at Woburn Abbey, or the Three Brethren tree at Cockermouth.

As a member and secretary of the Society of Antiquaries, William Stukeley was particularly absorbed with ruined structures. His *Drawings in a Journey with Mr Roger Gale* (1721) and *Iterarium Curiosum* (published the same year as Defoe's book) featured his own sketches made during his travels.

Defoe's were but the beginning of explorations of Britain. The churchman Richard Pococke kept a diary, now held in the British Library, of his *Travels through England* during 1750-57. He notes on September 1756, 'the ruins of Halesowen, commonly call'd the Manor: there remains of the large church only one of the north windows of the chancel, & two of the south Cross Isle... and six narrow windows of finer Gothic Workmanship'.

By the end of the 18th and early 19th century William Gilpin (*see* Extract 34) published a series of what he called *Observations* of various parts of England and Scotland – the Scottish Highlands in 1782, Wye Valley in 1789. Perhaps mainly concerned to aid travelers in their skills with sketching, ruins were a necessarily central element of the desired repertoire that Gilpin advocated.

William Stukeley, *The Ruins of Holdenby*, drawing, 1709. Bodleian Library, Oxford.
O. Neale, *The Three Brethren Tree*, engraving, 1779. Cumbria Record Office.
William Stukeley, *Ruins of Glastonbury Abbey*, engraving, from the 1745 edition of his *Iterarium Curiosum*.

25

ALEXANDER POPE

c.1724

Alexander Pope visited Sherborne, the former home of Sir Walter Raleigh, in Dorset, probably in 1724, and his visit was recounted for his friend, Martha Blount. His account of the grounds takes him upwards into the hills, where he finds several features in the landscape that suggest ruins, and then arrives at one that 'completes the solemnity of the scene'. The language of 'scene' suggests a theatrical experience, where the varied assemblage of garden and landscape 'entertains' him, as he hopes his letter will do for Martha Blount. He muses on what he might suggest to enliven the ruins with a more careful and deliberate acknowledgement of the genius of that place. In 1735, in another letter to Blount, he tells of a trip in a yacht down Southampton water to see Netley Abbey and Netley Castle, where he writes of the 'aspect of the Towers, & the high crumbling Battlements, overgrown with Ivy, with a Square room in the middle out of which at three large arches you saw the main sea...' Of the Abbey, as a Catholic he admired 'the Ruin of a large Monastery... very extensive, the Altar vastly high, & the whole wrought finely with old Gothic ornaments: one Part of the Roof, which seems to have been under the Steeple, was yet standing, but looked terribly, it was about 60 foot high, & hung like Net work, so thin & so fine...'

Letters to Martha Blount, 1724 and 1735,
in *The Works of Alexander Pope, Esq. in Verse and Prose*, vol.10
(London: J. Johnson, 1806)

On the left, full behind these old trees, which make this whole part inexpressively awful & solemn, runs a little, old, low wall, beside a trench, cover'd with elder trees and ivyes; which being crossed by another bridge, brings you to the Ruin, to compleat the solemnity of the scene. You first see an old tower penetrated by a large arch, and others above it thro which the whole country appears in prospect, even when you are at the top of the other ruins, for they stand very high, & the ground slopes down on all sides. These venerable broken walls, some arches almost entire 30 or 40 ft deep, some open like porticos with

J. Toms and J. Mason, after William Bellers, *Netley Abbey*, engraving, 1774. Private collection.

fragments of pillars, some circular or enclosed in three sides, but exposed at top, with steps which Time has made of disjointed stones to climb to the highest points of the ruin...

What should induce Lord D. the rather to cultivate these ruins and do honour to them, is that they do no small honour to his family; that Castle, which is very ancient, being demolished in the Civil wars after it was nobly defended by one of his ancestors in the cause of the King. I would set up at the entrance of 'em an Obelisk, with an inscription of the fact: which would be a monument erected to the very ruins; as the adorning & beautifying them in the manner I have been imagining... When I have been describing his agreeable seat, I cannot make the reflection I've often done upon contemplating the beautiful villas of other noblemen, rais'd upon the spoils of plundered nations, or aggrandiz'd by the wealth of the public. I cannot ask myself the question, 'What else has this man to be lik'd? What else has he cultivated or improv'd? What good or what desirable things appears of him without the walls?' ...

Another walk under this hill winds by the Riverside quite covered with high Trees on both banks, over hung with Ivy, where falls a natural Cascade with never-ceasing murmurs. On the opposite handing of the bank (which is a steep of 50 ft) is plac'd, with a very fine fancy, a Rustick Seat of stone, flagged and rough, with two urns in the same rude taste upon pedestals, on each side: from whence you lose your eyes upon the glimmering of the waters under the wood, & your ears in the constant dashing of the waves. In view of this, is a bridge that crosses the stream, built of the same ruinous taste: the wall of the garden handing over it, is humoured so as to appear the Ruin of another Arch or two above the bridge. Hence you mount the hill over the Hermits Seat (as they call it) described before, & so to the highest Terras, again.

26

WILLIAM KENT

1730s—40s

The landscape architect William Kent came away from nine years in Italy very '*Italianizzato*', and clearly knew both ancient ruins in Rome as well as the city's contemporary gardens. On his return, he was keen to put his acquired skills to bear in making gardens and buildings for contemporary Britain. He modeled the arched colonnade at his best surviving garden, Rousham in Oxfordshire, on memories of the sequence of descending terraces around the Roman baths at Palestrino (ancient Praeneste) to create what he, or his client, called the Praeneste. His eclectic absorption of not only Palladian motifs but also Chinese design and British Gothicism enabled him to deploy his visual skills around various sites such as the ruined gatehouse at Esher.

These were many Gothick allusions, such as the 'ruined' Hermitage at Stowe, which Kent designed with a missing tower, and at Richmond for Queen Caroline. At Rousham, an 'eye-catcher' set on the distant hillside looks from afar like one standing wall of a ruined church; seen from closer up, it appears like a stage setting,

The Orti Farnesiani, Palatine Hill, engraving from Bartolomeo Marliani, *Urbis Romae Topographia*, 1588, an engraving of a Roman antique garden terrace.

William Kent, the Gothick 'eye-catcher' and decorated mill at Rousham. Private collection.
The Arch at Rousham today. Photograph: John Dixon Hunt.

a one-dimensional fake ruin. The Rousham steward, William White, chose to see it as a triumphal arch.

Inviting the estate's owner, General James Dormer, to inspect the work, White wrote: 'On each side [of the bowling green] is a fine Green Terrace Walk, at the end of which is [sic] two open groves, backed with two Natural Hillocks planted with Scotch Firs, and two Minervas upon Terms stands before them, and in the middle stands a Lion devouring a Horse upon a very Large pedestal [copied from Ligorio's design at the Villa D'Este], you walk forward to view the Lion nearer, when your eye drops upon a very Concave slope, at the Bottom of which runs the Beautiful River Charvell... the most extensive part of it is but short, yet you see from hence five pretty Country villages, and the Grant [i.e. great] Triumphant Arch in Aston Field.'

That ruins served as eye-catchers, drawing the eye into a landscape, and to mark the termination of an alley or prospect, and as stage settings, suggests how much they were intended as imaginative promptings but rarely designed to stimulate much thought.

27

JOHN DYER

1740

The Welsh poet and painter John Dyer is best known for his poem 'Grongar Hill', in which he surveys a landscape from an elevation, ending:

> 'Tis now the raven's bleak abode;
> 'Tis now th' apartment of the toad;
> And there the fox securely feeds;
> And there the poisonous adder breeds,
> Conceal'd in ruins, moss and weeds;
> While ever and anon there falls
> Huge heaps of hoary, moulder'd walls...

It is to this early work that his lengthy poem *The Ruins of Rome* (1740) refers at its start. Although he saw his native Welsh hills as infinitely more congenial than the naked mountains of Italy, he liked that country's antiquities and, unable to find any good images, started sketching them himself: 'I am now about the ruins which are in Rome... I have a great deal of poetry in my head when I scramble among the hills of ruins, or as I pass through the arches along the Sacred Way.'[1]

Dyer spent two years in Rome and began work on the Roman verses on his return to England in 1726. He prefaced the 545-line poem with a Latin epigraph from the Renaissance writer Janus Vitalis that, translated, reads, 'Look at all the walls, the stone dislodged, the vast theaters brought low by the power of decay. That is Rome. And do you see how the very corpse of such a city is still imperial and seems to offer menaces.'

The Ruins of Rome (London: Gilliver, 1740)

> ENOUGH of Grongar, and the shady dales
> Of winding Towy, Merlin's fabled haunt,
> I sung inglorious. Now the love of arts,
> And what in metal or in stone remains

BOOK OF RUINS

Of proud Antiquity, thro' various realms
And various languag'es and ages fam'd,
Bears me remote o'er Gallia's woody bounds,
O'er the cloud-piercing Alps remote, beyond
The vale of Arno, purpled with the vine,
Beyond the Umbrian and Etruscan hills,
To Latium's wide champain, forlorn and waste,
Where yellow Tiber his neglected wave
Mournfully rolls. Yet once again, my Muse!
Yet once again, and soar a loftier flight;
Lo! the resistless theme, imperial Rome.
Fall'n, fall'n, a silent heap! her heroes all
Sunk in their urns; behold the pride of pomp,
The throne of nations, fall'n! obscur'd in dust;
Ev'n yet majestical: the solemn scene
Elates the soul, while now the rising sun
Flames on the ruins in the purer air
Tow'ring aloft upon the glittering plain,
Like broken rocks, a vast circumference!
Rent palaces, crush'd columns, rifled moles,
Fanes roll'd on fanes, and tombs on bury'd tombs!...
Yet here, advent'rous in the sacred search
Of ancient arts, the delicate of mind,
Curious and modest, from all climes resort,
Grateful society! with these I raise
The toilsome step up the proud Palatin,
Thro' spiry cypress groves, and tow'ring pine,
Waving aloft o'er the big ruin's brows,
On num'rous arches rear'd; and, frequent stopp'd,
The sunk ground startles me with dreadful chasm,
Breathing forth darkness from the vast profound
Of aisles and halls within the mountain's womb.
Nor these the nether works; all these beneath,
And all beneath the vales and hills around,
Extend the cavern'd sewers, massy, firm,
As the Sibylline grot beside the dead
Lake of Avernus; such the sewers huge,
Whither the great Tarquinian genius dooms
Each wave impure; and proud with added rains,

THE RUINS of ROME.

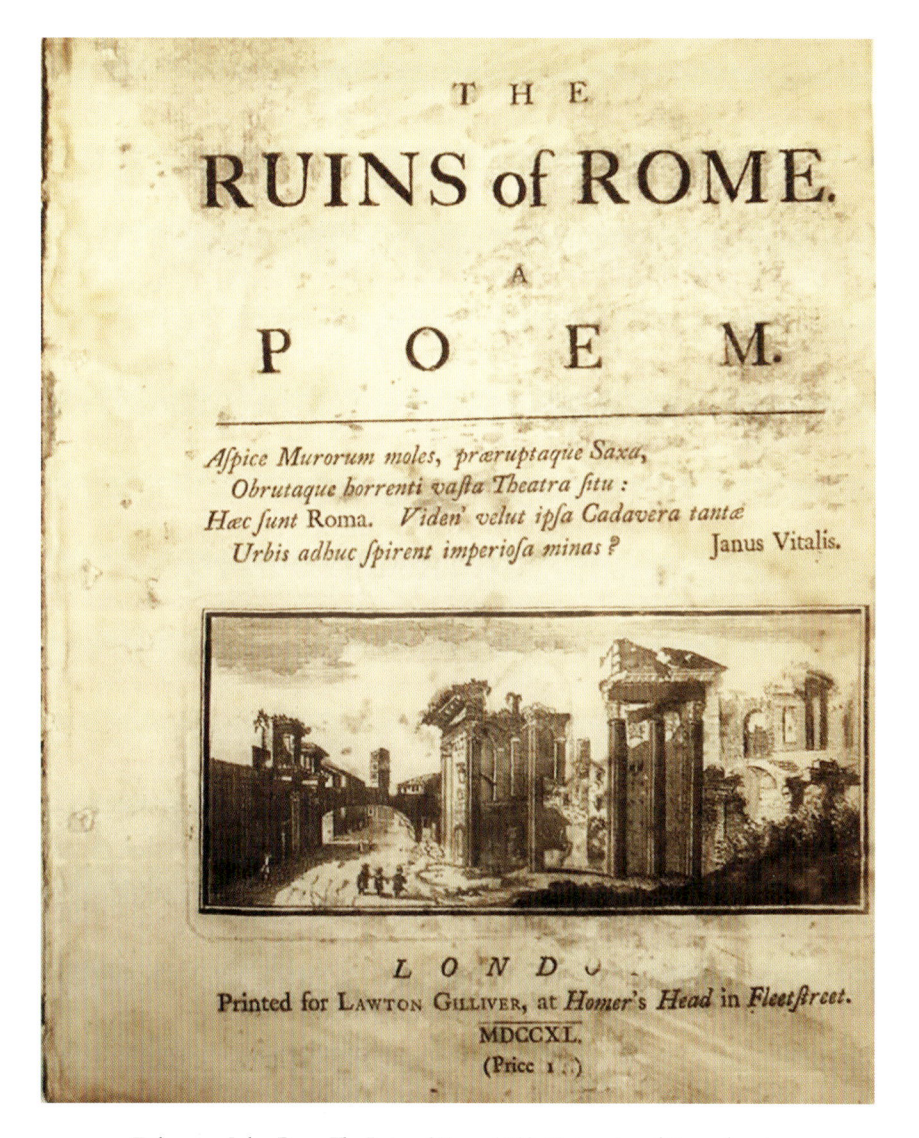

A POEM.

*Aspice Murorum moles, præruptaque Saxa,
Obrutaque horrenti vasta Theatra situ:
Hæc sunt Roma. Viden' velut ipsa Cadavera tantæ
Urbis adhuc spirent imperiosa minas?*   —Janus Vitalis.

LONDON.
Printed for LAWTON GILLIVER, at *Homer's Head* in *Fleetstreet*.
MDCCXL.
(Price 1s.)

Title page, John Dyer, *The Ruins of Rome*, 1740. University of Pennsylvania.

> Hark how the mighty billows lash their vaults,
> And thunder! how they heave their rocks in vain!
> Tho' now incessant time has roll'd around
> A thousand winters o'er the changeful world,
> And yet a thousand since, th' indignant floods
> Roar loud in their firm bounds, and dash and swell
> In vain, convey'd to Tiber's lowest wave...
> Amid the tow'ry ruins, huge, supreme,

Th' enormous amphitheatre behold,
Mountainous pile! o'er whose capacious womb
Pours the broad firmament its vary'd light,
While from the central floor the seats ascend
Round above round, slow wid'ning to the verge,
A circuit vast and high; nor less had held
Imperial Rome and her attendant realms,
When, drunk with rule, she will'd the fierce delight,
And op'd the gloomy caverns, whence out rush'd,
Before th' innumerable shouting crowd,
The fiery madded tyrants of the wilds,
Lions and tigers, wolves and elephants,
And desp'rate men, more fell. Abhorr'd intent!
By frequent converse with familiar death
To kindle brutal daring apt for war;
To lock the breast, and steel th' obdurate heart,
Amid the piercing cries of sore distress
Impenetrable. But away thine eye!
Behold yon' steepy cliff; the modern pile
Perchance may now delight, while that rever'd
In ancient days the page alone declares,
Or narrow coin thro' dim cerulean rust.
Behold by Tiber's flood, where modern Rome
Couches beneath the ruins: there of old
With arms and trophies gleamed the field of Mars:
There to their daily sports the noble youth
Rushed emulous; to fling the pointed lance;
To vault the steed; or with the kindling wheel
In dusty whirlwinds sweep the trembling goal;
Or wrestling, cope with adverse swelling breasts,
Strong grappling arms, closed heads, and distant feet;
Or clash the lifted gauntlets: there they formed
Their ardent virtues: lo the bossy piles,
The proud triumphal arches: all their wars,
Their conquests, honours, in the sculptures live.
And see from every gate those ancient roads,
With tombs high-verged, the solemn paths of Fame:
Deserve they not regard? O'er whose broad flints
Such crowds have rolled, so many storms of war!

JOHN DYER

Such trains of consuls, tribunes, sages, kings!
So many pomps! so many wondering realms!
Yet still through mountains pierced, o'er valleys raised,
In even state, to distant seas around,
They stretch their pavements. Lo the fane of Peace,
Built by that prince, who to the trust of power
Was honest, the delight of human kind.
Three nodding aisles remain; the rest an heap
Of sand and weeds; her shrines, her radiant roofs,
And columns proud, that from her spacious floor,
As from a shining sea, majestic rose
An hundred foot aloft, like stately beech
Around the brim of Dion's glassy lake,
Charming the mimic painter: on the walls
Hung Salem's sacred spoils; the golden board,
And golden trumpets, now concealed, entombed
By the sunk roof...

28

GIOVANNI BATTISTA PIRANESI

1743

Prima Parte di Architetture e Prospettive, the first of Piranesi's many publications, begins with an acknowledgement of the subject that was to dominate his prolific and influential career, the 'speaking ruins' of Rome. He was 23 years old, and had recently moved there from Venice, where he had trained himself in the technicalities of building construction, the several media of architectural representation, particularly etching, apprenticed in stage set design (largely influenced by the prints and publications of the Bibiena family), and familiarized himself with leading studies of architectural history and antiquities, particularly those of Filippo Juvarra and Fischer von Erlach, after whose *Entwurf einer historischen Architektur* of 1721 he made a number of careful studies. The etchings of the *Prima Parte* combine these formative studies, skills, and experiences in views that are equally theatrical, archaeological, and tectonic. They are, of course, also imaginative, but plausibly so. In a later publication that presented his reconstructed Campo Marzio, he defended his work as the outcome of *ragionevole congettura* (responsible or reasonable conjecture). Thus, ruins inspired and required both rigorous examination, an approximately philological reconstruction, and imaginative projection or fantasy. From the start to the end of his career Piranesi valued ruins less for the melancholic sentiments they provoked than for their capacity to prompt a vision of what once was and what might have been – architecture's ancient magnificence and its unrealized potential. John Soane's observation on the study of ruins (*see* Extract 43) is entirely *apropos*: it allowed architects to become 'intimately acquainted with not only what the ancients have done, but... what they would have done'. The wonder the young Piranesi describes in his first encounter with Rome fueled the fire of his imagination.

GIOVANNI BATTISTA PIRANESI

Dedicatory Letter to Nicola Giobbe, *Prima Parte di Architetture e Prospettive*
(Rome: Fratelli Pagliari, 1743)[2]

We are now at the close of the third year, most Revered Sig. Nicola, since I, moved by that noble desire which has drawn from the remotest parts of Europe the most able men of our age, and of the past, to admire, and to learn from the august relics, still extant, of the ancient majesty and magnificence of Rome, the greatest perfection ever achieved in architecture, I too left my native land, and by the same spirit was brought to this Queen of Cities.

I will not again tell you with what wonder I was filled when observing closely the most exact perfection of the architectural elements of the buildings, the rarity, or the immeasurable mass of marbles to be found everywhere, or even that vast space once occupied by circuses, fora, or imperial palaces; I will only tell you, that these speaking ruins have filled my spirit with such images the like of which I could never have been able to conceive from the drawings, although most accurate, of the same ruins by the immortal Palladio, even though I always kept them in front of my eyes.

Giovanni Battista Piranesi, engravings from *Prima Parte di Architetture e Prospettive*, 1743.
Fisher Fine Arts Library, University of Pennsylvania.

Therefore, having thought of revealing to the world some of these images, and since it is not to be hoped that an architect of our times could actually be able to execute any, the fault being either in architecture itself, fallen from that blessed perfection reached at the time of the highest grandeur of the Roman Republic, and that of the very powerful Caesars which came after it, or indeed the fault being of those who should make themselves patrons of this most noble faculty, the truth is that since in our days one cannot see buildings that would entail the expense needed, for example, for a Forum of Nerva, an Amphitheater of Vespasian, or a Palace of Nero, and not seeing either in princes or in private men an inclination to realize them, I do not see any other possibility left to me or to any other modern architect than to explain one's own ideas with drawings, and in this way to take away from sculpture and painting the advantage, that, as the great Juvara said, they have, in this respect, over architecture; and also to subtract her from the power of those who have great possessions, and believe themselves able to dispose at their pleasure of the creations of architecture.

To this aim I endeavored, during my sojourn in this great metropolis, to unite to whatever knowledge I have acquired of architecture not only the art of drawing my ideas but also of etching them on copper; how much I succeeded in each of these two things you, who are an excellent connoisseur of everything pertaining to each one of these liberal arts, will be able to judge.

In all these drawings you will see to what extent perspective has helped me to draw the attention of the viewer to certain parts which I rather wanted to be perceived by the beholder before others. Perspective, as Vitruvius, the great master of architecture, said very wisely, is essential to the architect, and indeed I believe one can add that whoever does not see the use of it and its need in architecture, does not yet know whence it derives its greatest and most solid beauty.

But it is now time, most revered Sir, that, putting my drawings aside, I come to the reasons which induced me to adorn them with your very honored name. And if I say that primarily I persuaded myself to do so in order to leave you before my departure [for Venice] a clear demonstration of the obligation I owe you for having always kindly welcomed me in your home during all my sojourn in Rome, and favored me in various ways with those things that a stranger in a foreign city often needs, it will be a poor thing compared with the special and frequent help received from you in the exercise of my profession; you have always left at my complete disposal the rich and select collection which you own of paintings, books, and engravings, perhaps the most abundant, or at least the one assembled with more exquisite taste and knowledge than any in Rome, allowing me not only to look repeatedly in your house at whatever I needed, but also to take it wherever I pleased.

But most of all I am grateful for what you have taught me; for you have made me examine in every detail not only the most particular beauties of every sort of rarity, either ancient or modern, which can be found in Rome: but through the examples of your excellent drawings you have also shown me how one, through new forms, can make laudable use of the architectonic inventions of our predecessors.

Therefore, Sir, if I have now decided to honor my drawings with your name, it is not so much in order to obtain for them that luster, which they do not in themselves have, as to, in some way, return to you that which, thanks to your teaching and example, my scarce talent has been able to produce.

And here, Sir, since we are talking about favors received from you, I cannot end this letter without reminding you, with my infinite pleasure, of the friendship acquired through you of the two most renowned architects of our time, Nicola Salvi and Luigi Vanvitelli. Their merit, since it will be sufficiently proved to posterity by the outstanding works they have built, and especially by the Trevi Fountain which the former is on the point of completing, and by the harbor and lazaret of Ancona, just finished by the latter, makes it therefore superfluous for me to say more in their praise. As far as I am concerned I cannot but say that to have become acquainted with them has not been the least of the advantages that you have procured me, and that I, with experience, have recognized these to be to my great profit...

29

FOUNTAINS ABBEY AND STUDLEY ROYAL

1744

The gardens at Studley Royal in Yorkshire were created by John Aislabie on land adjacent to the ruined Fountains Abbey. The report of his visit there by Philip Yorke, 2nd Earl of Hardwicke, in 1744 suggests that a Gothic ruin would be, if not the prime exhibit of its past and particularly apt for England, at the very least a magnificent addition to the associations of that place. The ruins were already famous, and celebrated in a poem of the 1730s: 'Where Prayers were read, and pious Anthems sung, / Now Heaps of Rubbish the Apartments throng. / Up roofless Walls the clinging Ivy creeps…'[3] The inclusion of the remains within the garden was achieved in 1768.

Fountains Abbey. Photograph: John Dixon Hunt.

FOUNTAINS ABBEY AND STUDLEY ROYAL

PHILIP YORKE
Visit to Studley Royal, 1744 (Bedfordshire Historical Society, 1940)

Spent six hours in riding over Mr Aislabie's park in Studley. The natural beauties of this place are superior to anything of the kind I ever saw, and improved with great taste both by the late and present owner... You have besides several agreeable views of Ripon, the adjacent country, and Fountains Abbey... [The] ruins of the Abbey lie just without the enclosure of the park. They are in the possession of a Roman Catholic gentleman, who has refused very large offers from the late Mr Aislabie. They would indeed have been a noble addition to the beauties of the place. This monastery was seated in a romantic vale, and, when entire, spread over 5056 acres. Its remains are remarkably well preserved and make a very venerable magnificent appearance. The church, which is 200 yards longs, wants little but its roof to be as perfect as ever; the tower, contrary to the usual manner, rises at the north end. The hall is 36 yards by 15; the dormitory, supported by cloisters, 106 yards. At the end of them runs the [River] Scheld under 4 arches. There are besides the ruins of the kitchen, a granary or common parlour over it, the abbot's lodge, and the principal gateway – all very distinguishable and entire. Over the west window of the church is a bird standing on a tun, probably the device of the builder or founder, and a date which is 1444 or 1449.

30

WILLIAM SHENSTONE

1764

The gardens at The Leasowes were William Shenstone's major achievement. Though Dr Johnson thought of landscape gardening was but an 'innocent sentiment', it was certainly more than that for Shenstone, in both his creation of the garden and his long mediation on landscaping, published in the second volume of his works in 1763. His 'Unconnected Thoughts on Gardening' deal fully and carefully with the scope of what by mid-century he saw as its potential, including the following passage on ruins. He believes that one crucial aspect of ruins is that, when carefully situated, their spaces can be fleshed out in a visitor's imagination.

D. Jenkins, *View from the Ruined Halesowen Priory Towards the Leasowes*, engraving, c.1750.

WILLIAM SHENSTONE

'Unconnected Thoughts on Gardening', 1764,
in *The Works in Verse and Prose* (London: J. Dodsley, 1791)

Ruinated structures appear to derive their power of pleasing, from the irregularity of surface, which is VARIETY; and the latitude they afford the imagination, to conceive an enlargement of their dimension, or to recollect any events or circumstances appertaining to their pristine grandeur, as concern grandeur and solemnity. The breaks in them should be as bold and abrupt as possible. If mere beauty be aimed at (which however is not their chief excellence) the waving line, with more than easy transitions, will become of greater importance. Events relating to them may be stimulated by numberless little artifices; but it is ever to be remembered, that high hills and sudden descents are most suitable to castles; and fertile vales, near wood and water, most imitative of the usual situation for abbeys and religious houses; large oaks, in particular, are essential to the latter.

Whose branching arms, and reverend height
Admit a dim religious light.

31

Denis Diderot

1767

What Denis Diderot once said of memory, that it is a sensation that endures, can perhaps be said of ruined monuments, that their fragments are what endure. His basic concern was with the impermanence of all existing things, their transience. Melancholy is a key term in his writings, one that registers the emotional impact of incessant change. But for Diderot, particularly when viewing the paintings of Hubert Robert, neither despair nor sadness dominated his feelings. Of course, one can see inevitable losses, of greatness, of beauty and achievement, but there is also an intuition of hope and affirmation, even of the triumph of justice when children and their mothers dance in the ruins of a tyrant's palace. In an age of revolutions, ruination was less a sign of fate than of moral force. Diderot insisted on the representation of transience in both a picture's main theme and what he called its accessories, not only fallen columns, wrecked walls, and broken vaults, but also tablets, ornaments, and sculptural works – the latter, perhaps, of a lonely figure, inwardly focused, alienated from others, deprived of lively association. Insofar as the mutability of works and lives was their main theme, ruin images replaced traditional reminders of death's inevitability. Instead of hubris being checked by an hourglass or skull, a perforated dome or smashed bridge would convey the same admonition: all will pass, *memento mori*. But for Diderot, ends were also beginnings; melancholy was *sweet*.

Hubert Robert was a man of the salons, at home among other sensitive souls who had spent enough time in Rome to absorb its lessons. Both past and future losses were depicted in his paintings, oscillating between the past and future anterior tenses. Fine detail is omitted, the surfaces are rather fuzzy, but the scale is often colossal, much grander than anything to be seen in Rome; sublime effect is achieved through magnitude, as Edmund Burke had advised. Once boundary walls and roofs were breached, interiors were absorbed into a continuous landscape, the 'all' that Diderot said will always remain.

Hubert Robert, *Imaginary View of the Grande Galerie in the Louvre in Ruins*, oil on canvas, 1796. Musée du Louvre, Paris.

The Salon of 1767, in *Oeuvres de Denis Diderot, Salons*,
vol.1 (Paris: J.L.J. Brière, 1831)[4]

What beautiful, sublime ruins! What decisiveness and at the same time what lightness, control, and facility with the brush. What an effect! What grandeur! What nobility!

The ideas ruins evoke in me are grand. Everything comes to nought, everything perishes, everything passes, only the world remains, only time endures. How old is this world! I walk between two eternities. Wherever I look my glance, the objects surrounding me announce death and compel my resignation to what awaits me. What is my ephemeral existence in comparison with that of a worn down rock, of a valley being formed, of a forest dying, of these deteriorating masses suspended above my head? I see the marble of tombs crumble into powder, and I don't want to die! And I begrudge the effect on weak tissues of fibers and flesh of a general law that even bronze can't contravene! A torrent drags each and every nation into the depths of a common abyss; myself, I resolve to make a solitary stand at the edge and resist the currents flowing past me.

If the site of a ruin seems perilous, I shudder. If I feel safe and secure there, I'm freer, more alone, more myself, closer to myself. It's there that I call out to my friend, it's there that I miss my friend; it's there that we enjoy ourselves without anxiety, without witnesses, without intruders, without those jealous of us. It's there that I probe my own heart; it's there that I interrogate his, that I take alarm and reassure myself. Between this place and the abodes of the city, the native ground of tumult, the seat of interest, passion, vice, crime, prejudice, and error, the distance is great.

If my soul were predisposed to tender feelings, I'd surrender to them without restraint, if my heart were calm, I'd savor the full sweetness of its quietude...

If... melancholy brought me back there, I'd surrender completely to my pain. The secluded spot would ring out with my lamentations, the silence and the darkness would be rent with my cries, and when my soul had regained its composure I would dry my tears and my hands and return to the world of men, and they'd never suspect I had wept.

If I have something more to say about the poetics of ruins, Robert will bring it to mind.

32

JOHN CUNNINGHAM

1766

This poem by John Cunningham, from his *Poems chiefly Pastoral* of 1766, prefaced Rose Macaulay's *Pleasure of Ruins*,[5] a book that all ruinists must acknowledge for its explorations, verbal and visual. Cunningham's poem is at once general in its gestures to ruins and specific in that this 18th-century poem announces the centrality of ruins to English culture at the time, with its fascination with the past that features in his pastoral poems; this was not incidental, since pastoralism was a poetic mode that sought to find a manner of speaking in the modern world.

Rose Macaulay does not comment on the poem, but we draw upon one of her illustrations that speaks to the poet's outlook at that moment of the picturesque: it is part of a sequence of ruin images in Batty Langley's *New Principles of Gardening* (1728), in which a ruin terminates a garden walk. There are also three pages with eight further close-up images of ruins. These are captioned, 'Views of Ruins after the Old Roman manner for the termination of walks, avenues, etc'. They were suggestions for painted views or invitations to garden makers to construct 'real' ones.

Even when Langley's introduction comments on the engravings, he does not take time to consider ruins in his text, which is mainly focused on the use of geometry in garden layout and on planting. Yet the gesture to Roman ruins does imply some sense that ancient culture of the pastoral played a role in the modern or 'new' garden of the picturesque.

Poems chiefly Pastoral, 1766 (London: Payne and Cropley, 1761)

Elegy on a Pile of Ruins

Aspice murorum moles, praeruptaque saxa! (Janus Vitalis)
Omnia teous edax depascitur, omnia carpit (Seneca)

In the full prospect yonder hill commands,
O'er barren heath and cultivated plains,
The vestige of an ancient abbey stands,
Close by a ruin'd castle's rude remains.

BOOK OF RUINS

Half bury'd there lie many a broken bust,
And obelisque, and urn, o'erthrown by Time;
And many a cherub there descends in dust
From the rent roof, and portico sublime...

Where rev'rend shrines in gothic grandeur stood,
The nettle, or the noxious night-shade spreads;
And ashlings, wafted from the neigh'ring wood,
Thro' the worn turrets wave their trembling heads...

I left the mantling shade in moral mood...
Sigh'd, as the mould'ring monuments I viewed.

Inexorably calm, with silent pace
Here Time hath pass'd – What ruin marks his way!
This Pile, now crumbling o'er its hallow'd base,
Turn'd not his step, nor could his course delay...

How solemn in the cell, o'ergrown with moss
That terminates the view, yon cloister'd way!
In the crush'd wall, a time-corroded cross
Religion-like, stand mould'ring in decay...

Near the brown arch, redoubling yonder gloom,
The bones of an illustrious chieftain lie,
As trac'd among the fragments of his tomb,
The trophies of a broken Fame imply...

Hither let Luxury lead her loose-robed train;
Here flutter Pride, on purple-painted wings:
And from the moral prospect learn – how vain
The wish, that sighs for sublunary things!

JOHN CUNNINGHAM

DAVID MACBETH MOIR ('DELTA')
Lines written at Kelburne Castle, Ayrshire, 1798

        Away
From the sea murmur ceaseless, up between
The green secluding hills, that hem it round,
As 'twere their favourite, Kelbourne Castle stands,
With its grey turrets in baronian state,
A proud memento of the days when men
Thought but of war and safety. Stately pile,
Magnificent, not often have mine eyes
Gazed o'er a scene more picturesque, or more
Heart-touching for its beauty. Thou wert once
The guardian of these mountains, and the foe
Approaching, saw, between himself and thee,
The fierce down-thundering, mocking waterfall;
While, on thy battlements, in glittering mail,
The warder glided, and the sentinel,
As near'd the stranger horseman to thy gate,
Pluck'd from his quiver the unerring shaft,

An Avenue in Perspective, from Batty Langley's *New Principles of Gardening*, engraving, 1728.
Fisher Fine Arts Library, University of Pennsylvania.

Which from Kilwinning's spire had oft brought down
The mock papingo.
          Mournfully, alas!
Yet in thy quietude not desolate,
Now, like a spectre of the times gone by,
Down from thin Alpine throne, upon the sea,
Which glitters like a sheet of molten gold,
Thou lookest thus at eventide, while sets
The day o'er distant Arran, with its peaks,
Sky-piercing, yet o'erclad with winter's snows
In desolate grandeur; while the cottaged fields
Of nearer Bute smile, in their vernal green,
A picture of repose.
On Edward's overthrow at Bannockburn
To olden times my reveries have roam'd.
To glory and war, red tumult, and the day
Of Scotland's renovation. Like a dream
Fitful and fair, yet clouded with a haze,
As if of doubt, to memory awakes
The bright heart-stirring past, when human life
Was half-romance; and, were it not that yet,
In stream and crag, and isle, and crumbling wall
Of keep and castle, still returns to us
Physical proof, that History is no mere
Hallucination, oftentimes the mind –
So different is the present from the past –
Would deem the pageant illusion all.
Sweet scenes of beauty and peace, farewell! The eyes
But of a passing visitor are mine
On thee; before this radiant eve, thou wert
Known but in name; but now thou art mind own,
Shrined 'mid the pictures, which find memory
In musing fantasy will ofttimes love
To conjure up, gleaning, amid the stir
And strife of multitudes, as 'twere repose,
By dwelling on the tranquil and serene!

33

THOMAS WHATELY

1770

Once England realized that the new 'landscape gardening' was different and in need of special analysis and explanation, ruins became a prominent item to explore. The remnants of abbeys ruined after the Reformation were everywhere, of course, and their Gothic architecture could seem more relevant to England than that of ancient Rome, although that remained a reference point for designers wishing to promote a modern culture based on the Roman architectural legacy.

Ruins had already been promoted as features of gardens and parks by earlier writers like Vanbrugh (*see* Extract 22), Addison, or Batty Langley, to form distant eye-catchers or the termination of walks and alleys. But it was with more substantial books such as Thomas Whately's *Observations on Modern Gardening* (1770) and William Gilpin's accounts of various districts in England that they emerged as major themes. For Whately, ruins were a crucial element to add variety to any design: 'They are a class by themselves,' he wrote, 'beautiful as objects, expressive as characters… and may be accommodated with ease to irregularity of ground.' He expanded on those ideas in section XLIII of *Observations*, where the final Latin quotation signals the site where Troy had been.

Observations on Modern Gardening (London: T. Payne, 1770)

XLIII. To this great variety must be added the many changes which may be made by the means of *ruins*; they are a class by themselves, beautiful as objects, expressive as characters, and peculiarly calculated to connect with their appendages into elegant groups; they may be accommodated with ease to irregularity of ground, and their disorder is improved by it; they may be intimately blended with trees and with thickets, and the interruption is an advantage; for imperfection and obscurity are their properties; and to carry the imagination to something greater than is seen, their effect. They may for any of these purposes be separated into detached pieces; contiguity is not necessary, nor even the appearance of it, if the relation be preserved; but straggling ruins have a bad effect, when the several parts are equally considerable. There should be one large mass to raise the idea of greatness, to attract the others about it, and to be a common centre of union for all: the smaller pieces then mark the original dimensions of one extensive structure; and no longer appear to be the remains of several little buildings.

All remains excite an enquiry into the former state of the edifice, and fix the mind in a contemplation on the use it was applied to; besides the characters expressed by their style and position, they suggest ideas which would not arise from the buildings, if entire. The purposes of many have ceased; an abbey, or a castle, if complete, can now be no more than a dwelling; the memory of the times, and of the manners, to which they were adapted, is preserved only in history, and in ruins; and certain sensations of regret, of veneration, or compassion, attend the recollection... Whatever building we see in decay, we naturally contrast its present to its former state, and delight to ruminate on the comparison...

The original construction of [Tintern Abbey] is perfectly marked; and it is principally from this circumstance that they are celebrated as a subject of curiosity and contemplation. The walls are almost entire; the roof only is fallen in; but most of the columns which divided the aisles are still standing; of those which have dropped down, the bases remain, every one exactly in its place; and in the midst of the nave, four lofty arches, which supported the steeple, rise high in the air above all the rest... The shapes even of the windows are little altered; but some of them are quite obscured, others partially shaded, by tufts

William Gilpin, *Tintern Abbey*, engraving from *Observations on the River Wye*, 1792.

of ivy, and those which are most clear, are edged with its slender tendrils and lighter foliage, wreathing about the sides and the divisions; it winds round the pillars; it clings to the walls; and in one of the aisles, clusters at the top in bunches so thick and so large, as to darken the space below. The other aisles, and the great nave, are exposed to the sky; the floor is entirely overspread with turf; and to keep it clear from weeds and bushes, is now its highest preservation. Monkish tomb-stones, and the monuments of benefactors long since forgotten, appear above the greensward; the bases of the pillars which have fallen, rise out of it; and maimed effigies, and sculpture worn with age and weather... Other shattered pieces, though disjointed and mouldering, still occupy their original places; and a staircase much impaired, which led to a tower now no more, is suspended at a great height, uncovered and inaccessible. Nothing is perfect; but memorials of every part still subsist; all certain, but all in decay; and suggest, at once, every idea which can occur in a seat of devotion, solitude, and desolation.

Upon such models, fictitious ruins should be formed; and if any parts are entirely lost, they should be such as the imagination can easily supply from those which are still remaining. Distinct traces of the building which is supposed to have existed, are less liable to the suspicion of artifice, than an unmeaning heap of confusion. Precision is always satisfactory; but in the reality it is only agreeable; in a copy, it is essential to the imitation. A material circumstance to the truth of the imitation, is, that the ruins appear to be very old; the idea is besides interesting in itself; a monument of antiquity is never seen with indifference; and a semblance of age may be given to the representation, by the hue of the materials; the growth of ivy, and other plants; and cracks and fragments seemingly occasioned rather by decay, than by destruction. An appendage evidently more modern than the principal structure will sometimes corroborate the effect; the shed of a cottage amidst the remains of a temple, is a contrast to the former and the present state of the building; and a tree flourishing among ruins, shows the length of time that have lain neglected. No circumstance so forcibly marks the desolation of a spot once inhabited, as the prevalence of nature over it:

Campos ubi Troja fuit

is a sentence which conveys a stronger idea of a city totally overgrown, than a description of its remains; but in a representation to the eye, some remains must appear; and then the perversion of them to an ordinary use, or an intermixture of a vigorous vegetation, intimates a settled despair of their restoration.

34

WILLIAM GILPIN

1772

From his earliest publication in 1748 to the last of his *Observations* of English and Welsh counties in 1809, William Gilpin was interested in theoretical formulations of the picturesque, giving advice on how to read picturesque opportunities and searching for suitable and promising sites to sketch. While his work did not dwell exclusively on ruins, in his early account of a visit to the garden at Stowe he was quick to see the possibility that ruins offered the crucial need for variety in designed landscapes. *A Dialogue upon the Garden at Stowe* (1748) remarks at the very start of the visit that the 'old Ruin upon the left of the Canal' contributed 'a fine Variety of Objects' to the site. So did the 'fine Effect that old Ruin has at the Head' of the lake, and he would have seen William Kent's quasi-ruined Hermitage there, too (*see* Extract 26). The *Dialogue*'s two fictional visitors debate what was valuable to see there, with rather more emphasis given to its 'various prospects' than to a discussion of ruins, which go to 'make a considerable Variety'. One visitor sees its Hermitage as a ruin (Kent designed it with a deliberately missing turret) and thought it 'romantick', with 'a good effect'; his companion wants to know what ruins mean.

Twenty-five years later in 1772, when Gilpin visited the gardens at Painshill in Surrey, he drew their ruined abbey, Hermitage (made from thatch and tree roots), and Roman Arch (now termed the Mausoleum). The abbey overlooked the lake, and the other two, the River Mole. The 'ruined' abbey was constructed in 1772 on the site of a brick works that had proved a financial disaster, and its inclusion was in line with the incorporation of the genuinely ruined abbeys of Fountains and Rievaulx into gardens at Studley Royal and Duncombe Park in Yorkshire. The 'Roman Arch' was based on the estate owner Charles Hamilton's recollection of his visit to Rome, and included niches for the display of his collection of statuary. These ruins augmented an extremely busy landscape dotted with other elements of the picturesque repertoire, including a grotto, a Gothic temple, and a Chinese bridge.

Gilpin's later writings, as he toured the different parts of England, were mainly concerned with ruins that sustained his picturesque interest and were objects worthy of a sketch, such as Tintern Abbey. Yet often he was to notice ruins without the need to sketch them; in his two-volume *Observations on Westmoreland and Cumberland*, the ruins of castles and the occasional abbey that caught his eye are described in detail that the picturesque draftsman would not have been able to capture. On his way back from Cumberland, he takes in other ruins, including Furness Abbey in Lancashire (now Cumbria) and Fountains Abbey in Yorkshire.

Gilpin was less concerned to promote the creation of fake ruins: in his *Remarks on Forest Scenery* (1791) he cautioned against them: 'If there be a natural river, or a real ruin in the scene, it may be a happy circumstance: let the best be made of it: but I should be cautious in advising the *creation* of either...'

Observations on...Cumberland, and Westmoreland
(London: T. Cadell and W. Davis, 1808)

To these natural features, which are, in a great degree, peculiar to [this] landscape of England, we may lastly add another, of the artificial kind – the ruins of abbeys; which, being naturalized to the soil, might indeed, without much impropriety, be classed among its natural beauties...

[Furness Abbey] lies about twenty miles from Ambleside, beyond those mountains, which range on the western side of Windermere... About a mile within the valley, in the widest part, stands the abbey. From the drawings I have seen of it, it seems to have been constructed in the good style of Gothic architecture; and has suffered, from the hand of time, only such depredations as picturesque beauty requires. The *intire* plan of the abbey-church, and a large

William Gilpin, *Penrith Castle*, engraving from
Observations on Westmoreland and Cumberland, 1786.

William Gilpin, *The Ruined Arch and Hermitage at Painshill*, pen and ink, c.1772. Surrey Heritage.

Anonymous, *Ruined Kitchens at Fountains Abbey*, engraving. Private collection.

fragment of it, still remains. The tower in the centre, which seems never to have been lofty, is perforated with large arches. At the end of the western aisle stands the ruins of a low, simple tower, where the bells of the abbey are supposed to have hung; and from the south aile projects a building, which is the chapter-house. The cloysters are continued in the same direction; one wall of which, and all the internal structure are gone. At the end of the cloysters arises a very rich and picturesque fragment, which is called the *School*. Round the whole runs an irregular wall, the boundary of the abbey, which crossing the valley in two places, and mounting its sides, makes a circuit of about two miles. In many parts it is hid with trees, or shrubs: in some parts, when it is discovered, it is beautiful; and in a very few, displeasing...

From Keswick we mounted a hill, on the great turnpike to Penrith. At the summit we left our horses; and went to examine a Druid temple... The diameter of this circle is thirty-two *paces*; which, as nearly as could be judged from so inaccurate a mode of mensuration, is the diameter of Stonehenge... But the structures are very different: tho the diameters may be nearly equal. The stones here are diminutive in comparison with those on Salisbury-Plain. If Stonehenge were a cathedral in its day, this circle was little more than a country church... These structures, I suppose, are by far the most antique vestiges of architecture (if we may call them architecture) which we have in England. Their rude workmanship hands down the great barbarity of the times of the Druids: and furnishes strong proof of the savage nature of the religion of these heathen priests. Within these magical circles we may conceive any incantations to have been performed: and any rites of superstition to have been celebrated. It is history, as well as poetry, when Ossian mentions the *circles of stones*, where our ancestors, in their nocturnal orgies, invoked the spirits which rode upon the winds – the awful forms of their deceased forefathers...

One of those fortresses, which is known by the name of Penrith-castle, presented us with a very noble ruin; and under the most interesting circumstances... A grand broken arch presented itself first in deep shadow. Through the aperture appeared a part of the internal structure, thrown into perspective to great advantage; and illuminated by the departing ray [of the setting sun]. Other fragments of the shattered towers, and battlements were just touched with the splendid tint: but the body of light rested on those parts, which were seen through the shadowed arch... The valley, in which Fountain's abbey stands, is not of larger dimension than the other, we have just described [i.e. Studley Royal]... Its sides are composed of woody hills sloping down in varied declivities; and uniting with the trees at the bottom, which adorn the river.

At one end of this valley stand the ruins of the abbey, which formerly overspread a large space of ground. Besides the grand remains of ruin, there appeared in various parts, along the trees and bushes, detached fragments, which were once the appendages of this great house...

A few fragments scattered around the body of a ruin are *proper*, and *picturesque*. They are *proper*, because they account for what is defaced; and they are *picturesque* because they unite the principal pile with the ground; on which union the beauty of composition, in a good measure, depends...

35

GEORGES LOUIS LE ROUGE

1775–89

The engravings of Georges Louis Le Rouge form one of the most comprehensive publications on the 'new' gardening in 18th-century Europe. Le Rouge published a series of illustrations in 21 *cahiers* between 1775 and 1789. The number of engravings in each *cahier* differed; some were of various sites in different countries, but the emphasis was on how France, England, and China contributed to this new idea of design, in which ruins inevitably played a role.

Ruined Château near Nogant, engraving in George Louis Le Rouge's *Les jardins anglo-chinois*, vol.11, 1775-89.

As his overall title indicates, the new gardening was – for the French, at least – not solely an invention of the English, but had been importantly sustained by knowledge of the tradition of Chinese gardening: hence several *cahiers* were devoted to China, where the incidence of ruins was of little consequence. It was England and France that supplied Le Rouge with his best examples, and France itself the most (France, of course, did not undergo a Reformation, so examples of ruined abbeys and monasteries were virtually absent, but castles were there).

The examples of ruins represented were the ruined arch at Kew (*cahier* IV), some in gardens at Pelham in Surrey (III), a ruined mill for the Duc de Chartres (X) and the fake ruined column at the Désert de Retz and a former Gothic church there (XIII), a temple at Ermenonville, ruins at the Chateau of Moussean (X), another near Nogent sur Seine (XI), ruins of the Temple of Mars in Parc Monceau (X), and a ruined bridge at Château de la Chapelle-Godefoy, Aude (XII). They are noted, almost as a routine element, in any new garden.

A facsimile of the series was published in individual *cahiers* by Connaissance et Mémoires in Paris in 2004; the image on p.141 is reproduced from this edition. It was accompanied by a volume, edited by Véronique Royer, in which all the engravings are catalogued and described, simultaneously published by the Bibliothèque Nationale de France.

36

J. W. von Goethe

1786

The background of the well-known portrait of Goethe on p.145 shows the open expanse of the Campagna bathed in golden light, the end of the day approaching, with the Alban hills in the remote distance, architectural ruins (probably the ancient city Tusculum) in the middle ground, and in the foreground, fragments of a composite column capital and temple frieze, enriched with high-relief carving. Presumably the idea and design for the painting were developed when the artist and writer traveled together from Rome to Naples. The carving depicts Iphigenia meeting her brother, a scene in Goethe's verse drama *Iphigenia in Tauris*, on which he was working at the time, and drafts of which he read aloud to the artist Tischbein. Goethe himself sits astride an emblem of the most remote of antiquities, a broken obelisk, pensively gazing into the distance – toward what we don't know – and silent.

Words and images: their relationship is no less interesting in the case of Goethe's encounter with ruins than in any other. Like all travelers of his day, he had read about the ruins, and seen images of them. His disappointment with the buildings of Palladio and the ruins of Rome is perhaps no more significant than the fact that a comparison between kinds of representation arose as an issue. Before his *Italian Journey*, he had come to know Italian architecture as a boy, thanks to engravings on the walls of his family home. In *Poetry and Truth* he explained that within his 'house my gaze was drawn most to a row of Roman prospects with which my father had decorated an antechamber. They had been etched by some adept predecessors to Piranesi who understood architecture and perspective well [probably views of Rome by Giovanni Battista Falda, 1665]... Every day I saw here the Piazza del Popolo, the Coliseum, St Peter's Piazza, the Church of St Peter's from within and without, Castel Sant Angelo, and other places.' Years later, he endeavored to learn still more through the study of publications, especially works of Palladio and Piranesi. And while visiting Padua en route to Rome, he purchased a copy of Palladio's treatise.

Character evokes emotion for Goethe, in much the same way that it was supposed to in the experience of architecture and landscape set out by early and mid-18th century English writers (the Third Earl of Shaftesbury, Robert Morris, and William Chambers), and by more recent French theorists such as Le Camus de Mésières. But

Goethe's encounters also provoked a sense of identification with the objects or places in view, the poet's fatigue and age, for example, being echoed by the tectonic failure and antiquity of the ruins. But the encounter also suggested a possible renewal. Once he set foot in Rome, the images of his youth and the teachings of his father were recalled amid a flood of feelings. Gaps between remembered images and present reality were both acknowledged and bridged in his written account.

> *Travels in Italy*, translated by A. J. W. Morrison, in *Goethe's Works*,
> vol.7, edited by F. D. Hedge (Boston: S.E. Cassino, 1884)

At last I can speak out and greet my friends with good humour. May they pardon my secrecy, and what has been, as it were, a subterranean journey hither. For scarcely to myself did I venture to say whither I was hurrying – even on the road I often had my fears, and it was only as I passed under the Porta del Popolo that I felt certain of reaching Rome.

And now let me also say that a thousand times – aye, at all times, do I think of you, in the neighbourhood of these objects which I never believed I should visit alone. It was only when I saw everyone bound body and soul to the north, and all longing for those countries utterly extinct among them that I resolved to undertake the long solitary journey, and to seek that centee towards which I was attracted by an irresistible impulse. Indeed, for the few last years it had become with me a kind of disease, which could only be cured by the sight and presence of the absent object. Now, at length I may venture to confess the truth: it reached at last such a height, that I durst not look at a Latin book, or even an engraving of Italian scenery. The craving to see this country was over ripe. Now, it is satisfied; friends and country have once more become right dear to me, and the return to them is a wished for object – nay, the more ardently desired, the more firmly I feel convinced that I bring with me too many treasures for personal enjoyment or private use, but such as through life may serve others, as well as myself, for edification and guidance.

Rome, November 1, 1786.
Well, at last I am arrived in this great capital of the world. If fifteen years ago I could have seen it in good company, with a well-informed guide, I should have thought myself very fortunate. But as it was to be that I should thus see it alone, and with my own eyes, it is well that this joy has fallen to my lot so late in life.

Over the mountains of the Tyrol I have as good as flown. Verona, Vicenza, Padua, and Venice I have carefully looked at; hastily glanced at Ferrara, Cento,

J. W. VON GOETHE

Johann Heinrich Tischbein, *Goethe in the Roman Campagna*, oil on canvas, 1787. Städel Museum, Frankfurt.

Bologna, and scarcely seen Florence at all. My anxiety to reach Rome was so great, and it so grew with me every moment, that to think of stopping anywhere was quite out of the question; even in Florence, I only stayed three hours. Now I am here at my ease, and as it would seem, shall be tranquillized for my whole life; for we may almost say that a new life begins when a man once sees with his own eyes all that before he has but partially heard or read of. All the dreams of my youth I now behold realized before me; the subjects of the first engravings I ever remember seeing (several views of Rome were hung up in an ante-room of my father's house) stand bodily before my sight, and all that I had long been acquainted with through paintings or drawings, engravings, or woodcuts, plaister-casts, and cork models are here collectively presented to my eye. Wherever I go I find some old acquaintance in this new world; it is all just as I had thought it, and yet all is new; and just the same might I remark of my own observations and my own ideas. I have not gained any new thoughts, but the older ones have become so defined, so vivid, and so coherent, that they may almost pass for new ones.

When Pygmalion's Elisa, which he had shaped entirely in accordance with his wishes and had given to it as much of truth and nature as an artist can, moved at last towards him, and said, 'I am!' – how different was the living form from the chiseled stone.

In a moral sense, too, how salutary is it for me to live awhile among a wholly sensual people, of whom so much has been said and written, and of whom every stranger judges according to the standard he brings with him. I can excuse everyone who blames and reproaches them; they stand too far apart from us, and for a stranger to associate with them is difficult and expensive...

Rome, November 5, 1786.
I have now been here seven days, and by degrees have formed in my mind a general idea of the city. We go diligently backwards and forwards. While I am thus making myself acquainted with the plan of old and new Rome, viewing the ruins and the buildings, visiting this and that villa, the grandest and most remarkable objects are slowly and leisurely contemplated. I do but keep my eyes open and see, and then go and come again, for it is only in Rome one can duly prepare oneself for Rome.

It must, in truth, be confessed, that it is a sad and melancholy business to prick and track out ancient Rome in new Rome; however, it must be done, and we may hope at least for an incalculable gratification. We meet with traces both of majesty and of ruin, which alike surpass all conception; what the barbarians spared, the builders of new Rome made havoc of.

When one thus beholds an object two thousand years old and more, but so manifoldly and thoroughly altered by the changes of time, but sees nevertheless, the same soil, the same mountains, and often indeed the same walls and columns, one becomes, as it were, a contemporary of the great counsels of Fortune, and thus it becomes difficult for the observer to trace from the beginning Rome following Rome, and not only new Rome succeeding to the old, but also the several epochs of both old and new in succession. I endeavor, first of all, to grope my way alone through the obscurer parts, for this is the only plan by which one can hope fully and completely to perfect by the excellent introductory works which have been written from the fifteenth century to the present day. The first artists and scholars have occupied their whole lives with these objects.

And this vastness has a strangely tranquillizing effect upon you in Rome, while you pass from place to place, in order to visit the most remarkable objects. In other places one has to search for what is important; here one is oppressed and borne down with numberless phenomena. Wherever one goes and casts a look around, the eye is at once struck with some landscape – forms of every kind and style; palaces and ruins, gardens and statuary, distant views of villas, cottages and stables, triumphal arches and columns, often crowding so close together, that they might all be sketched on a single sheet of paper. He ought to have a hundred hands to write, for what can a single pen do here; and, besides, by the evening one is quite weary and exhausted with the day's seeing and admiring.

Rome, November 7, 1786.
Pardon me, my friends, if for the future you find me rather chary of my words. On one's travels one usually rakes together all that we meet on one's way; every day brings something new, and one then hastens to think upon and to judge of it. Here, however, we come into a very great school indeed, where every day says so much, that we cannot venture to say anything of the day itself. Indeed, people would do well if, tarrying here for years together, they observed awhile a Pythagorean silence.

37

C. C. L. HIRSCHFELD
1779—89

In the five volumes of Hirschfeld's *Theorie der Gartenkunst* (1779-89), he refers to ruins, or sometimes to memorials for dead personages. In volume 3, quoted here, he devotes several pages to the principles behind creating convincing artificial ruins, and elsewhere illustrates 'ruins of majestic structures' in 'solemn gardens'; in volume 4 he expounds on a hermitage near Hannover; he sees 'ruined dwellings, their cracked walls open to the wind [on a lakeshore], enhance still further the concept of poverty' and Gothic castles are impressive when 'time and tempests have left traces of their fury'. He also includes quotations from the British authors Joseph Heeley, William Home, and Whately's *Observations* (*see* Extract 33).

Theory of Garden Art, translated by Linda Parshall
(Philadelphia: University of Pennsylvania Press, 2001)

It is primarily the effects of ruins that not only justify but even recommend their imitation. Their general effects are the recollection of past times and a certain feeling of regret mixed with melancholy. Yet these can be considerably modified by various things: by the particular character of a ruin or by its former purpose, by its age, by its often clear, sometimes vague arrangement and form, by the occasional, half eradicated inscription on a collapsed building, by the site itself, and by other indications of past events and customs. Thus the ruins of a mountain fortress, a monastery, or an old country estate all awaken very different emotions, each heightened by contemplating the era and other circumstances that in themselves can be so very diverse. One moves back into the past. For a few moments one lives again in the centuries of barbarism and feuding, but also of strength and courage, in the centuries of superstition but also of piety, in the centuries of savagery and lust for the hunt but also of hospitality. Aside from a mountain fortress, monastery, or old country estate, the ruins of other building types can also have their special effect. With all ruins, however, the mind makes an unnoticed comparison between past and present; the memory of events or customs of an earlier world is renewed, and the extant monuments incite the

C. C. L. HIRSCHFELD

Image, uncaptioned, in C. C. L. Hirschfeld's *Theorie der Gartenkunst*, vol.4, 1779-85. Fisher Fine Arts Library, University of Pennsylvania.

imagination to go further than our gaze alone can reach, to be caught up in ideas that contain a secret yet fertile source of pleasure and sweet melancholy.

These are the effects of true ruins; and if imitations are successfully deceptive, they can have much the same power...

A ruin's location is determined by these effects. It is of utmost importance to remove any appearance of art... This implies that there be masses of considerable size, and that, no matter how separated and destroyed everything might be, some relationship among the parts, even if indistinct, be still recognizable. In the meantime, it is not absolutely essential for everything to be in fragments; whole sections of wall can be left complete, still holding together to allow a glimpse of its bygone function. And if the intent is to engender a certain effect, then some trace of the building's former purpose must remain... For artificial ruins to achieve their intended effect, the deception must be immediate and the soul allowed no opportunity to ponder at length, to question whether it is genuine, to find room for doubt. The deception, if given much consideration, is weakened, and once the imitation is discovered, the illusion will inexorably disappear... Nothing gives more visible proof to the passage of time than when a building and its setting are overrun with moss, grass, and other greenery. Ivy growing from inside a crumbling tower, a solitary, bowed cherry tree blooming beside decaying masonry, vegetation trailing down from its windows, a stream murmuring past the stones of a scarcely recognizable staircase – all these often accompany actual ruins and vividly announce the power of time...

What feelings of nostalgia, melancholy, and sorrow often overwhelmed those admirers of antiquity who, traveling in what were once magnificently developed parts of Greece, came upon shepherds' sleeping places and the caves of wild animals amid the temple fragments! Chandler describes such a solemnly moving scene in the ruins of the Temple of Apollo at Ura, not far from Miletus...

Home insists that ruins should be in the Gothic and not the Grecian form, because the former 'exhibits the triumph of time over strength, a melancholy but not unpleasant thought. A Grecian ruin suggests rather the triumph of barbarity over taste, a gloomy and discouraging thought.'

Yet there is an even more important reason for Gothic ruins which did not occur to Lord Home, namely that in our countries they have a plausibility which Greek ruins lack. We know that the Goths built structures in our clime, or at least disseminated their building style, whereas Greek architecture never became so common in northern Europe that we could expect to find remains... We are happy to accompany Riedesel or Chandler as they lead us to ruins at actual classical sites. But in an English park, what a contradiction there is between object and location when we find the affected fragment of a building the remains of which could only be found in Greece! The deception is soon exposed, and our distaste plagues a failed endeavor.

Assuming, then, that the ruins do not contradict the indigenous architecture, they must be situated in a way that befits their character and does not distort their effects. They appear most natural in desolate hollows or on barren, rocky heights... For ruins are a component of regions that are solitary, gently melancholic, grave, and solemn... They cannot, therefore, be used in a way contrary to their nature and effect; they cannot, as people have oddly attempted, be made into dining rooms or music halls; they cannot be abodes of pleasure, since their exteriors announce nothing but frailty and melancholy...

In addition, depending on their location and their association with vegetation and trees, ruins can be more successful in creating picturesque scenes than brand new or well preserved buildings... It was doubtless a sensitivity to these advantages that moved many great painters to incorporate ruins rather than entire buildings in their landscapes.

It will always be more difficult for a garden artist to imitate ruins in a totally convincing way. And since even experts have so often failed in their attempts, one feels it might be better to discourage further efforts. Occasionally a garden artist may come upon real ruins of a significant size and character in his territory; this is admittedly a rare coincidence, but it is of much greater value than the most successful works of imitation. We would like to look first at a relevant British example that demonstrates the progress of good taste; then we will turn to two descriptions of actual ruins in England that can serve as models...

> The ruin [of the castle] at Hagley Park, solemn and venerable, rears its gothic turret among the bushy trees. Upon the first glimpse of this becoming object, one cannot resist an involuntary pause – the mind naturally falls into reflections, while curiosity is on the wing, to be acquainted with its history. An Antiquarian would sigh to know in what aera it was founded, and by whom: – what sieges it had sustained; – what blood had been spilt upon its walls: – and would lament that all-mouldering time should so rapaciously destroy it. This antique pile has the power of stamping these impressions on the mind, so masterly is it executed. Although it was designed, and raised, here, by the late noble possessor, it maintains, even on the nearest approach, the face of having been, some centuries ago, strong and formidable. This gothic ruin is very judiciously situated on the boldest eminence in the whole domain; and commands a most unbounded prospect: particularly so, from a neatly fitted-up room in the tower, which intentionally is left in a perfect state. And to keep the whole design in its purity – to wipe away any suspicion of its being any otherwise than a real ruin, the large and massy stones, which have seemingly tumbled from the tottering and ruinous walls, are suffered to lie about the different parts of the building, in the utmost confusion. To throw a deeper solemnity over it, and make it carry a stronger face of antiquity, ivy is encouraged to climb about the walls, and turrets; and it now so closely embraces those parts with its gloomy arms, that it is impossible to look upon it without a suggestion of its being as ancient as it really appears.[6]

According to Young's report, there was an attempt made to connect Sandbeck Park with the real ruins of Roche Abbey. For this purpose a new section of land was added.

> The spot at present is one of the most striking that is to be seen: It is a narrow winding valley full of wood; a stream takes an irriguous course through it over a bed of stones and fragments of rock shivered from the steep cliffs that bound the vale on either side; in the middle of it are the ruins of the abbey. – A few massy buttresses remain, with some lofty arches; trees have grown from the rubbish, and spread their branches among the ruin'd columns; the walls are half covered with ivy, which breaks in some

places from its support, and hangs among the trees in thick groups of foliage; the surface of the vale is half covered with thorns and briars; irregular and broken – with here and there a rocky fragment that has forced its way through them – the stream murmurs over the rock – and the cliffs, which hang almost perpendicular over the vale and look down on the ruin, are spread with thick woods that throw a solemn gloom over the whole; and *breathe a browner horror* on every part of the scene – all is wild, and romantic: every object is obscure; – every part unites to raise melancholy ideas; perhaps the most powerful, of which the human soul is capable.

38

BERNARDIN DE SAINT-PIERRE

Bernardin de Saint-Pierre's *Etudes de la Nature* (1784–97) included a chapter, 'Plaisir des ruines', which followed immediately upon his account of the 'Sentiment of Melancholy'. He was of the opinion that 'the passive taste for ruin is universal', noting how gardens were embellished with fake ruins. He considered that ruins were not architectural remnants, nor 'a source of forms, techniques and ornaments for new architectural endeavors', but (as Susan Steward observes in *The Ruins Lesson*) 'a projected state of mind'. He visited Dresden in 1765, where he discussed the destruction recently wrought on the city by the Prussian armies during the Seven Years' War.

Etudes de la Nature, 1784–97 (*Studies of Nature*, translated by Henry Hunter, London: J. Mayman, 1801)

Of the Sentiment of Melancholy

Beneficent Nature converts all her phenomena into so many sources of pleasure to man; and if we attend to her procedure, it will be found that her most common appearances are the most agreeable. I enjoy pleasure, for example, when I see old mossy walls dripping, and hear the whistling of the wind, mingled with the clattering of rain. These melancholy sounds, in the night-time, throw me into a soft and profound sleep.

I cannot tell to what physical law philosophers may refer the sensations of melancholy; I consider them as the most voluptuous affections of the soul. Melancholy is dainty; it proceeds from its gratifying at once the body and the soul; the sentiment of our misery and of our excellence.

In bad weather, the sentiment of my human misery is tranquillized by seeing it rain, while I am under cover; by hearing the wind blow violently, while I am comfortably in bed. I, in this case, enjoy a negative felicity. With this are afterwards blended some of those attributes of the Divinity, the perceptions of which communicate such exquisite pleasure to the soul. It looks as if Nature were then conforming to my situation, like a sympathizing friend. She is besides at all times so interesting, under whatever aspect she exhibits herself, that when it rains I think I see a beautiful woman in tears. She seems to me more beautiful the more that she wears the appearance of affliction. In order to be impressed with these sentiments, which I venture to call voluptuous, I must have no project in hand of a pleasant walk, of visiting, of hunting, which perhaps would put me into bad humour to enjoy bad weather; the soul must be traveling abroad, and the body at rest. From the harmony of those two powers of our constitution, the most terrible revolutions of Nature frequently interest us more than her gayest scenery.

The Pleasure of Ruin

I for some time believed man had an unaccountable taste for destruction. If a monument is within reach of the populace, they are sure to destroy it. I have seen at Dresden beautiful statues of females, mutilated by the Prussian soldiery, when in possession of that city. The common people have a turn for slander, and take pleasure in levelling the reputation of all that is exalted. This malevolent instinct is not of Nature; it is infused by the misery of individuals, whom education

Bernardo Bellotto, *Ruins of the old Kreuzkirche, Dresden,* oil on canvas, 1765.
Gemäldegalerie, Dresden.

inspires with an ambition interdicted by society, and which throws them into a negative ambition. Incapable of rising, they are impelled to lay everything low. This taste for ruin is not natural, but simply the exercise of the power of the miserable. Man in a savage state destroys the monuments only of his enemies; he preserves those of his own nation; he is naturally much better than man in a state of society, for he never slanders his compatriots.

The passive taste for ruin is, however, universal. Our voluptuaries embellish their gardens with artificial ruins; savages delight in melancholy repose by the brink of the sea, especially during a storm, or in the vicinity of a cascade surrounded by rocks. Magnificent destruction presents new picturesque effects; and this curiosity, combined with cruelty, impelled Nero to set Rome on fire, to enjoy the spectacle of a vast conflagration. This kind of affection, by no means connected with our physical wants, has induced certain philosophers to allege that our soul, being in a state of agitation, took pleasure in all extraordinary emotions; but they have advanced their axiom as slightly as many others with which their works abound. First, the soul takes pleasure in rest as in commotion; it is a harmony very gentle, and easily disturbed by violent emotions; and granting it to be in its own nature a movement, I do not see that it ought to take pleasure in those which threated it with destruction. Lucretius has come much nearer to the truth, when he says, tastes of this sort arise from the sentiment of our own security, heightened by the sight of danger to which we are not exposed. It is a pleasant thing, says he, to contemplate a storm from the shore...

But there is a more sublime sentiment within us, which derives pleasure from ruin independently of all picturesque effect, and every idea of personal security; it is that of Deity, which ever blends itself with our melancholy affections, and constitutes their principal charm.

The heart of man is so naturally disposed to benevolence, that the spectacle of a ruin which brings to recollection only the misery of our fellow-men, inspires us with horror, whatever may be the picturesque effect it presents. It is not so much with ruins effected by time. These give pleasure by launching us into infinity; they carry us several ages back, and interest us in proportion to their antiquity. Hence the reason why the ruins of Italy affect us more than those of our own country; the ruins of Greece more than those of Italy; and the ruins of Egypt more than those of Greece. The ruins in which Nature combats with human art inspire a gentle melancholy. In these she discovers to us the vanity of our labours, and the perpetuity of her own. A fine style of architecture always produces beautiful ruins, the plans of art, in this case, forming an alliance with the majesty of those of Nature. The interest of ruin, however, is greatly heightened when some moral sentiment is blended with it.

39

Constantin-François de Chasseboeuf, Comte de Volney

1789

The Ruins, by Constantin-François de Chasseboeuf, Comte de Volney, with the additional title of *Meditation on the Revolutions of Empires: And the Law of Nature*, was first published in 1789 and represented a key element of the 18th century's rationalist historical and political thought. Benjamin Franklin, the first ambassador from the newly formed United States to France, had formed a close enough friendship with Volney to establish a relationship between the French aristocrat and the new country's Minister for Treaties and Commerce, Thomas Jefferson. The friendship was, it seems, doubly consequential: Jefferson secretly translated 20 chapters of Volney, and helped to secure the book's wide distribution, while the Frenchman's arguments helped Americans see more clearly the ruinous consequences of excessive self-interest, as well as the need for a sharp distinction between matters of church and state.

Volney – who derived his title by combining *Vol* from Voltaire with *ney* from Voltaire's home at Ferney – had traveled widely in the Near East in 1782, where he studied Arabic, before he published this major book. In *The Ruins* he writes that he embarked on a tour of ancient remains, and describes his meditations on that experience. His perspective was formed less from searching how ruins might allow us glimpses into the past than by focusing on many religions – 'Indians, Persians, Jews, Christans, Musslemans' – and to ask 'what concerns the happiness of mankind... in human history'? Therefore he wondered whether ancient ruined civilizations might be the future of mankind, and imagined how some traveler could sit down on the banks of any famous river, be it the Seine or the Thames, and amid that solitude and silent ruins to lament 'a people injured, and their gestures changed into an empty name'. The 1872 engraving by Gustave Doré (see p.159), based on one in Volney's *Ruins*, was noted in a footnote on Volney in Susan Stewart's *The Ruins Lesson*.

CONSTANTIN-FRANÇOIS DE CHASSEBOEUF

The Ruins: or Meditation on the Revolutions of Empires
(Boston: Charles Gaylord, 1840)

In the eleventh year of the reign of Abd-ul Hamid, son of Ahmed, emperor of the Turks; when the Nogaian Tartars were driven from the Crimea, and a Mussulman prince, of the blood of Gengis Khan, became the vassal and *guard* of a woman, a Christian, and a queen... I journeyed in the empire of the Ottomans, and traversed the provinces which formerly were kingdoms of Egypt and of Syria.

Directing all my attention to what concerns the happiness of mankind in a state of society, I entered cities, and studied the manners of their inhabitants; I gained admission into palaces, and observed the conduct of those who govern; I wandered over the country, and examined the condition of the peasants: and no where perceiving aught but robbery and devastation, tyranny and wretchedness, my heart was oppressed with sorrow and indignation.

Every day I found in my route fields abandoned by the plough, villages deserted, and cities in ruins. Frequently I met with antique monuments; wrecks of temples, palaces, and fortifications; pillars, aqueducts, sepulchres. By these objects my thoughts were directed to past ages, and my mind absorbed in serious and profound meditation.

Arrived at Hamsa on the borders of the Orontes, and being at no great distance from the city of Palmyra, situated in the desert, I resolved to examine for myself its boasted monuments. After three days travel in barren solitude, and having passed through a valley filled with grottoes and tombs, my eyes were suddenly struck, on leaving this valley and entering a plain, with a most astonishing scene of ruins. It consisted of a countless multitude of superb columns standing erect, and which, like the avenues of our parks, extended in regular files farther than the eye could reach. Among these columns magnificent edifices were observable, some entire, others in a state half demolished. The ground was covered on all sides with fragments of similar buildings, cornices, capitals, shafts, entablatures, and pilasters, all constructed of a marble of admirable whiteness and exquisite workmanship. After a walk of three quarters of an hour along these ruins, I entered the inclosure of a vast edifice which had formerly been a temple dedicated to the sun; and I accepted the hospitality of some poor Arabian peasants, who had established their huts in the very area of the temple. Here I resolved for some days to remain, that I might contemplate, at leisure, the beauty of so many stupendous works.

Every day I visited some of the monuments which covered the plain; and one evening that, my mind lost in reflection, I had advanced as far as the *Valley*

A Traveler Contemplating the Ruins of Palmyra, engraving from C. F. Volney's *The Ruins*, 1791. Cornell University Library.

of Sepulchres, I ascended the heights that bound it, and from which the eye commands at once the whole of the ruins and the immensity of the desert... The sun had just sunk below the horizon; a streak of red still marked the place of his descent, behind the distant mountains of Syria: the full moon, appearing with brightness upon a ground of deep blue, rose in the east from the smooth bank of the Euphrates: the sky was unclouded; the air calm and serene; the expiring light of day served to soften the horror of approaching darkness; the refreshing breeze of the night gratefully relieved the intolerable sultriness of the day that had preceded it; the shepherds had led the camels to their stalls; the grey firmament bounded the silent landscape; through the whole desert every thing was marked with stillness, undisturbed but by the mournful cries of the bird of night, and of some *chacals* [jackals]... The dusk increased, and already I could distinguish nothing more than the pale phantoms of walls and columns... The solitariness of the situation, the serenity of evening, and the grandeur of the scene, impressed my mind with religious thoughtfulness. The view of an illustrious city deserted, the remembrance of past times, their comparison with the present state of things, all combined to raise my heart to a strain of sublime meditations. I sat down on the base of a column; and there, my elbow on my knee, and my head resting on my hand, sometimes turning my eyes towards the desert, and sometimes fixing them on the ruins, I fell into a profound reverie.

HERE, said I to myself, an opulent city once flourished; this was the seat of a powerful empire. Yes, these places, now so desert, a living multitude formerly animated, and an active crowd circulated in the streets which at present are so solitary. Within those walls, where a mournful silence reigns, the noise of the arts and the shouts of joy and festivity continually resounded. These heaps of

Gustave Doré, *A Visitor from New Zealand Gazing at St Paul's*,
engraving, after Volney, 1872.

marble formed regular palaces, these prostrate pillars were the majestic ornaments of temples, these ruinous galleries present the outlines of public places. There a numerous people assembled for the respectable duties of its worship, or the anxious cares of its subsistence: there industry, the fruitful inventor of sources of enjoyment, collected together the riches of every climate, and the purple of Tyre was exchanged for the precious thread of Serica; the soft tissues of Cassimere for the sumptuous carpets of Lydia; the amber of the Baltic for the pearls and perfumes of Arabia; the gold of Ophit for the pewter of Thule...

And now a mournful skeleton is all that subsists of this opulent city, and nothing remains of its powerful government but a vain and obscure remembrance! To the tumultuous throng which crowded under these porticos, the solitude of death has succeeded. The silence of the tomb is substituted for the hum of public places. The opulence of a commercial city is changed into hideous poverty. The palaces of kings are become the receptacle of deer, and unclean reptiles inhabit the sanctuary of the Gods... What glory is here eclipsed, and how many labors are annihilated!... Thus perish the works of men, and thus do nations and empires vanish away!

The history of past times strongly presented itself to my thoughts. I called to mind those distant ages when twenty celebrated nations inhabited the country around me. I pictured to myself the Assyrian on the banks of the Tygris, the Chaldean on those of the Euphrates, the Persian whose power extended from the Indus to the Mediterranean. I enumerated the kingdoms of Damascus and Idumea; of Jerusalem and Samaria; and the warlike states of the Philistines; and the commercial republics of Phenicia. This Syria, said I to myself, now almost depopulated, then contained a hundred flourishing cities, and abounded with towns, villages, and hamlet. Every where one might have seen cultivated fields, frequented roads, and crowded habitations. Ah! what are become of those ages of abundance and of life? What are become of so many productions of the hand of man? Where are those ramparts of Nineveh, those walls of Babylon, those palaces of Persepolis, those temples of Balbec and of Jerusalem? Where are those fleets of Tyre, those dockyards of Arad, those work-shops of Sidon, and that multitude of mariners, pilots, merchants, and soldiers? Where those husbandmen, those harvests, that picture of animated nature of which the earth seemed proud? Alas! I have traversed this desolate country, I have visited the places that were the theatre of so much splendour, and I have nothing beheld but solitude and desertion! I looked for those ancient people and their works, and all I could find was a faint trace, like to what the foot of a passenger leaves on the sand. The temples are thrown down, the palaces demolished, the ports filled up, the towns destroyed, and the earth, stript of inhabitants, seems a dreary burying-place... Great God! from whence proceed such melancholy revolutions? For what cause is the fortune of these countries so strikingly changed? Why are so many cities destroyed? Why is not that ancient population re-produced and perpetuated?

40

UVEDALE PRICE AND RICHARD PAYNE KNIGHT

1794

Price and Knight were the two prominent expounders of the picturesque by the end of the 18th century. Yet they differed, as Humphry Repton noticed, often quite sharply. The first saw picturesque as something that pertained to the site itself; the latter saw it as a theory of association, a function of the individual's imagination, albeit a rather mechanical one. Gainsborough painted some aged beech trees at Price's family home at Foxley in Herefordshire, where Price admitted 'some little sacrifice of picturesque beauty to neatness near the house'; Thomas Hearne painted the rustic bridge in the densely wooded glen at Downton Castle for its owner Knight, who enjoyed a more rigorous and painterly inspired estate there, realizing, à la Salvator Rosa, an 'awful precipice' and 'wild but pleasant horrors' in its valley. Those localities may have sustained their differing perspectives on the picturesque. But ruins, though an apt ingredient, did little to obtain their preferred picturesque.

Price's *An Essay on the Picturesque* (1794) chose to expand Edmund Burke's concepts of the sublime and the beautiful by inserting the picturesque between them, and the styles of architecture that gave him the opportunity to do so. Grecian buildings were 'too perfect' and complete, but time and weather helped to render them picturesque. 'Gothic architecture is generally considered as more picturesque, though less beautiful, than Grecian; and upon the same principle that a ruin is more so than a new edifice,' and his third chapter expands upon that distinction. In 'Decorations near the House' he is flexible to the extent that he finds painterly examples hard to find, because their representation of 'embellishments of *gardens*... are comparatively few'. Moreover, under the influence of Lancelot 'Capability' Brown, the effects of 'time and accident' in older gardens have been largely eliminated: the contemporary 'affectation of simplicity, or mere nature' defeats any opportunity of picturesque: where there are few buildings, there is less ruin.

Knight's *The Landscape, A Didactic Poem*, also from 1794, did recognize 'tow'rs and temples, mould'ring to decay', but related them to paintings of Rosa, Hobbema, and Ruisdael; buildings will be 'harsh and cold' until they can be

> soften'd down by long revolving years;
> Till time and weather have conjointly spread
> Their mould'ring hues and mosses o'er its head.
> Bless'd is the man, in whose sequester'd glade,
> Some ancient abbey's walls diffuse their shade;
> With mould'ring windows pierc'd, and turrets crown'd,
> And pinnacles with clinging ivy bound.

And if the owner cannot enjoy an ancient abbey, then 'some ruin'd castle' can be glimpsed above woodlands on the far hillside, as Gilpin (*see* Extract 34) found at Blaise Castle. In *An Analytical Inquiry into the Principles of Taste* 11 years later Knight was far too concerned with enunciating general principles to have time for anything as specific as ruins.

Price, however, did explore the topic in *Essays on Artificial Water, on Decorations, and on Architecture and Buildings*, the second part of his *Essay on the Picturesque*, where he advanced ideas on how 'time and decay convert a beautiful building into a picturesque one'.

Essay on the Picturesque, 1794
(London: J. Robson, 1794)

I have shown in an early part of my first Essay, how time and decay convert a beautiful building into a picturesque one, and by what process the change is operated. That the character of every building must be essentially changed by decay, is very apparent; and, likewise, that the alteration must be in proportion as the original character or design is obliterated by that decay; a building, however, does not immediately change its original character, but parts with it by degrees; and seldom, perhaps, loses it entirely. It will probably be acknowledged, that a beautiful building is in its most beautiful state, when the columns are in every part round and smooth, the ornaments entire, and the whole design of the artist in every part complete. If this be granted, then from the first moment that the smoothness, the symmetry, and the design of such a building suffers any injury, it is manifest that its beauty is thereby diminished; and it may be observed, that there is a state of injury and decay, in which we only perceive and lament the diminution of beauty, without being consoled for it by any other character. In proportion as the injury increases, in proportion as the embellishments that belong to architecture, the polish of its columns, the highly finished execution of its capitals and mouldings, its urns and statues, are changed for what may be called the embellishments of ruins, for incrustations and weather

Two engravings from Uvedale Price's *Essay on the Picturesque*, 1794. Fisher Fine Arts Library, University of Pennsylvania.

stain, and for the various plants that spring from, or climb over the walls – the character of the picturesque prevails over that of the beautiful; and at length, perhaps, all smoothness, all symmetry, all trace of design are totally gone. But there may still remain an object which attracts notice. Has it then no character when that of beauty is departed? Is it ugly? is it insipid? is it merely curious? Ask the painter, or the picturesque traveller; they never abandon a ruin to the mere antiquity, till none but an antiquary would observe it. Whatever then has strong attractions as a visible object, must have a character; and that which has strong attractions for the painter, and yet is neither grand nor beautiful, is justly called picturesque.

Take, again, a building, the sole character of which is grandeur. On that, the changes are less sensible than on the delicate qualities of beauty; but, when the walls begin to lose their firmness, and in parts to totter – when large cracks and breaches appear, that species of architectural grandeur which is derived from one of its greatest sources, solidity, is diminished in proportion. It is long, however, before the picturesque prevails over that original grandeur; from the first approaches of decay they are indeed in some degree mixed and combined with each other, but the ruins of Agrigentum and Selinus will testify, that though beauty in buildings may be destroyed by time and decay, grandeur resist their power; and, by a singular agreement, these most solid bodies resemble what Milton says of immaterial substances, and cannot, but by annihilating, die.

The chaste and noble style of Grecian architecture does not admit of a number of sudden breaks and variations of form, or of enrichments over a large part of the surface; it therefore never displays a marked picturesque character till in ruin. But Gothic buildings are full of breaks and divisions, and the parts highly and profusely enriched; the correspondence between the parts being also much less obvious than in Grecian architecture, the whole has often an apparent irregularity, and from these circumstances many Gothic structures, even in their entire and perfect state, display a marked picturesque character. That character, however, cannot but be increased by decay. Abruptness and irregularity are two of its principal sources, and consequently every building must be more picturesque in a ruinous state than it was when entire; for, in a perfect habitable building, however abruptly and irregularly the lines of the walls and roofs may cross each other, yet each break which decay occasions in them at once increases both their irregularity and their abruptness...

Of all ruins, those of ancient Greek and Roman buildings are on many accounts the most intresting; – in no other buidings are the rival qualities of grandeur and beauty so happily united, and to that union is added the prejudice in favour of their high antiquity, and of their being the productions of two peoples, renowned for every art and accomplishment that can raise or adorn our nature.

Next to them, and in some points of view to us more interesting, are the ruins of abbeys and castles. I have named them together, though nothing can be more contrasted than their two characters. The abbey, built in some sequestered spot, and surrounded by woods, announces religious calm and security – its sanctity, even in those early times of turbulence, but likewse of superstition, was thought a sufficient safeguard, and its structure, though solid and massive, seems designed for ornament, not for defence...

In the castle, every thing proclaims suspicious defiance – the security of strength and precaution. A commanding, or at least an uncommanded situation – high solid wall and towers; the draw-bridge, the portcullis; few apertures, and those small; no breaks nor projections that would interfere with strength and solidity. The ruins of these once magnificent edifices are the pride and boast of this island; we may well be proud of them, not merely in a picturesque point of view; we may glory that the abodes of tyranny and superstition are in ruin...

In the third degree are old mansion-houses... Where any of them are sufficiently preserved to be capable of being repaired, and are intended to be made habitable, too much caution cannot be used in clearing away those disguises and intricacies which the hand of time has slowly created, lest, with those accompaniments, their ancient and venerable character should be destroyed.

41

HUMPHRY REPTON

1795–6

As a designer of gardens and landscapes, Humphry Repton was far less interested in providing fake ruins than, when necessary, dealing with existing ones, whether genuine or more recently devised by others. His concern was always to provide comfort and convenience on both larger properties and small villa sites, sketched out in plans and drawings in the 'Red Books' he compiled as suggestions for potential clients; 'propriety', not the 'picturesque', was his aim, as he wrote in his *Sketches and Hints on Landscape Gardening*. In his Red Book for Rug in North Wales he wrote that he sought 'to preserve... every vestige of ancient or hereditary dignity; and I should feel it a kind of sacrilege in taste, to destroy an atom of that old, ruinous, and almost uninhabitable mansion at Rug, if it were to be replaced by one of these gaudy scarlet houses, which we see spring up like mushrooms, in the neighbourhood of large manufacturing towns'. So in that case, he found that an appeal to 'modern comfort and convenience' was needed. However, he retained an existing Norman archway for the entrance to Scrivelsby in Lincolnshire, while in the Red Book for Anthony House, Cornwall, he drew the distant Tremuton Castle to terminate a scenic walk.

At Blaise Castle, near Bristol, in 1795-6 he was called upon to organize the approaches and vistas both within it and alongside the River Avon. But the castle that gave the place its name was a recent erection, and Repton had some problems: 'Some difficulty occurs with respect to Blaise Castle, and as the house neither does nor

Humphry Repton's Red Book for Blaise Castle, near Bristol; distant view of castle (at left) and cottage from the main house, watercolor, 1795-96. Bristol Museums.

Humphry Repton, *Old Trees at Cobham Hall*, captioned 'Enemy of Vegetation', from his Red Book, watercolor, c.1814. J. Paul Getty Museum, Los Angeles.

ought to partake of the castle-character, there may perhaps appear a little incongruity in making the entrance in that style, yet I cannot propose an entrance-lodge of Grecian architecture...' So it was designed (and remains) in Gothick form. In his Red Book he drew the castle and an adjacent cottage as a view from the classical mansion.

What he did admire and hail, as a natural equivalent of a ruin, were the old and venerable trees, relics of ancient woodland, at Cobham Hall in Kent. And in an Appendix to *Sketches and Hints* he does cite (facetiously perhaps) Uvedale Price's hope that 'Mr Repton will have a nobler ambition; – that of having his artificial rivers and lakes mistaken for real ones.' Yet he never seems to have mistaken the status of ruins; indeed he rarely, if at all, addresses them.

42

PERIODICAL VERSES ON RUINS

1776–1832

While poets such as Du Bellay in France or Dyer in Britain wrote whole poems on the idea of ruins and their most conspicuous sites, like Rome, 18th-century periodicals such as the *London Chronicle*, the *Universal Magazine*, and *Blackwood's Edinburgh Magazine* frequently published poems on specific British sites, such as 'Lines Written at Kelburne Castle' by 'Delta' (*see* Extract 32). Others were published independently, such as the Rev. Joseph Jefferson's *The Ruins of Temple, a Poem...* in 1793. The authors were either anonymous, or wrote under initials; none, it must be confessed, were probably worth naming. They raise both conventional and occasionally more unusual perspectives, as individual visitors found in ruins either historical or personal and highly sentimental reflections. It was usually castles that attracted these writers – at Pomfret, Winchelsea, Donnington, and Kenilworth in England, at Kelbourne Castle and 'the celebrated' Dornadilla in Srathnaver in Scotland, or Conway Castle in Wales.

'Spontaneous thoughts written in the Ruins of
Winchelsea Castle, near Rye, in Sussex',
in *The Universal Magazine*, 1776

Within this spot, where obscene birds of night
Nestle, and nod, and screech, alternate, round,
Soft Music: floated once, whilst with delight
The distant Sailors caught the dying sound.

No more the warlike drum founds o'er these plains,
Nor the shrill trumpets pierce the ambient air;
Where stood the Centinel, now silence reigns,
And Desolation murmurs, 'Who comes there!'

Declining Commerce now, methinks, I see
In tears, reclin'd against the time-shook wall;

BOOK OF RUINS

Com'st thou, O Youth, she cries, to pity me
Com'st thou to mourn, or to withstand my fall?

Perhaps, in ancient times, when Rother's flood,
Roll'd swift and dreadful by those ruins wild,
Upon this very spot some parent stood,
And wept, with joy, to see her long-lost child...

Yon grove, deserted, ruinous, and wild,
Whose brown top bends beneath the ev'ning breeze,
Is still the nurse of Fancy's airy child,
And seems, to whisper how it once could please.

Imagination paints the flow'ry bed,
The stream below, the shady bow'r above;
Where some fond youth reclin'd his pensive head,
And spent the hours betwixt the Muse and Love.

His shade, methinks, now stalks majestic by,
Behold it glides beneath yon mould'ring wall;

The Iron Age broch Dun Dornadilla (Dun Dornaigil), Strathnaver, Scotland.

His hand he waves, lo! now he seems to sigh,
And thus Imagination hears him call:

'Dear Youth, whose lonely feet those ruins tread;
Whose down-cast eye lets fall the gen'rous tear.
Regard not transient life, which soon is fled;
Reflect on Heav'n and all the glories there...

'Reflection cease,' – methinks some voice replies,
'I solemn thoughts and groaning numbers hate;
Forsaken walls and ruins I despise;
Have me to banquetings and rooms of state.'

'To balls and banquets unmolested stray,
Let me in peace my wayward path pursue;
In viewing these I see my own decay;
If walls thus perish – I must perish too.'

Struck by this thought, Reflection sallies forth
Thro' ev'ry path of life she trod before,
Weighs ev'ry action, views its spring and growth,
And what 'twill yield, when time shall be no more.

'Lines written at Kenilworth Castle, Warwickshire',
in *The Universal Magazine*, c.1760

Here whilst I linger, midst the mouldering pile,
The fallen archways, and the fretted aisle,
And pensive view, with mind intent to scan
The short-lived glories of unthanking man,
Thy crumbling walls, where many a ruin'd tower
Gives kindly shelter to the straggling flower,
And many a child, escaped from school to play,
Pursues its gambols in the sunny ray,
Sad sinks my heart, to think how chang'd the scene,
Since courtly Leicester led the virgin Queen
With all her train, to grace his festive halls,
And loud rejoicings shook the massy walls:
Then spoke the clarion loud, the trumpet bray'd,

Sweet sang the choir, and soft the minstrels play'd;
Now sadly trembling, sighs the whispering breeze,
And sinks in gentle murmurs o'er the trees.
There where the Gothic windows' long array,
Enwreathed with Ivy, scarce admits the day,
The banquet stood: and many a stripling page,
And many a trusty squire of riper age,
Submissive gave, to crown their rising glee,
The sparkling goblet on his bended knee.
Great was the feast, with kingly pride display'd,
The gorgeous pageant and the high parade;
Bright beamed the lamps, enchanting strains resound,
Knights' tales of love, and jesters' jokes went round.
Now hush'd their mirth! The moping owl alone
Pours to the moon her solitary moan:
The wint'ry blast its driving torrents pours,
And groans and thunders thro' the trembling towers.
When great Eliza's gracious smile beheld
Th' aspiring favourite, high his bosom swell'd,
And little deemed he, man so soon should see
Laid low in dust the mighty pageantry.
But turn, my Muse a sadder theme pursue:
The royal Edward's gloomy dungeon view:
Here, ere to Berkeley's lofty walls he went,
Full many a sigh his tortur'd bosom rent,
He steeps his chains in unavailing tears,
And wrapt in frantic woe, the howling blast he hears:
And now autumnal breezes seem to bring
The groans and anguish of the captive king.
But hark! the trumpet's clang, the thundering drums,
And shouts proclaim, 'Victorious Cromwell comes':
Then the loud cannon, with rebellowing sound,
Shakes the huge pile, and spreads destruction round:
Vain is the ponderous gateway's guardian power,
And vain the bulk of Caesar's mighty tower:
Long lasts the siege, and rock the crumbling walls,
Till, quite o'erwhelm'd, the tottering fabric falls,
Should man with power, with pomp of wealth elate,
Exult and glory in his high estate,

PERIODICAL VERSES ON RUINS

Here let the proud one turn, and start to see
The sad remains of fallen majesty,
And stamp those truths upon his conscious heart,
Thy faded glories, Kenilworth, impart.

CHRISTOPHER SMYTH
'Ruins at Kenilworth',
in the *Literary Magazine and British Review*, 1790

How chang'd the scene – black Winter's storm
Waves the high grass that crowns the wall;
And red-ey'd Horror's giant form
Stalks, rudely thro' the desert hall.

The ivy pale shall spread its shade,
And twining round, each arch sustain,
Long as the tottering piles decay'd,
Look scornful on the barren plain.

Yet Grandeur here diffus'd his ray,
And Pleasure once her reign began;
Where now gaunt Time, with ruthless sway,
Laughs at the baseless, hopes of man...

'Lines written on the celebrated
Castle of Dornadilla, in Strathnaver,
a district in the Shire of Sutherland',
in the *Scots Magazine*, 1804

HAIL! venerable dome! whose mould'ring brow
Nods, sternly tow'ring, o'er the vale below;
Tow'ring above the tempest's sweeping course,
And struggling still with time's resistless force!
A solemn stillness meets me on the gale,
And spreads a secret terror o'er the vale;
My fluttering bosom, hush'd in silent awe,
Shrinks with a holy dread as near I draw;
As through thy halls, all naked and despoil'd,
I hear the passing blast sad and wild;

A secret voice comes whisp'ring to my ear,
'Avaunt, frail worm! the mighty once were here!'
Thrice, venerable pile some monarch's pride,
Ere yet the muse her infant powers had tried;
Whose grey towers mock the transient race of man,
And look sublime beyond his narrow span;
A long survivor of his fame and song,
To speak while time shall roll his tide along,
How desolate and waste thy grandeur now!
Without a trace thy founder's name to shew!
Speaks not thy age what mighty hand began
To rear thy height, to mete thy spacious plan?
To bind the rocky barrier round thy halls,
And plant the mystic chamber, in thy walls.

Yes! Dornadilla's sacred name appears;
He o'er thee first his streaming ensign rears:
Methinks I see his banner's gaudy pride
Athwart the lonely hills his warriors guide.
I see them croud with stern intrepid eye
Where thy proud towers aspire amid the sky;
Th' assembled chiefs of many distant land
Move to the chase beneath his high command;
When rosy morn the joyful huntsman calls,
They pour, unnumber'd, from the spacious halls;
Pursue the bounding wand'rer of the wild,
Through all his lonely haunts, midst rocks fantastic pil'd;
O'er hills and dales, thro' forest-glooms they fly,
The quenchless arrows glance, the herded tremblers die...

T. H.
'Donnington Castle Near Newbury',
in *The Gentleman's Magazine*, 1808

'Twas then to Donnington's ruin, I stray'd,
Whose grandeur the sickle of Time has laid low;
And the battlements where once the sentinel staid,
The grey moss and bramble and ivy o'er-grow.
Yonder tower, where the standard of War was once rear'd,

PERIODICAL VERSES ON RUINS

Is a nest for the young of the night-screeching owl;
And those walls where the trumpet's shrill clarion was heard,
Re-echo alone to the noise of the fowl.
The sun has long set, and the glimmerings of day
Had departed to yield to fair Cynthia's beams;
And her mild lustre marks out the devious way,
Whilst clearly reflected on yon rippling stream.
'Twas an hour when all Nature was hush'd in repose,
And a pleasing serenity stole on the mind,
When the soul on contemplative pinions arose,
And left all Earth's follies and trifles behind.
Ah! where, I exclaim'd, ah! where are the hands
That made yonder edifice proudly arise;
And where are the num'rous victorious bands
That oftimes in triumph with shouts rent the skies?
And where is the Bard [Chaucer] who so sweetly could sing,
And tell of the warriors of Britain of old?
But no more shall the walls with loud merriment ring
And no more shall the tale of old times be there told.
Now silent in death is the tongue of the Bard,
And nought from Time's ruin his mansion could save;
And the hands which younger proud edifice rear'd,
Have long since been mould'ring away in the grave.

43

ALEXANDRE DE LABORDE

1808

Alexandre de Laborde's massive 1808 survey of new 18th-century French gardens and parks in the neighborhood of Paris, *Description des Nouveaux Jardins de la France et de ses anciens châteaux*, highlights two sites with ruins – the Gardens of Betz and the much better-known Désert de Retz in Chambourcy. Laborde's notes and descriptions were published in French, German, and English, the last of which is used here. The volume was determined to make the case for new gardens in contrast to the earlier, 17th-century style; its multilingual text was also a determined challenge to the *jardin anglais* that seemed to have dominated landscape design throughout Europe by the end of the 18th century. Both ruins are shown to be situated in the larger landscape, and both are illustrated. Betz had earlier been celebrated in a rare poem of 1792 with notes on its composition and meaning; Retz has been discussed more widely in early modern and recent writings (*see* Extract 64). Laborde deems other unruined ancient structures, such as the genuine Gothic Gabrielle Tower at Ermenonville, to be 'without either unity or elegance', redeemed by being pleasantly surrounded with shrubs and ivy. A modern edition of Laborde's book, with an introduction by Michel Baridon, was published by Éditions Connaissance et Mémoires in Paris in 2004.

Description des Nouveaux Jardins de la France et de ses anciens châteaux
(Paris: Delance, 1808)

Gardens of Betz

At the distance of ten leagues from Paris, in the midst of an agreeable country, is situated the castle of Betz, formerly a seat belonging to the princess of Monaco. All that is majestic in vegetation, whatever art can add to the beauties of nature, were united in this narrow space. Even now, in its present forlorn state, this place is yet admirable by the remains of its past grandeur. The trees have reared their heads, as if they would protect the dwelling of their former masters. They have unfolded all their vigour near those habitations fallen into ruins; like them they are covered with moss and ivy, an ornament for the one, but a sign of decline for the others. It is thus that the hand of time employs the same means

Le Désert de Retz, Chambourcy, France. Photograph: John Dixon Hunt.

to embellish the productions of nature, and to destroy the labour of men. There is nothing more left at Betz, but a castle in ruins, some traces of buildings, and a fine vegetation...

There is nothing more interesting, no aspect more noble than the ruins of the old castles which raise their heads over the country, and seem to preserve yet the pride of their ancient inhabitants. These dark dwellings form a striking contrast with the smiling landscape around them; and, when their imitation is executed on a large scale, and in a garden, it produces a remarkable effect... Betz, though less considerable [than some German sites] is large enough to excite curiosity and interest.

Le Désert de Retz

This garden is a league and a half distant from Saint-Germain, at the extremity of an agreeable and fruitful valley. Two roads lead to it; the first in the midst of the fields bordered by willows and poplars, through which we discover an unknown horizon [i.e spread out – '*un horizon très-étendu*'], and, now and then, pretty houses. The second through the forest.

The chief entry is represented by a rustic gate composed of huge stones in the form of toothings [sic], surmounted by a beam on which is a little reconstruction of unhewed stone band, with a band or square projection; the higher part is crowned with shrubs and herbs that grow there naturally. There is no knowing what it means, it is neither a ruin nor an edifice. A prodigious quantity of trees have just been felled which formed a little forest at the entry, the greater part were beech-trees; in advancing we discover a Temple, half circular, and half square, of the Tuscan order, on a slope, and breaks from a ground of the richest verdure. We afterwards meet with a kind of farm composed of rustic buildings and inhabited by the keeper or gardener.

At the extremity of a vast meadow is the principal building; the idea of the architect has been to represent the remains of a doric column, channelled, of an immense proportion, that is to say of a circumference of two and twenty fathoms...

The column has gutter-work six feet high, the sides are two feet six inches broad; all worked with partition stone. The first story has doors, the second square windows, and the third oval windows; the light falls in afterwards through clinks, which appears to be natural accidents in the construction [a crack shown in the engraving on the top of the column suggests rather some subsequent fracture]... In the thickness between the circumference of the stairs and the diameter of the column, small apartments have been contrived, so it seems advantage has been taken of this ruin to construct an habitation in it...

44

John Soane

1815

When John Soane lectured on architecture at the Royal Academy he addressed ruins in his presentation on gardens. His claim that they added variety to a garden was hardly new; nor was his assertion that they deepened its historical meaning, exciting both memory and melancholy. Less common was his insistence on the appearance of truth in the constructed fictions – fabrications, or *fabriques*. Ruins, he maintained, should be contrived to look as if they belonged in their location, having survived injuries to a complete building that had once been there, and were therefore capable of telling their own story, the story of that place. A ruin in London that made use of ancient Greek fragments would be unacceptable. Only objects that seemed real could ignite the association of ideas and the emotions that follow. The same is true when ruins are built into new buildings, which is to say when the garden landscape is taken as the model for an interior landscape, as was the case with Soane's own house at Lincoln's Inn Fields, London.

What Soane's house is to a garden, the 'Monk's Yard' that adjoins it is to a ruin: artificial but seemingly real, forecasting the building's demise while recalling what preceded it. Equipped with both practical and representational elements, it is intended to be used and thought about. The Yard includes the representation of a tomb, as well as a real grave for Mrs Soane's pet dog Fanny. Soane wanted the fragments to be seen and understood as the remains of some monastic settlement. In point of fact, they are *spolia* from recently demolished parts of the medieval Palace of Westminster. Other elements include a well and pump, a few urns, and other architectural odds and ends, all of which rest on a pavement made from pebbles said to be found in the gravel of the monastery. Not everything was fictional, however. Nearby was the furnace for heating the house's water. On pleasant afternoons Soane and his friends had tea there, reportedly on silk-upholstered chairs.

The unusual conjunction of representational and practical themes is likewise vivid in the more famous *Bird's-Eye View of the Bank of England* by Soane's assistant Joseph Gandy. The watercolor shows the roofless building surrounded by encroaching vegetation, creating a humbling sense of loss, not only of the building but of all that it represented in English culture – maybe the country itself – but the image can also be read as a study in architectural construction, thanks to the combination of plan, section, and elevation views, as well as construction details – a Renaissance precedent for which is a famous drawing of the interior of St Peter's in Rome by Baldassare Peruzzi. The remarkable revelation made possible by this view of building and unbuilding was stressed in a quotation from the French writer Alain-René Lesage's 1707 novel *Le Diable Boiteux* that Soane included in the caption to the catalogue for the 1830 Royal Academy Exhibition: '*Je vais enlever les toits de cette superbe édifice national... le dedans va se découvrir à vos yeux de même qu'on voit le dedans un pâté dont on vient d'ôter la croute*' (I want to lift the roof of that wonderful national building. The interior will be revealed to you like a meat pie with the crust removed).

'Gardens and City Plans', Lecture X (1815), *Lectures*, 1810–20

Besides entire buildings of different kinds, Ruins are frequently introduced into Ornamental Gardening. When congenial with the scenery of the place, and its historical character, Ruins increase the variety and cause a pleasing diversity. In Italy or Greece, we constantly see the mouldering remains of Mausolea, Temples, Amphitheatres, and Aqueducts, and when the scene is enriched with 'nodding Arches and broken Temples spread', such objects fill the mind with the most serious and awful reflections. The Mausolea of Hadrian, of Cecilia Metella, and Plautus, point out most forcibly the departed grandeur of their former magnificence and dazzling splendour. Works that might have defied the efforts of Time are now with their battlements and embrasures, become mere monuments of the insufficiency of our endeavours, and of the mutability of all human expectations.

The Monument of the Horatii and Curatii fills us with respect for the Patriotic and Heroic deeds to which it refers. The remains of many towering Structures, broken arches, and massive Walls, bring back to our recollections interesting, important, and instructive incidents of History, calling forth all the noblest feelings of a sympathetic mind. The mighty ruins of a Column, whose enormous dimensions excite our attention, point out the fatal spot where the unhappy Nicias threw himself at the feet of the Conqueror, beseeching Gyllippus to stop the further slaughter of the brave Athenians, his comrades in defeat, thousands of whom were then bleeding before his eyes. When Ruins of buildings bring the recollection of such deeds fresh to the mind, as if then acting, we are truly anxious for Time to spare such Monuments, that the same effect may be produced to the latest Ages. Here there is no delusion, no imaginary colouring, and the effect on the mind is complete. If artificial Ruins of rocks and buildings are so cunningly contrived, so well-conceived, as to excite such reflections and

Joseph Gandy, *View of the Court of the Monk's Grave*, watercolour, c.1824.
Sir John Soane's Museum, London.

convey such useful, tho' melancholy lessons, then too much cannot be said in favour of their introduction on every occasion. Like the buildings of the Egyptians, covered with their hieroglyphics, such Ruins may be considered as Histories open to all the world.

Ruins, to please the Beholder, must present to the mind the recollection of some particular event, or some known fact of importance. They must appear

Joseph Gandy, *A Bird's Eye View of the Bank of England*, 1830.
Sir John Soane's Museum, London.

to be the remains of what once really existed in the very place, or at least be analogous to it. They must tell their own story, or they will appear trivial and uninteresting. The remains of a Castle seen in a valley or plain cannot by any stretch of the imagination be supposed to have been placed there for any other purpose than mere decoration.

From representations of Roman Buildings seen in places that were not known to the Romans, no emotion of satisfaction can be produced. If, however, instead of Roman Buildings remains of Gothic towers rise majestically among Forest Trees, 'whose high tops are bald with dry antiquity', they can be pleasing features. The superb remains of an old Baronial Castle, an Abbey, a Cloister, or the Tower of a Church (as at Coventry), so situated as to present to the mind the idea that they are really part of something of great extent, which time and circumstance has spared, lead us to enquire into their history and induce the proper emotions of respect and reverence. We experience effects similar to that noble enthusiasm, which the sight of Roman Buildings in ruins, in the pictures of Claude and Salvator Rosa, creates in the mind. Recollections are aroused of former struggles for power, and of those revolutions in religious thinking, which have caused the destruction of so many noble efforts of superior greatness, as recorded in many of the pages of our past history.

In order that these artificial Ruins, mimic representations and portraits of objects, shall produce pleasing sensations there must be an appearance of Truth. A picture of any kind to please must be correct as to what it proposes to represent. In like manner a ruin should not be so strikingly out of character, in respect of form and situation, as to show at once that is but a representation and not a reality. In a word, a Ruin must recall to the mind the idea of a real object and not be considered as a mere picture.

Nor is it sufficient that objects are picturesque in their forms and combinations, and enriched with a variety of tints, softened and harmonized into each other by the end of Time. Ruins, evidently constructed for decoration only, in situation and character, where they cannot pretend to represent anything more than a heap of materials, broken into a great variety of agreeable forms, can never produce the requisite sensation. It is from the association of ideas that ruins excite in the mind that our feelings are aroused... When in our Parks and Pleasure Grounds we see representations of Buildings in ruins, with all the evidence of a laboured, artificial construction, perceiving immediately that they are there merely for embellishment, our minds revolt at once at the impropriety and we are unable to restrain a smile at the futility of the imitation.

Ruins representing the remains of Grecian or Roman buildings, however beautiful and picturesque, can never be introduced into the Decorative Gardening of the country. Nor perhaps can any other style of composition be so effectively used as the Gothic, of which we have so many striking examples in the mouldering ruins of Castles, religious Houses, magnificent Priories, and extensive Cathedrals, still existing in so many parts of England.

IV

THE 19TH CENTURY

George Beaumont, frontispiece to Wordsworth's *The White Doe of Rylstone*, 1815.
University of Pennsylvania.

45

WILLIAM WORDSWORTH

1835

William Wordsworth wrote variously about ruins throughout his life, so the references are scattered through his work. In need of money, he published his *Guide to the Lakes* anonymously in 1810 as part of Joseph Wilkinson's *Select Views in Cumberland, Westmoreland, and Lancashire,* alongside a collection of engravings (which Wordsworth came to dislike). There were several subsequent, augmented editions, with the last and final version, *A Guide through the District of the Lakes*, published in Kendal in 1835. This was yet another response to the vogue for touring and observing Britain (*see* Extract 24), and its recent editor Peter Bicknell details the context of many other excursions in that area.[1]

Given the location, Wordsworth is less concerned with ruins than with the cottages of local inhabitants and the discovery of routes, poor roads, and paths to mountain summits. Some small ruins are identified, but usually as landmarks by which explorers can navigate unfamiliar territory. Nonetheless, on his approaches to the central lakes, he notes Kirkstall Abbey and the 'much celebrated' Furness Abbey, the castle at Lowther near Pooley Bridge, and some Roman remains in Eskdale.

One topic he does pursue occasionally is Neolithic remains which, like many of his contemporaries, he attributed to Druids, considering them the 'only vestiges that remain upon the surface of the country, of these ancient occupants', who 'officiated at… the mimic arrangement of stones, with its *sanctum sanctorum*'. In his ode 'The Pass of Kirkstone' (1817), he sees 'Altars for Druid service fit'. This 'druidical circle' near Keswick (now known as Castlerigg Stone Circle) was not unique, for he notes in a long footnote how a friend unearthed 'a perfect circle of stones, from two to three feet high… the whole a complete place of Druidical worship', which since 'has been destroyed'. He also observes that such circles can be reinvented as follies (what he calls 'puerilities') in a landscape. On Vicar's Island on Windermere an earlier proprietor had once established a 'Druidical Temple' created from stones excavated from a nearby house: this, its eccentric owner asserted, was 'the most compleat & last built Temple in Europe'.

Wordsworth's poems evoke useful, picturesque settings, where ruins are central. At the age of 17 in 'The Vale of Esthwaite' he had described a Gothick mansion with a rusted door that 'shield[s] from death the wandering poor'. *Descriptive Sketches Taken during a Pedestrian Tour Among the Alps*, written in 1790–91 and published in 1793, are not, as the title might suggest, sketched descriptions, but discuss how a scene might be thought about. These included lines on the 'wretched fane' and 'troubled walls' of the Abbey of Ensiedeln, and the pilgrims who originally visited it. And some years later, in the unfinished poem 'Insipient Madness' (1797), he writes of a decayed hut:

> I entered in, but all was still and dark,
> Only within the ruin I beheld
> At a small distance, on the dusky ground
> A broken pain, which glittered in the gloom
> And seemed akin to life...

Wordsworth always found ruins an invitation to think on their former inhabitants, as in his 'Address to Kilchurm Castle, upon Loch Awe': there, in his sister's words, he 'poured out these verses [while] looking on the castle and the huge mountain opposite'. The poem begins with the line 'Child of loud-throated War!' because the rumor was that it was built by a lady when her husband was on the Crusades. As the address proceeds, it is the ruined and abandoned castle, the 'Majestic pile' that signaled the later 'fury uncontrollable' of the Crusades. Yet he prefixed to his verses a prose extract from his sister's diary; she was more attentive to its formal appearance and landscape setting:

> From the top of the hill a most impressive scene opened upon our view, - a ruined castle on an Island (for an Island the flood had made it) at some distance from the shore, backed by a Cove of the Mountain Cruaclan, down which came a foaming stream. The Castle occupied very foot of the Island that was visible to us, appearing to rise out of the water, - mists rested upon the mountain side, with spots of sunshine; there was a mild desolation in the low grounds, a solemn grandeur in the mountains, and the Castle was wild, yet stately - not dismantled of turrets - nor the walls broken down, though obviously a ruin.

An early devotee of the picturesque, Wordsworth could adopt and mold ruins into his excursions, though it was never topography alone that tempted him when possessed with a reverence for elegiac themes. In 1807 he visited Bolton priory in Yorkshire, and there wrote 'The White Doe of Rylstone', based on a local legend, where his heroine, Emily, frequenting 'Bolton's sacred Pile, / On favouring nights, she loved to go; / There ranged through cloister, court, and aisle. /Attended by the soft-pac'd Doe', and an engraving of that setting became the frontispiece to his long poem.

WILLIAM WORDSWORTH

Even in natural landscapes he could see them as somehow formed by an unknown force, 'the wreck of IS and WAS': so in the amphitheater of Malham Cove, in Yorkshire, he saw that 'Things incomplete and purposes betrayed / Make sadder transits o'er thought's optic glass / Than noblest objects utterly decayed'. He found many occasions on which to ground his thoughts on ruins. In lines 'Composed among the Ruins of a Castle in North Wales' (possibly Carnarvon, which he visited in 1824), the place was less significant than what he termed the 'Thralls of Destiny': 'Relic of Kings! Wreck of forgotten wars, / To winds abandoned and the prying stars, / *Time* loves thee!'

One ruin he knew well was Furness Abbey. In his *Guide* he wrote that those who 'wish to see the celebrated ruins of Furness Abbey, and are not afraid of crossing the Sands [of Morecambe Bay], may go from Lancaster to Ulverston'. He also mentions the Abbey in *The Prelude*, and wrote two sonnets on it during the 1840s. In one of these, he notes that casual visitors are moved by the ruins, including some railway engineers taking their noonday rest within the walls. The workmen sit, walk, indulge in no 'idle talk', but instead listen as 'a Hymn with tuneful sound / Hallows once more the long-deserted Choir', while others 'admire / That wide-spanned arch, and wondering how it was raised...'

It is an odd encounter in that Wordsworth, like John Ruskin after him, found the intrusion of railway lines into the Lakes intolerable. In December 1844 he wrote from his home at Rydal Mount a long letter to the editor of the *Morning Post* in which

Hand tinted lithograph by Thomas Pinken, after James Baker Pyne, *Druid circle near Keswick*. Photo: Wikicommons.

he inveighed against any thought that the railway, which had now reached Bowness, might be extended beyond into the vales of Ambleside and Grasmere and spoil the essential character of the country.

A Guide through the District of the Lakes
(Bloomington: Indiana University Press, 1952)

These lakes and inner vallies are unadorned by any remains of ancient grandeur, castles, or monastic edifices, which are only found upon the skirts of the country, as Furness Abbey, Calder Abbey, the Prior of Lannercost, Glenston Castle, – long ago a residence of the Flemings, – and the numerous ancient castles of the Cliffords, the Lucys, and the Dacres...

'At Furness Abbey', in *Miscellaneous Sonnets*, 1845

>Here, where, of havoc tired and rash undoing,
>Man left this Structure to become Time's prey,
>A soothing spirit follows in the way
>That Nature takes, her counter-work pursuing.
>See how her Ivy clasps the sacred Ruin,
>Fall to prevent or beautify decay;
>And, on the mouldered walls, how bright, how gay,
>The flowers in pearly dews the blooms renewing!
>Thanks to the place, blessings upon the hour;
>Even as I speak the rising Sun's first smile
>Gleams on the grass-crowned top of yon tall Tower
>Whose cawing occupants with joy proclaim
>Prescriptive title to the shattered pile,
>Where Cavendish, *thine* seems nothing but a name![2]

46

FRANÇOIS-RENÉ DE CHATEAUBRIAND

1802

The French diplomat and writer Chateaubriand was, in the words of Roland Mortier, 'a virtuoso of ruins'. Indeed, he wrote widely and enthusiastically about ruins and, unlike Volney (see Extract 39), found support in Christianity for a consideration of ruins. In the fifth book of his *Génie de Christianisme* (1802), chapters 3 to 5 – from which these passages are taken – he explores the relation of paganism to Christian religion.

Genius of Christianity, translated by Charles I. White, (Philadelphia: J.B. Lippincott & Co., 1884)

Chapter III: Of Ruins in General

Ruins are of two kinds

From the consideration of the sites of Christian monuments, we proceed to the effects of the ruins of those monuments. They furnish the heart with magnificent recollections and the arts with pathetic compositions.

All men take a secret delight in beholding ruins. This sentiment arises from the frailty of our nature, and a secret conformity between these destroyed monuments and the caducity of our own existence. We find moreover something consoling to our littleness in observing that whole nations, and men once so renowned, could not live beyond the span allotted to our own obscurity. Ruins, therefore, produce a highly moral effect amid the scenery of nature; and, when they are introduced into a picture, in vain does the eye attempt to stray to some other object; they soon attract it again, and rivet it upon themselves. And why should not the works of men pass away, when the sun which shines upon them must one day fall from its exalted station in the heavens? He who placed it in the firmament is the only sovereign whose empire knows no decay.

There are two species of ruins, the one the work of years, the other that of men. In the former there is nothing disagreeable because the operations of nature keep pace with those of time. Does time bring forth a heap of ruins? Nature bestrews them with flowers. Does time cause a rent in a tomb? Nature places within it the nest of a dove. Incessantly engaged in the work of reproduction, she surrounds death itself with the sweetest illusions of life.

The ruins of the second class are rather devastations than ruins; they exhibit nothing but the image of annihilation, without any reparative power. The effect of calamity, and not of years, they resemble hoary hair on the head of youth. The destructions of men are, besides, much more violent and much more complete than those of time: the latter undermine, the former demolish. When God, for reasons unknown to us, decrees the acceleration of ruin in the world, he commands time to lend his scythe to man; and time with astonishment beholds us lay waste in the twinkling of an eye what it would have taken him whole ages to destroy.

Chapter IV: Picturesque Effect of Ruins

Ruins of Palmyra, Egypt, &c.
Ruins, considered under the aspect of scenery, produce a more magical effect in a picture than the uninjured and entire monument. In temples which the hand of time has not shaken, the walls intercept the view of the surrounding scenery and prevent you from distinguishing the colonnades and arches of the edifice; but when these temples crumble into ruins, nothing is left but detached masses between which the eye discerns, above and in the distance, the stars, the clouds, mountains, rivers, and forests. Then, by a natural effect of optics, the horizon recedes and the galleries suspended in the air appear painted on the ground of the sky and of the earth. These beautiful effects were not unknown to the ancients; if they erected a circus, it was not an uninterrupted mass of masonry, but constructed with such openings as to admit the illusions of perspective.

Ruins have, in the next place, particular conformities with their desert localities, according to the style of their architecture and the character of the places in which they are situated.

In hot climates, unfavorable to herbage and mosses, they are destitute of those grasses which decorate our Gothic mansions and ancient castles; but then larger vegetables are intermixed with the more massive proportions of their architecture. At Palmyra the date-tree cleaves the heads of the men and the lions which support the capitals of the *Temple of the Sun*; the palm, with its column, supplies the place of the broken pillar, and the peach-tree, consecrated by the ancients to Harpocrates, flourishes in the abode of silence. Here, too, you see a different kind of trees, which, by their dishevelled foliage and fruit hanging in crystals, harmonize admirably with the pendent ruins. A caravan, halting in these deserts, heightens their picturesque effects. The dignity of the oriental dress accords with the dignity of these ruins, and the camels seem to swell their dimensions, when, reposing between fragments of masonry, they exhibit only their russet heads and their protuberant backs.

In Egypt ruins assume a different character; there, in a small space, are frequently comprised various styles of architecture and various kinds of recollections. The pillars in the ancient Egyptian style rise by the side of the elegant Corinthian column; a fabric of the Tuscan order stands contiguous to an Arabic tower, a monument of the pastoral age near a structure of the Roman period. Fragments of the Sphinx, the Anubis, with broken statues and obelisks, are rolled into the Nile and buried in the earth amid rice-grounds, bean-fields, and plains of clover. Sometimes, in the overflowing of the river, these ruins have the appearance of a large fleet on the water; sometimes clouds, pouring like waves over the sides of the ruins, seem to cut them in halves; the jackal, mounted on a vacant pedestal, stretches forth his wolf-like head behind the bust of a Pan with a ram's head; the antelope, the ostrich, the ibis, the jerboa, leap among the rubbish, while the sultana-hen stands motionless upon them, like a hieroglyphic bird of granite and porphyry.

The vale of Tempe, the woods of Olympus, the hills of Attica and of the Peloponnesus, are everywhere bestrewed with the ruins of Greece. There the mosses, the creeping plants, and the rock-flowers, flourish in abundance. A flaunting garland of jessamine entwines an antique Venus, as if to replace her cestus; a beard of white moss hangs from the chin of Hebe; the poppy shoots up on the leaves of the book of Mnemosyne, a lovely emblem of the past renown and the present oblivion of these regions. The waves of the Aegean Sea, which only advance to subside beneath crumbling porticos; Philomela chanting her plaintive notes; Alcyon heaving his sighs; Cadmus rolling his rings around an altar; the swan building her nest in the lap of a Leda – all these accidents, produced, as it were, by the Graces, pour a magic spell over these poetic ruins. You would say that a divine breath yet animates the dust of the temples of Apollo and the Muses, and the whole landscape bathed in the sea resembles a beautiful picture of Apelles, consecrated to Neptune and suspended over his shores.

Chapter V: Ruins of Christian Monuments

The ruins of Christian monuments have not an equal degree of elegance, but in other respects will sustain a comparison with the ruins of Rome and Greece. The finest of this kind that we know of are to be found in England, principally toward the north, near the lakes of Cumberland, on the mountains of Scotland, and even in the Orkney Islands. The walls of the choir, the pointed arches of the window, the sculptured vaultings, the pilasters of the cloisters, and some fragments of the towers, are the portions that have most effectually withstood the ravages of time.

In the Grecian orders, the vaults and the arches follow in a parallel direction the curves of the sky; so that on the gray hangings of the clouds or in a darkened landscape they are lost in the grounds. In the Gothic style, the points universally form a contrast with the circular arches of the sky and the curvatures of the horizon. The Gothic being, moreover, entirely composed of *voids*, the more readily admits of the decoration of herbage and flowers than the *fulness* of the Grecian orders. The clustered columns, the domes carved into foliage or scooped out in the form of a fruit-basket, afford so many receptacles into which the winds carry with the dust the seeds of vegetation. The house-leek fixes itself in the mortar; the mosses cover some rugged parts with their elastic coating; the thistle projects its brown burrs from the embrasure of a window; and the ivy, creeping along the northern cloisters, falls in festoons over the arches. No kind of ruin produces a more picturesque effect than these relics. Under a cloudy sky, amid wind and storm, on the coast of that sea whose tempests were sung by Ossian, their Gothic architecture has something grand and sombre, like the God of Sinai of whom they remind you. Seated on a shattered altar in the Orkneys, the traveller is astonished at the dreariness of those places: a raging sea, sudden fog, vales where rises the sepulchral stone, streams flowing through wild heaths, a few reddish pine-trees scattered over a naked desert studded with patches of snow, – such are the only objects which present themselves to his view. The wind circulates among the ruins, and their innumerable crevices are so many tubes which heave a thousand sighs. The organ of old did not lament so much in these religious edifices. Long grasses wave in the apertures of the domes, and beyond these apertures you behold the flitting clouds and the soaring sea-eagle. Sometimes, mistaking her course, a ship, hidden by her swelling sails, like a spirit of the waters curtained by his wings, ploughs the black bosom of ocean. Bending under the northern blast, she seems to bow as she advances, and to kiss the seas that wash the relics of the temple of God.

On these unknown shores have passed away the men who adored that *Wisdom* which walked beneath the waves. Sometimes in their sacred solemnities they marched in procession along the beach, singing, with the Psalmist, *How vast is this sea which stretcheth wides!* At others, seated in the cave of Fingal on the brink of ocean, they imagined they heard that voice from on high which said to Job, *Who shut up the sea with doors when it brake forth as issuing out of the womb?* At night, when the tempests of winter swept the earth, when the monastery was enveloped in clouds of spray, the peaceful cenobites, retiring within their cells, slept amid the howling of the storm, congratulating themselves on having embarked in that vessel of the Lord which will never perish.

Sacred relics of Christian monuments, ye remind us not, like so many other ruins of blood, of injustice and of violence! Ye relate on a peaceful history, or at most the mysterious suffering of the Son of Man! And ye hold hermits, who, to secure a place in happier regions, exiled yourselves to the ices of the pole, ye now enjoy the fruit of your sacrifices; and if, among angels, as among men, there are inhabited plains and desert tracts, in like manner as ye buried your virtues in the solitudes of the earth, so ye have doubtless chosen the celestial solitudes, therein to conceal your ineffable felicity!

47

LORD BYRON

1818

Byron's Childe Harold came to Italy to meditate, 'a ruin amidst ruins', first to Venice, then to Rome. In this he was preceded, or echoed, by many visitors: Samuel Rogers noticing that paintings on its palace facades were 'half ruined', Henry James later finding Tintorettos settling fast into 'incurable blackness' and that the city itself was but a 'mausoleum with a turnstile'. Ruskin learnt to lament the loss of a great Byzantine-Gothic cityscape. Maurice Barrès' *Mort de Venise* of 1903, Thomas Mann's *Death in Venice* of 1912 – all contributed to a sense of *La Serenissima* as a place of crumbling palaces, distressed gentlefolk, or the lagoon ossuary where Baron Corvo saw snakes crawling through the empty eye sockets of Austrian soldiers. In all these instances, the recognition of ruin also meant that its empty spaces could be filled or 'completed' by the visitor's imagination: 'There Harold gazes on a work divine, / A blending of all beauties; streams and dells, / Fruit, foliage, crag, wood, cornfield, mountain, vine / And chiefless castles breathing stern farewells / From gray but leafy walls, where Ruin gravely dwells'.

It is in Italy, and at Rome, that the poet and his hero in 1818 encounter the loss and vision of ruins most completely.

Childe Harold's Pilgrimage
(London: John Murray, 1812)

CXXVIII

I stood in Venice, on the Bridge of Sighs;
A palace and a prison on each hand:
I saw from out the wave her structures rise
As from the stroke of the enchanter's wand:
A thousand years their cloudy wings expand
Around me, and a dying Glory smiles
O'er the far times, when many a subject land
Look'd to the winged Lion's marble piles,
Where Venice sate in state, throned on her hundred isles!

CXXVIII

Arches on arches! As it were that Rome,
Collecting the chief trophies of her line,
Would build up all her triumphs in one dome,
Her Coliseum stands; the moonbeams shine
As 'twere its natural torches, for divine
Should be the light which streams here, to illume
This long-explored but still exhaustless mine
Of contemplation; and the azure gloom
Of an Italian night, where the deep skies assume

CXXIX

Hues which have words, and speak to ye of heaven,
Floats o'er this vast and wondrous monument,
And shadows forth its glory. There is given
Unto the things of earth, which time hath bent,
A spirit's feeling, and where he hath leant
His hand, but broke his scythe, there is a power
And magic in the ruin'd battlement,
For which the palace of the present hour
Must yield its pomp, and wait till ages are its dower.

CXXX

Oh Time! The beautifier of the dead,
Adorner of the ruin, comforter
And only healer when the heart hath bled –
Time! The corrector where our judgements err,
The test of truth, love, – sole philosopher,
For all beside are sophists, from thy thrift,
Which never loses though it doth defer –
Time, the avenger! Unto thee I lift
My hands, and eyes, and heart, and crave of thee a gift:

CXXXI

Amidst this wreck, where thou hast made a shrine
A temple more divinely desolate,
Among thy mightier offerings here are mine,
Ruins of years – though few, yet full of fate: –
If thou hast ever seen me too elate,

Hear me not; but if calmly I have borne
Good, and reserved my pride against the hate
Which shall not whelm me, let me not have worn
This iron in my soul in vain – shall they not mourn?

CXXXII

And thou, who never yet of human wrong
Left the unbalanced scale, great Nemesis!
Here, where the ancient paid thee homage long –
Thou, who didst call the Furies from the abyss,
And round Orestes bade them howl and hiss
For that unnatural retribution – just,
Had it but been from hands less near – in this
Thy former realm, I call thee from the dust!
Dost thou not hear my heart? – Awake! Thou shalt, and must.

CXXXVIII

The seal is set. – Now welcome, thou dread power!
Nameless, yet thus omnipotent, which here
Walk'st in the shadow of the midnight hour
With a deep awe, yet all distinct from fear;
Thy haunts are ever where dead walls rear
Their ivy mantles, and the solemn scene
Derives from thee a sense so deep and clear
That we become a part of what has been,
And grow unto the spot, all-seeing but unseen.

CXXXIX

And here [the Coliseum] the buzz of eager nations ran,
In murmur'd pity, or loud-roar'd applause,
As man was slaughter'd by his fellow man.
And wherefore slaughter'd? wherefore, but because
Such were the bloody Circus' genial laws,
And the imperial pleasure. – Wherefore not?
What matters where we fall to fill the maws
Of worms – on battle-plains or listed spot?
Both are but theatres where the chief actors rot...

48

Percy Bysshe Shelley

1818

Shelley's famous sonnet 'Ozymandias' speaks for itself. The title is a transliteration of the Greek Οσυμανδύας, ultimately derived from ancient Egyptian, part of the prenomen of Rameses II of Egypt, of whom a colossal 57-foot statue, now surviving only in fragments, once stood at Thebes. Shelley's source was apparently the Greek historian Diodorus Siculus, who records the inscription on the statue. The word was later invoked by Thomas Hardy and others to signal an oppressive tyrant.

'Ozymandias', in *Rosalind and Helen*
(London: C. and J. Ollier, 1819)

I met a traveller from an antique land,
Who said— 'Two vast and trunkless legs of stone
Stand in the desert... Near them, on the sand,
Half sunk a shattered visage lies, whose frown,
And wrinkled lip, and sneer of cold command,
Tell that its sculptor well those passions read
Which yet survive, stamped on these lifeless things,
The hand that mocked them, and the heart that fed;
And on the pedestal, these words appear:
My name is Ozymandias, King of Kings;
Look on my Works, ye Mighty, and despair!
Nothing beside remains. Round the decay
Of that colossal Wreck, boundless and bare
The lone and level sands stretch far away.

49

VICTOR HUGO AND CHARLES MARVILLE

1832

Victor Hugo is perhaps best known for his novel *The Hunchback of Nôtre Dame*, known on its first publication in 1831 simply as *Notre-Dame de Paris*, but his interest in ancient structures and cultures was part of a larger concern to preserve the long and rich architectural history of France. In the years that followed the Revolution, it was inevitable that the French sought to establish a new material expression of the Republic, and then of the Empire under Napoleon from 1804 to 1814; and from 1852 to 1870, a second Empire under Napoleon III saw a further radical remodeling of Paris, before republicanism was restored.

Hugo's protests against the wholesale destruction of French monuments in response to the needs of a new regime were proclaimed in essays of 1825 and 1832, pleas to '*arrêter le marteau* [the sledgehammer] *qui mutilait la face du pays*'. The first essay simply listed the vandalism and neglect of ancient French monuments, while the second, published the year after *The Hunchback of Notre-Dame*, expressed his anger at this unthinking and ignorant demolition at greater length. In 1837 France created the Commission Supériéure des Monuments Historiques.

Bossu in Hugo's novel means hunchback, and the very year it was published, Charles-Francois Bossu (1813–79) adopted the pseudonym Charles Marville, under which he became, over the next 30-odd years, one of the most famous photographers of old Paris and its modern refurbishments, including Viollet le Duc's (*see* Extract 52) spire on Notre-Dame. He also supplied prints for Victor Hugo.[3] His photographs of suburbs (described by Hugo as 'amphibian') and his images of destruction, repair, and remodeling captured exactly the concerns that Hugo had voiced earlier. Hugo would later proclaim that the Universal Exhibition of 1867, which Marville photographed, would crown Paris as the capital of Europe. Marville's careful attention to restorations marked his keen architectural concerns, albeit in a somewhat less censorious spirit than Hugo's.

VICTOR HUGO AND CHARLES MARVILLE

Dessins et Pamphlets (Apt: Editions L'Archange Minotaure, 2003), translated by Emily T. Cooperman

Guerre aux démolisseurs! (1825)

What is needed is a crying universal appeal to the new France to save the ancient one. All sorts of profanation, degradation, and ruin already threaten what little remains of the admirable monuments of the Middle Age, where the old national glory is enshrined, linked to both the memory of kings and popular traditions. Meanwhile, costly constructions, I know not what, of bastard edifices with French pretensions of being Greek or Roman, are neither; and other buildings, admirable and original, fall without anyone daring to inform us and their only error, however, is that they are French by origin, history, and use. At Blois, the chateau of the States is now a barracks, the beautiful octagonal tower of Catherine de Medici crumbles, shrouded by the cavalry stables. At Orleans, the last vestige of the defensive walls of Joan have just disappeared. In Paris, we know what has happened to the old towers of Vincennes that made a magnificent adjunct to the castle keep. The abbey of the Sorbonne, so elegant and ornamented, is currently falling under the sledgehammer. The beautiful Romanesque church of Saint-Germain-des-Prés, whence Henri IV

Victor Hugo, *The Abbey*, engraved by Paul Chenay, 1858.

Charles Marville, *Troyes Cathedral Under Restoration*, photograph, 1863.

had observed Paris, once had three spires, the only kind that embellished the cityscape. Two of their pinnacles were threatened; it meant either shoring them up or demolishing them, and it was quickly decided to demolish them. Then, to link, as much as possible, the venerable monument with the dreadful portico in Louis XIII style that hid the portal, the restoration people have replaced several of the little chapels with little bonnet-like Corinthian capitals in the style of Saint-Sulpice; and the remainder is painted a beautiful canary yellow… I write this in haste, without preparation, and choosing randomly some of the souvenirs which remain after a rapid excursion through a small portion of France…

1832

It must be said, and said loudly, this demolition of the old France, which we have denounced on many occasions during the restoration of the Empire [under Napoleon I], continues with even more tenacity and barbarity than before. Since the July Revolution, an ignorant democracy has encroached, as well as brutality. In many places, local authority, municipal influence, communal cultural care has passed from gentlemen who don't know how to write to peasants who cannot read. We have fallen down there. While waiting for these wonderful people who know to spell, they just govern. The blundering administration, the natural and normal machine of Marly that is called centralization, passes the buck – as in the past – from mayor or sub-prefect, from sub-prefect to prefect, from prefect to the minister. But more and more grossly.

Our intervention is to envisage only the innumerable forms under which they can do something for an astonished people. We do not want to have to deal with this blundering administration on the question of monuments, and further have no inclination to contribute to the immense publication in 25 volumes that will still not exhaust the subject.

We suppose then that there is now nowhere in France, no single town, no director of district organization, no single head of a district, that does not propose, or not begin, to achieve the destruction of some historical monument of national importance, either by central authority, or by local decisions with approval from the center, committed by individuals under the eyes of and with the tolerance of the locality.

We proceed here with the profound conviction of never making mistakes, and invoke the fact of somebody's decision, on some point relevant to France, without the least artistical or antiquarian expertise. Each day some old memory of France disappears with the stones on which it was written. Each day we tear some leaf of the venerable book of tradition. And soon, when the ruin of all the ruins is achieved, we are left simply with crying out with the Trojan, who at least could carry off his gods: *Fuit Ilium, et ingens. Gloria!*[4]

50

ARTHUR HUGH CLOUGH

1858

First published in the *Atlantic Monthly* in 1858, Clough's verse novel *Amours de Voyage* is one of his finest works, though its use of hexameters, an unfamiliar meter in English, makes it sometimes hard to read; but in *Amours* it works well, partly because it suits the epistolary tone and format, partly because its protagonist Claude uses it best to set out his often dyspeptic, sarcastic view of the world, as in this early letter from Italy.

Amours de Voyage, 1858
(London: Macmillan and Co., 1890)

Rome disappoints me still; but I shrink and adapt myself to it.
Somehow a tyrannous sense of a superincumbent oppression
Still, where I go, accompanies ever, and makes me
Feel like a tree (shall I say?) buried under a ruin of brick-work.
Rome, believe me, my friend, is like its own Monte Testaco,[5]
Merely a marvelous mass of broken and castaway wine-pots.
Ye gods! what do I want with this rubbish of ages departed,
Things that Nature abhors, the experiments that she had failed in?
What do I find in the Forum? An archway and two or three pillars.
Well, but St Peter's? Alas, Bernini has filled it with sculpture!
No one can cavil, I grant, at the size of the great Coliseum.
Doubtless the notion of grand and capacious and massive amusement,
This the old Romans had; but tell me, is this an idea?
Yet of solidity much, but of splendour little is extant:
'Brickwork I found thee, and marble I left thee' their Emperor vaunted;
'Marble, I thought thee, and brickwork I find thee!' the Tourist may answer.

51

JOHN RUSKIN

1843–60

Ruskin scattered reflections and notes on ruins through his many volumes, though they do not always seem central to his ideas. One of his earliest responses was to draw, at age ten, the ruins of Dover Castle. In his writings, he compared English and continental examples; saw them as 'conventional' images in the picturesque; and found delight in the plants that grew upon them. His remarks, scattered through the five volumes of his *Modern Painters*, begin with a critical view of the way artists had depicted ruins in their paintings.

Modern Painters, in The Works of John Ruskin: Modern Painters, vols 1–5 (London: J. Wiley, 1890)

Modern Painters I (1843), Ch.7, sec 31: What ruins they drew looked as if broken down on purpose; what weeds they put on seemed put on for ornament. Their domestic buildings had never any domesticity; the people looked out of their windows evidently to be drawn, or came into the street only to stand there for ever. A peculiar studiousness infected all accident; bricks fell out methodically, windows opened and shut by rule; stones were chipped at regular intervals; everything that happened seemed to have been expected before; and above all, the street had been washed and the houses dusted expressly to be painted in their best. We owe to Prout, I believe, the first perception, and certainly the only existing expression, of precisely the characters which were wanting to old art; of that feeling which results from the influence, among the noble lines of architecture, of the rent and the rust, the fissure, the lichen, and the weed, and from the writing upon the pages of ancient walls of the confused hieroglyphics of human history. I suppose, from the deserved popularity of the artist, that the strange pleasure which I find myself in the deciphering of these is common to many. The feeling has been rashly and thoughtlessly contemned as mere love of the picturesque; there is, as I have above shown, a deeper moral in it, and we owe much, I am not prepared to say how much, to the artist by whom pre-eminently it has been excited…

John Ruskin, *The Roman Tower, Dover Castle*, sketch, c.1819. The Ruskin Foundation, University of Lancaster.

Modern Painters II (1856), Ch.1, sec. 7: There is need, bitter need, to bring back into men's minds, that to live is nothing, unless to live be to know Him [God] by whom we live; and that He is not to be known by marring His fair works, and blotting out the evidence of His influences upon his Creatures... [Ruskin here adds a long footnote on what European buildings have been defaced, and therefore ruined, by modern renovations.]

Modern Painters IV (1856), Ch.1, secs. 2-3: I cannot find words to express the intense pleasure I have always in first finding myself, after some prolonged stay in England, at the foot of the old tower of Calais church. The large neglect, the noble unsightliness of it; the record of its years written so visibly, yet without sign of weakness or decay; its stern wasteness and gloom, eaten away by the Channel winds, and overgrown with the bitter sea grasses; its slates and tiles all shaken and rent, and yet not falling; its desert of brickwork full of bolts, and holes, and ugly fissures, and yet strong, like a bare brown rock; its carelessness of what any one thinks or feels about it, putting forth no claim, having no beauty or desirableness, pride, nor grace; yet neither asking for pity; not, as ruins are, useless and piteous, feebly or fondly garrulous of better days; but useful still, going through its own daily work, as some old fisherman beaten grey by storm, yet drawing his daily nets: so it stands, with no complaint about its past youth, in blanched and meagre massiveness and serviceableness, gathering human souls together underneath it; the sound of its bells for prayer still rolling through its rents; and the grey peak of it seen far across the sea, principal of the three that rise above the waste of surfy sand and hillocked shore, – the lighthouse for life, and the belfry for labour, and this for patience and praise.

I cannot tell the half of the strange pleasures and thoughts that come about me at the sight of that old tower; for, in some sort, it is the epitome of all that makes the Continent of Europe interesting, as opposed to new countries; and, above all, it completely expresses that agedness in the midst of active life which binds the old and the new into harmony. We, in England, have our ruin emergent from it, a mere *specimen* of the Middle Ages put on a bit of velvet carpet to be shown, which, but for its size, might as well be on a museum shelf at once, under cover. But, on the Continent, the links are unbroken between the past and present, and, in such use as they can serve for, the grey-headed wrecks are suffered to stay with men; while, in unbroken line, the generations of spared buildings are seen succeeding each in its place. And thus in its largeness, in its permitted evidence of slow decline, in its poverty, in its absence of all pretence, of all show and care for outside aspect, that Calais tower has an infinite of symbolism in it, all the more striking because usually seen in contrast with English scenes expressive of feelings the exact reverse of these.

Modern Painters V (1860), Ch.10, sec. 14: It is yet more worthy of note that the proper duty of these 'rent' [lobed or serrated] leaves, which catch the eye so clearly and powerfully, would appear to be to draw the attention of man to spots where his work is needed, for they nearly all habitually grow on ruins or neglected ground: not noble ruins, or on wild ground, but on heaps of rubbish, or pieces of land which have been indolently cultivated or much disturbed.

52

EUGENE-EMMANUEL VIOLLET LE DUC

1868

Ruins reach their end in one of two ways: razed to the ground or raised up when completely restored. Viollet le Duc advocated for the latter, more influentially than perhaps any other 19th-century figure, in both writings and projects, the latter including most famously Notre-Dame in Paris, the Abbey Church of La Madeleine at Vézelay, the medieval town of Carcassonne, and the Pierrefonds Château. Ruins prompting restoration are often examined in his voluminous writings, most emphatically in the 20th chapter on 'Restoration' in the eighth volume of his massive *Dictionnaire raisonné de l'architecture française du XIe au XVe siècle*. Ruins fascinated Viollet from the time of his Italian journey to has last days, when he was preparing his publication on the restoration of the Alps, *Le massif du Mont Blanc*, 1868-76, under the premise that mountains, no less than buildings, suffer and can be saved from 'the ravages of time'.

His approach was forensic: no detail, fragment, or trace was to be overlooked or omitted from the survey. Though completeness of a work was surely not in evidence, always only projected, a complete accounting was required if 'the jigsaw puzzle' were to be put together. He admitted that the room, building, or town that resulted might be unprecedented. The incomplete evidence ruins supply requires of restoration work as much imagination as documentation.

'Restoration', from *Dictionnaire raisonné de l'Architecture Française*
(Paris: A. Morel, 1854-68)[6]

Both the word and thing are modern. To restore an edifice means neither to maintain it, nor to repair it, nor to rebuild it; it means to reestablish it in a finished state, which may in fact never have actually existed at any given time. The idea that constructions of another age can actually be restored is an idea that dates only from the second quarter of our own century, and it is not clear that this kind of architectonic restoration has ever been clearly defined. Perhaps this is an opportune occasion for us to get a clear idea of exactly what is meant and what ought to be meant by *restoration*. For it would seem that many ambiguities have come to surround the meaning that we assign and ought to assign to this particular activity.

We have said that both the word and the thing are modern; and, in fact, neither any civilization nor any people in history has ever carried out restoration in the sense in which we understand that term today.

In Asia, in the past as still today, whenever a temple or a place fell into ruin or decay as a result of the ravages of time, either it was simply rebuilt or else another one was built in its place. This does not mean the ancient edifice itself even had to be destroyed; that was normally left to the action of time itself; time would surely not fail to wear it down little by little as if the edifice belonged to time. The Roman rebuilt: they did not restore. The proof of this is that there is not even a Latin word that corresponds to our word *restoration* in the sense in which we understand the word today. *Instaurare*, *reficere*, *renovare*—none of these words means 'to restore' but rather 'to reestablish' or 'to rebuild anew'...

The Middle Ages no more had any idea of restoration than antiquity did...

Our era, and our era alone, since the beginning of recorded history, has assumed toward the past a quite exceptional attitude as far as history is concerned. Our age has wished to analyze the past, classify it, compare it, and write its complete history, following step-by-step the procession, the progress, and the various transformations of humanity...

The Château of Pierrefonds, before restoration by Viollet le Duc, 1858-79.
Fisher Fine Arts Library, University of Pennsylvania.

The Château of Pierrefonds, after restoration, engraving, c.1830. Fisher Fine Arts Library, University of Pennsylvania.

If you happen to be the one responsible for restoring an edifice already partly in ruins, you must, before beginning to do any actual restoration work at all, excavate everything, examine everything, and bring everything together, including the smallest fragments, taking care to note exactly where they were discovered. You can begin your actual restoration work only when the purpose of everything in all this debris has been determined and everything has been put into its proper logical place, like pieces of a jigsaw puzzle.

53

WILLIAM MORRIS

1877, 1893, AND 1895

William Morris was an eager and enthusiastic reinventor of medieval design, best known these days as the creator of fabrics and illuminated manuscripts. He saw Gothic architecture as 'the most completely organic form of Art which the world has ever seen', and thought Roman work was engineering not architecture, and that it exercised an appalling influence on 'the restless nightmare of modern engineering'.

While not a spokesman for ruins, he was nevertheless ferocious in his attacks on architects and city planners who sought 'ruination' in the interests of 'improving' places with 'uptodate' work. In 1877 he founded the Society for the Protection of Ancient Buildings, known as 'Anti-Scrape' (i.e. against the demolition or scrapping/scraping of old buildings). In support, he delivered a lecture on 'The Lesser Arts of Life', subsequently published as an essay. He also wrote endlessly to newspapers, of which two examples are given here.

Letter to *The Athenaeum*, 10 March 1877

My eye just now caught the word 'restoration' in the morning paper, and on looking closer, I saw that this time it is nothing less than the minster of Tewkesbury that is to be destroyed by Sir Gilbert Scott. Is it altogether too late to do something to save it – and whatever else of beautiful or historical is still left to us on the sites of the ancient buildings we were once famous for? Would it not be of some use once for all, and with the least delay possible, to set on foot an association for the purpose of watching over and protecting these relics, which, scanty as they have now become, are still wonderful treasures, all the more priceless in this age of the world, when the newly-invented study of living history is the chief joy of so many or our lives?

Your paper has so steadily and courageously opposed itself to those acts of barbarism which the modern architect, parson, and squire call 'restoration', that it would be waste of words to enlarge here on the ruin that has been wrought by their hands; but, for the saving of what is left, I think I may write a word of encouragement, and say that you by no means stand alone in the matter, and

Pages from William Morris's *Gothic Architecture*, 1893. Fisher Fine Arts Library, University of Pennsylvania.

that there are many thoughtful people who would be glad to sacrifice time, money, and comfort in defence of those ancient monuments: besides, though I admit that the architects are, with very few exceptions, hopeless, because interest, habit, and ignorance bind them, and that the clergy are hopeless, because their order, habit, and an ignorance yet grosser, bind them; still there must be many people whose ignorance is accidental rather than inveterate, whose good sense could surely be touched if it were clearly put to them that they were destroying what they, or more surely still, their sons and sons' sons, would one day fervently long for, and which no wealth or energy could ever buy again for them.

What I wish for, therefore, is that an association should be set on foot to keep a watch on old monuments, to protect against all 'restoration' that means more than keeping out wind and weather, and, by all means, literary and other, to awaken a feeling that our ancient buildings are not mere ecclesiastical toys, but sacred monuments of the nation's growth and hope.

Letter to the *Daily News*, 20 November 1885

I have just read your true article on the vulgarization of Oxford, and wish to ask if it is too late to appeal to the mercy of the 'dons' to spare the few specimens of ancient town architecture which they have not yet had time to destroy, such, for example, as the little plaster houses in front of Trinity College or the beautiful houses left on the north side of Holywell Street… For my part I do not think this a lofty conception of the function of a University; but if it be the only admissible one nowadays, it is at least clear that it does not need the history and art of our forefathers which Oxford still holds to develop it. London, Manchester, Birmingham, or perhaps a rising city in Australia would be a fitter place for the experiment, which it seems to me is too rough a one for Oxford. In sober truth, what specialty has Oxford if it is not to the genius loci which our modern commercial dons are doing their best to destroy?

54

Thomas Hardy

1870 and 1922

Though best known as a novelist and poet, Thomas Hardy trained and worked as an architect until his early thirties, and that early interest showed in several of his novels: there is 'Mellstock Church' in *Under the Greenwood* Tree, and 'Knapwater House' in *Desperate Remedies*, each probably modeled on buildings Hardy knew. *The Architectural Notebook of Thomas Hardy*[7] charts some of his exploration and technical work, and displays a Ruskinian attention to ancient structures. This does little, obviously, to touch upon ruinations as opposed to building, and his notions in the notebook are usually details of construction, Victorian Gothic details and floor plans, and notes on the changes to and conservation of St Juliet's Church in Cornwall.

Among the exceptions are his drawing of Glastonbury Abbey in 1861, and a poem in *Late Lyrics* (1922) on an ancient 'pile', not ruined at all, but still eloquent of loss. Yet he can just as much declare how 'Vain is the wish to try rhyming it, writing it! / Pen cannot weld into words what it was.' In the same way, he despised fake work, and even found some restorations wrong. His poetry, even if not focusing on ruins *per se*, hints at the absences they imply, for ruins are often emptied of what had once filled them. He barely notices the fragment of a 12th-century motte-and-bailey fortress 'At Castle Boterel', for it is his memories of 'myself and a girlish form' in a 'dry March weather' that he recalls. At 'An Aging House' – 'When the walls were red /That now are seen / To be overspread / With a mouldy green' – it is the now aged head of a girl he once saw leaning out of a casement that holds him. The faded green on a 'Garden Seat' is what its early users will reflect on when it is broken down. Drawing details in an old church, he hears the 'bell-rope sawing / And the oil-less axle grind' only to wonder if, when he's dead, a congregation will hear the same bells tolling for him. In Rome 'At the Pyramid of Cestius near the Graves of Shelley and Keats', he asked who Cestius could possibly have been ('I can recall no word / Of anything he did'). For an old house 'with ivied walls? And mullioned windows' he strives to recall the 'long dwellers in these halls'.

BOOK OF RUINS

'A Spellbound Palace (Hampton Court)' in *Human Shows, Far Phantasies, Songs and Trifles*
(London: Macmillan, 1925)

On this kindly yellow day of mild low-travelling winter sun
The stirless depths of the yews
Are vague with misty blues:
Across the spacious pathways stretching spires of shadow run,
And wind-gnawed walls of ancient brick are fired vermilion.

Two or three sanguine finches tune
Some tentative strains, to be enlarged by May or June:
From a thrush or blackbird
Comes now and then a word,
While an enfeebled fountain somewhere within is heard.

Our footsteps wait awhile,
Then draw beneath the pile,
When an inner court outspreads
As 'twere History's own asile,
Where the now-visioned fountain its attenuate crystal sheds

Thomas Hardy, *Glastonbury Abbey*, sketch in his *Architectural Notebook*, 1861.
Dorset Natural History and Archaelogical Society.

In passive lapse that seems to ignore the yon world's clamorous clutch,
And lays an insistent numbness on the place, like a cold hand's touch.

And there swaggers the Shade of a straddling King, plumed, sworded,
	with sensual face,
And lo, too, that of his Minister, at a bold self-centred pace:
Sheer in the sun they pass; and thereupon all is still,
Save the mindless fountain tinkling on with thin enfeebled will.

V

Modern and Contemporary

Caspar David Friedrich, *The Abbey in the Oak Wood*, oil on canvas, 1809. Alte Nationalgalerie, Berlin.

55

ALOIS RIEGL

1903

Alois Riegl wrote his famous article on the modern cult of monuments the year he joined Austria's Central Commission for the Research and Preservation of Artistic and Historical Monuments. Although it is plainly a theoretical text, with sharp definition of terms for carefully considered concepts and distinct categories of artistic phenomena, it was also meant to serve commissioners and historians as a practical guide for the classification and valuation of monuments, old and new, authored and anonymous. It seems to have been useful then, certainly became widely influential both in and outside Austria, and continues to guide practices and prompt debates about historic preservation. Among the many important distinctions made in the text, the one that is pertinent to ruins is the distinction between historical-value and age-value.

When viewing ruins, Riegl argued that we naturally focus not on their broken or incomplete state – what is no longer there – but on the density of historical substance in what we see. The past to which age-value refers is the one without dates or chapters, the unchronicled time of slow and steady sequence, cumulatively evident in the parts of works that just-so-happen-to remain – who knows why or how. This past could be called artifactual, as opposed to narrative time, continually subsuming temporal passage into the work's physical body, broken though it may be, saturated with historical sense, rather more like an atmosphere than an object or identifiable place. So defined, age-value recognizes no real distinction between significant and inconsequential remnants, nor high and low art because palaces and peasant houses are equally subject to time's corrosive and constructive effects. Age-value also places brackets around the indexical meaning of historical artifacts, indications of the designer responsible for what we see, its exact location, and the culture in which it served specific purposes. Even if they are located somewhere, their value is non-localized.

What then do ruins reveal? In short, finitude, the fate or tragedy of time's passing. Each new work shelters within itself the promise of its end. All artifacts, Riegl maintained, are at their core outgrowths of the natural world; they live and die like plants and animals, coming into being and passing away with the cultures and individuals who made them. But not completely – ruins remain.

A useful representation of this conception might be the Gothic ruin painted a century earlier by Caspar David Friedrich, *The Abbey in the Oak Wood*. The tree trunks and ruins are remnants of archaic and Christian pasts, grove-cults in the woods and churchgoers before the cross. Both have come to an end. A soil-colored blanket of fog absorbs everything we see under a cloud-and-sun-less sky, including the monks – probably there for a winter-time burial – who amplify the sense of endings expressed by the leafless branches and buckled buttresses. Time traces its rhythms across the skin of the stone and soil, free from narrative history's dead weight, free for the fluctuations of nature, which Friedrich has gathered together in a site saturated with fog.

'The Modern Cult of Monuments: Its Character and Its Origin',
from *Gesammelte Aufsätze* (Augsburg and Vienna: Dr Benno Filser, 1928)[1]

The Meaning of Monuments and Their Historical Development

A monument in its oldest and most original sense is a human creation, erected for the specific purpose of keeping single human deeds or events (or a combination thereof) alive in the minds of future generations. Monuments can be either artistic or literary, depending on whether the event to be remembered is brought to the viewer's consciousness by means of the visual arts or with the help of inscriptions. Most of the time both genres are used simultaneously. The erection and care of such 'intentional' monuments, which can be traced back to the beginnings of human culture, have not ceased. But when we talk about the modern cult and preservation of monuments, we are thinking not about 'intentional' monuments, but about *Kunst- und historische Denkmale*, monuments of art and history as they are officially designated in Austria. This designation, which proved adequate from the 16th through the 19th century, today could give rise to misunderstandings as a result of the modern perception of art and its value. For this reason, we will have to examine above all how monuments of art and history have been understood up until now.

A work of art is generally defined as a palpable, visual, or audible creation by man which possesses an artistic value; a historical monument with the same physical basis will have a historical value. We will eliminate aural creations for our purposes, as they can be classified with written documents. With respect to the visual arts (and in the broadest sense, all artifacts), therefore, the question is, what is artistic value and what is historical value?

Historical value is apparently the broader issue and therefore we will give it priority. Everything that has been and is no longer we call historical, in accordance with the modern notion that what has been can never be again, and that everything that has been constitutes an irreplaceable and irremovable link in a chain of development. In other words: each successive step implies its predecessor and could not have happened as it did without that earlier step. The essence of every modern perception of history is the idea of development. In these terms, every human activity and every human event of which we have knowledge or testimony may claim historical value; in principle, every historical event is irreplaceable. But since it is not possible to consider the vast quantity of occurrences and events of which we have direct or indirect evidence and which multiply to infinity, we have of necessity limited our attention to that testimony which seems to represent a conspicuous phase in the development of a specific branch of human activity. This testimony could be written, activating a series of mental processes, or it could be a work of art whose content can be apprehended directly through the senses. It is important to realize that every work of art is at once and without exception a historical monument because it represents a specific stage in the development of the visual arts. In the strictest sense, no real equivalent can ever be substituted for it. Conversely, every historical monument is also an art monument, because even a secondary literary monument like a scrap of paper with a brief and insignificant note contains a whole series of artistic elements – the form of the piece of paper, the letters, and their composition – which apart from their historical value are relevant to the development of paper, writing, writing instruments, etc. To be sure, these are such insignificant elements that for the most part we neglect them in many cases because we have enough other monuments which convey much the same thing in a richer and more detailed manner. But were this scrap of paper the only surviving testimony to the art of its time, we would consider it, though trivial in itself, an utterly indispensable artifact. To the extent that it is present, the artistic element of such a document interests us only from a historical point of view: such monuments are indispensable links in the development of art history. The 'art monument' in this sense is really an 'art-historical monument'; its value from this point of view is not so much artistic as historical. It follows that the differentiation of 'artistic' and 'historical' monuments is inappropriate because the latter at once contains and suspends the former.

But do we really appreciate only the historical value of a work of art? If this were so, then all the art from all epochs would have the same value in our view and would only increase in value by virtue of rarity or age. In reality, we admire some recent works more than earlier ones, e.g., a Tiepolo of the 18th century more than a Mannerist work of the 16th century. In addition to historical interest, there is, then, something else which resides in a work's specifically artistic properties, namely conceptual, formal, and coloristic qualities. Apart from the art-historical value, there is also in all earlier art a purely artistic value independent of the particular place a work of art occupies in the chain of historical development. Is this 'art-value' equally as present as the historical value in the past, so that it may claim to be an essential and historically independent part of our notion of monument? Or is this 'art-value' merely a subjective one invented by and entirely dependent on the changing preferences of the modern viewer? Were this the case, would such art-value have no place in the definition of the monument as a commemorative work?

There are two fundamentally different responses to this question today: an older one which has not entirely disappeared, and a newer one. From the Renaissance – when, as we shall argue later, historical value was first recognized – until the 19th century, an inviolable artistic canon prevailed which claimed an absolute and objective validity to which all artists aspired, but never achieved with complete success. Initially, ancient art seemed to conform to this canon most closely, even to the point of representing its very ideal. The 19th century definitively abolished this exclusive claim, allowing virtually all other periods of art to assume their own independent significance, but without entirely abandoning the belief in an objective artistic ideal. Only around the beginning of the 20th century have we come to recognize the necessary consequences of the theory of historical evolution, which declares that all artifacts of the past are irrecoverable and therefore in no way canonically binding. Even if we do not limit ourselves to appreciating modern works of art but also admire the concept, form, and color of older works, and even if we prefer the latter, we must realize that certain historic works of art correspond, if only in part, to the modern *Kunstwollen*. It is precisely this apparent correspondence of the modern *Kunstwollen* and certain aspects of historical art which, in its conflicting nature, exerts such power over the modern viewer. An entirely modern work, necessarily lacking this background, will never wield comparable power. According to current notions, there can be no absolute but only a relative modern art-value.

With this in mind, one must define the term art-value in different ways, depending on whether one adopts the earlier or the modern point of view. According to the former, a work of art possesses *art-value* insofar as it corresponds to a supposedly objective but never satisfactorily defined aesthetic. In the modern view, the art-value of a monument is established by the requirements of the modern *Kunstwollen*, but these requirements are even less well defined and in the strictest sense can never be defined because they vary from subject to subject and moment to moment.

For our task, it is indispensable to clarify this difference in the perception of art-value because it influences fundamentally all aspects of the preservation of monuments. If there is no such thing as an eternal art-value but only a relative, modern one, then the art-value of a monument ceases to be commemorative and becomes a contemporary value instead. The preservation of monuments has to take this into account, if only because it may have a practical and topical significance quite apart from the historical and commemorative value of a monument. Strictly speaking, contemporary appreciation will have to be excluded from the notion of the monument itself. If one agrees with the understanding of art-value as it has emerged from the entire complex of 19th-century art-historical research, then one may no longer speak of 'artistic historical monuments' but only of 'historical monuments.' This is the meaning given to the term in the text.

In contrast to intentional monuments, historical monuments are unintentional, but it is equally clear that all deliberate monuments may also be unintentional ones. Since those who fashioned the works which we have subsequently termed 'historical monuments' wanted primarily to satisfy their own practical and ideal needs – those of their contemporaries and, at most, those of their immediate progeny – without as a rule intending to leave testimony of their artistic and cultural life to later centuries, when we call such works of art 'monuments' it is a subjective rather than an objective designation. It is not their original purpose and significance that turn these works into monuments, but rather our modern perception of them. Both intentional and unintentional monuments are characterized by commemorative value, and in both instances we are interested in their original, uncorrupted appearance as they emerged from the hands of their maker and to which we seek by whatever means to restore them. In the case of the intentional monument, its commemorative value has been determined by the makers, while we have defined the value of the unintentional ones.

Historical value does not exhaust the interest and influence that artworks from the past arouse in us. Take, for instance, the ruins of a castle, which betray little of the original form, structure, internal disposition of rooms, and so forth, and with which the visitor has no sentimental association. The castle's historical value alone fails to account for the obvious interest which it excites in the modern observer. When we look at an old belfry we must make a similar distinction between our perception of the localized historical memories it contains and our more general awareness of the passage of time, the belfry's survival over time, and the visible traces of its age. The same distinction may be observed in a written testimony. A piece of parchment from the 15th century recording no more than the purchase of a horse evokes in us not only a dual commemorative value, but also, because of its written contents, a historical one established by the nature of the transaction (economic and legal history), by the names mentioned (political history, genealogy, land use) and so forth, and by the unfamiliar language, the uncommon expressions, concepts, and decisions which even someone unschooled in history would immediately recognize as old-fashioned and belonging to the past. Modern interest in such an instance is undoubtedly rooted purely in its value as memory, that is, we consider the document an involuntary monument; however, its value as memory does not interfere with the work as such, but springs from our appreciation of the time which has elapsed since it was made and which has burdened it with traces of age. We have distinguished historical monuments from intentional ones as a more subjective category which remains nonetheless firmly bound up with objects, and now we recognize a third category of monuments in which the object has shrunk to a necessary evil. These monuments are nothing more than indispensable catalysts which trigger in the beholder a sense of the life cycle, of the emergence of the particular from the general and its gradual but inevitable dissolution back into the general. This immediate emotional effect depends on neither scholarly knowledge nor historical education for its satisfaction, since it is evoked by mere sensory perception. Hence it is not restricted to the educated (to whom the task of caring for monuments necessarily has to be limited) but also touches the masses independent of their education. The general validity, which it shares with religious feelings, gives this new commemorative (monument) value a significance whose ultimate consequences cannot yet be assessed. We will henceforth call this the *age-value*.

From these reflections it is clear that the modern cult of monuments is not restricted to caring for historical monuments; it also requires consideration for monuments of mere age-value. Just as intentional monuments are part and parcel of historical monuments, so all historical ones can be categorized as monuments having an age-value. Outwardly these three classes of monuments can be thought of as contained within one another, while the scope of their memory-value widens. To the class of intentional monuments belong only those works which recall a specific moment or complex of moments from the past. The class of historical monuments is enlarged to include those which still refer to a particular moment, but the choice of that moment is left to our subjective preference. Finally, the category of monuments of age-value embraces every artifact without regard to its original significance and purpose, as long as it reveals the passage of a considerable period of time. These classes form three consecutive phases of the generalization of what a monument means. A cursory glance at the history of preservation up to this time reveals how these three classes have arisen in identical sequence over historical time.

56

LE CORBUSIER

1911

Le Corbusier's confrontation with the Acropolis in Athens came at the end of a six-month journey, when he was 24. His time there was immediately preceded by an inspiring stay at Mount Athos and followed by visits to Eleusis, Delphi, Naples, Rome, and Pompeii. In Athens, he visited the Acropolis daily for several weeks, until he was finally exhausted – crushed – by the place. He was accompanied by his friend William Ritter, and carried a camera, pencils, paints, and paper, as well as a vivid recollection of a short text by the religious writer Ernst Renan, *Prayer on the Acropolis*. Le Corbusier's text makes it plain that he agreed with the theologian's notion that the Pentelicus marble of the Parthenon 'crystallized the ideal of beauty', despite the fact that the 'spotless stones' were broken fragments that attested as much to the forces of nature and the violence of men as to the highest achievements of art.

A key point for the architect was the monochrome character of the stone, its whiteness. Later, after his visit to the United States in 1935, he charged the word with polemical meaning in *When the Cathedrals were White* (*Quand les Cathédrales étaient Blanches*, 1937). Less a color like red or blue, white served as an emblem of architectural form that was both legible and pristine: 'The cathedrals were white because they were new. The cities were new; they were constructed all at once, in an orderly way, regular, geometric, in accordance with plans. The freshly cut stone of France was dazzling in its whiteness, as the Acropolis in Athens had been white and dazzling, as the Pyramids of Egypt had gleamed with polished granite... White, limpid, joyous, clear, and without hesitations, the new world was opening up like a flower among the ruins.'

All this is fiction, of course (ancient temples were originally brightly painted), but it suggests a unique view of ruins, that there are two types: the odd and ends of uninspired design and construction, and the precious reminders of enduring beauty. The white stone of the Acropolis ruins was thus both (factually) ancient and (conceptually) modern, seen by him as an emblem of architecture that was no longer and not yet. It is hardly surprising that architectural details, so often the subject matter of archaeological study, are largely absent from his sketches and hardly noted in his text. They would have been distracting.

What is perhaps most remarkable about this song to Western architecture's most sacred site is his description of the relationship between the buildings and their vicinity, not only the hill on which they stand, but the landscape that extends toward the city port in one direction and nearby hills in the others. As the text unfolds, he attempts to stabilize a tension between the Parthenon's singularity (as the site's 'sovereign cube') and both the *temenos* (temple enclosure or precinct) and the wider terrain to which it adheres: land, sea, sun, and sky. The topography is continuous, the chronology contrasting; despite the depredations of nature and war, the Parthenon remains.

By contrast with the planar geometry, level horizons, and simple volumes, the language used to describe the site is hardly plain and simple, his metaphors verging on the excessive. The Parthenon is 'the marble pilot of a disabled hull', a 'stone brow', 'sovereign cube', 'gigantic apparition', and a 'terrible machine'. Given the pulsations, emanations, and vibrations he describes, one doesn't puzzle long about what binds these images together; it is their surprising and irrepressible vitality, a quality that's rather unexpected in ruins, but decisive for their continued relevance. Ruins are thus doubly architectural: windows into a past world and thresholds that lead *towards a new architecture*.

'Parthenon', from Le Voyage d'Orient
(Paris: Forces Vives, 1966)[2]

The uniformly red landscape is reflected by the temples. Their marbles have the luster of new bronze against the azure sky. Closeup, they really seem as reddish brown as terracotta. Never in my life have I experienced the subtleties of such monochromy. The body, the mind, the heart gasp, suddenly overpowered.

Here, the rectitude of the temples, the impeccable structure and the brutality of the site were confirmed. The strong spirit triumphs. Too lucidly the herald blows a brazen trumpet and proffers a jarring blast. The entablature of a cruel rigidity crushes and terrorizes. The feeling of a superhuman fatality seizes you. The Parthenon, a terrible machine, grinds and dominates; seen from as far as a four-hour walk and one hour by boat, alone it is a sovereign cube facing the sea...

As by the violence of a combat, I was stupefied by this gigantic apparition. Beyond the peristyle of the sacred hill, the Parthenon appeared alone and square holding high up above the thrust of its bronze-colored shafts its entablature, its stone brow. The steps below served as its support and increased its height by their twenty rises. Nothing existed but the temple, the sky, and the surface of paving stones damaged by centuries of plundering...

At the very moment the sun touches the earth... Pausing before the stairwell and impressed by this abyss of darkness, [visitors] hunch their shoulders as they sense, sparkling and elusive above the sea, a spectral past, an ineluctable presence…

Physically, the impression is that of a most profound inspiration that expands your chest. It is like an ecstasy that pushes you onto the bare rock devoid of its old slab paving and, out of joy and admiration, throws you from the Temple of Minerva to the Temple of Erechtheum, and from there to the Propylaea. From beneath this portico, the Parthenon can be seen on its domineering block, casting in the distance its horizontal architrave and facing this concerted landscape with its front like a shield…

I had thought it possible to compare this marble to new bronze, hoping that, in addition to the color so described, this word would suggest the pronounced luster of this substantial mass fixed in place with the inexorability of an oracle. In the face of the unexplainable intensity of this ruin, increasingly an abyss separates the soul which feels from the mind which measures.

It is good that we other builders know and meditate on this place. Today, the temples of the Acropolis are twenty-five hundred years old. They have not been maintained for the last fifteen centuries. Not only have storms loosed their unusual downpours, but, more harmful than earthquakes, men, troglodytes, have inhabited the hill certainly amazed by their good luck. And they have torn away whatever they needed, the marble slabs and the huge blocks, and have built any old way with mud and rubble shanties for swarms of children. The Turks used it as a fortress. What a target for an assault! One fine day in 1687 the Parthenon was used as a depository for explosives. During an attack an artillery shell hit the roof and ignited the gunpowder. Everything blew up.

Le Corbusier, *The Acropolis of Athens*, pencil on paper, 1911. Fondation Le Corbusier.

The Parthenon has remained, torn apart but not jostled...

Many an evening from a side of Lycabettus that overlooks the Acropolis, I could see beyond the modern city lighting up, the disabled hull and its marble vigil – the Parthenon – dominating it, as if it were taking it toward the Piraeus, to the sea that had been the sacred route by which so many conquered treasures came to be laid out beneath the porticoes of the temples. Like a rocky hull, a giant tragic carcass in the dying light above all this red earth. A fading light upon the aridity of the red earth coagulates black blood about the Acropolis and its temple – the impassive pilot that maintains the course with all the movement of its outstretched sides. A serpentine light that ignites an open boulevard winding around the giant carcass and runs on the right toward the public squares animated by modern life.

57

GEORG SIMMEL

1911

Georg Simmel's topographical essays, including among others 'The Ruin' (1911), 'The Philosophy of Landscape', and his city essays, 'Venice', 'Florence', and especially 'Rome', demonstrate his unique sense of the dialectical relationships between culture and nature, reciprocal involvements that are alternately cooperative and conflictual. The instance of cooperation he adduced in 'The Ruin' is the work of architecture, when antagonisms between 'the will of the spirit' and the 'necessity of nature' come to a temporary truce, disturbed when the work begins to crumble, attesting to Nature's rightful claim over materials once taken from her. With respect to meaning and emotions, some destructive forces are more effectual than others – natural more than human – because they signify a truly 'cosmic tragedy'. Trees and hillsides, having submitted to the aims of art, become through ruination materials of a new form, this time made by nature, again, it should be noted, for the materials out of which they have been (re)made never renounced their birthright.

'The Ruin' from *Philosophische Kultur. Gesammelte Essays*
(Leipzig: Alfred Kröner, 1919)[3]

Architecture is the only art in which the great struggle between the will of the spirit and the necessity of nature issues into real peace: that in which the soul in its upward striving and nature in its gravity are held in balance... This unique balance – between mechanical, inert matter which passively resists pressure, and informing spirituality which pushes upward – breaks, however, the instant a building crumbles. For this means nothing else than that merely natural forces begin to become master over the work of man: the balance between nature and spirit, which the building manifested, shifts in favor of nature. This shift becomes a cosmic tragedy which, so we feel, makes every ruin an object infused with our nostalgia; for now the decay appears as nature's revenge for the spirit's having violated it by making a form in its own image...

The moment its decay destroys the unity of the form, nature and spirit separate again and reveal their world-pervading original enmity – as if the artistic formation had only been an act of violence committed by the spirit to which the stone unwillingly submitted; as if it now gradually shook off this yoke and returned once more into the independent lawfulness of its own forces.

But this makes the ruin a more meaningful, more significant phenomenon than are the fragments of other destroyed works of art. A painting from which particles of paint have fallen off, a statue with mutilated limbs, an ancient text of poetry from which words or lines are lost – all of these have effect only according to what is still left in them of artistic formation or what the imagination can construe of it from these remnants. Their immediate appearance is no artistic unity; it offers us nothing but a work of art imperfect through the reductions it has undergone. The ruin of a building, however, means that where the work of art is dying, other forces and forms, those of nature, have grown; and that out of what of art still lives in the ruin and what of nature already lives in it, there has emerged a new whole, a characteristic unity. To be sure, from the standpoint of that purpose which the spirit has embodied in palace and church, castle and hall, aqueduct and memorial column, the form in which they appear when decayed is a meaningless incident. Yet a new meaning seizes on this incident, comprehending it and its spiritual form in a unity which is no longer grounded in human purposiveness but in that depth where human purposiveness and the working of non-conscious natural forces grow from their common root. For this reason a good many Roman ruins, however interesting they may be otherwise, lack the specific fascination of the ruin – to the extent, that is, to which one notices in them the destruction *by man*; for this contradicts the contrast between human work and the effect of *nature* on which rests the significance of the ruin as such.

Such a contradiction is engendered not only by man's positive action but also by his passivity when (and because) he strikes us as an element of mere nature. This characterizes a good many urban ruins, like those, still inhabited, often found in Italy off the main road. In these cases, what strikes us is not, to be sure, that human beings destroy the work of man – this indeed is achieved by nature – but that men *let it decay*. From the standpoint of the idea of man, such indifference is, so to speak, a positive passivity, whereby man makes himself the accomplice of nature and of that one of its inherent tendencies which is dramatically opposed to his own essential interests. Here the inhabited ruin loses for us that sensuous–suprasensuous balance of the conflicting tendencies of existence which we see in the abandoned one. This balance, indeed, gives it its problematical, unsettling, often unbearable character. Such places, sinking from life, still strike us as settings of a life.

In other words, it is the fascination of the ruin that here the work of man appears to us entirely as a product of nature. The same forces which give a

Ehrenberg Castle, Reutte, Austria.

mountain its shape through weathering, erosion, faulting, growth of vegetation, here do their work on old walls. Even the charm of alpine forms – which for the most part, after all, are clumsy, accidental, artistically insipid – rests on the felt counterplay of two cosmic tendencies: volcanic eruptions or gradual stratification have built the mountain upward; rain and snow, weathering and landslides, chemical dissolution and the effect of gradually intruding vegetation have sawed apart and hollowed out the upper ledge, have cast downward parts of what had been raised up, thus giving the contour its form. In this form, we thus feel the vitality of those opposing tendencies – and, instinctively sensing these antitheses in ourselves, we notice, beyond everything merely formal and aesthetic, the significance of the configuration in whose serene unity they have their synthesis.

In the ruin, these antitheses are distributed over even more widely segmented parts of existence. What has led the building upward is human will; what gives it its present appearance is the brute, downward-dragging, corroding, crumbling power of nature. Still, so long as we can speak of a ruin at all and not of a mere heap of stones, this power does not sink the work of man into the formlessness of mere matter. There rises a new form which, from the standpoint of nature, is entirely meaningful, comprehensible, differentiated. Nature has transformed the work of art into material for her own expression, as she had previously served as material for art.

According to its cosmic order, the hierarchy of nature and spirit usually shows nature as the substructure, so to speak, the raw material, or semi-finished product; the spirit, as the definitely formative and crowning element. The ruin reverses this order: what was raised by the spirit becomes the object of the same forces which form the contour of the mountain and the bank of the river. If in this way there emerges an aesthetic significance, it also ramifies into a metaphysical one, in the manner revealed by patina on metal and wood, ivory and marble. In patina, too, a merely natural process is set off on the surface of a human product and makes for the outgrowth of a skin which completely covers up the original one. That the product becomes more beautiful by chemical and physical means; that what is willed becomes, unintentionally and unenforceably, something obviously new, often more beautiful, and once more self-consistent: this mysterious harmony is the fantastic fascination of patina which cannot be wholly accounted for by analyzing our perception of it.

This is the fascination of the ruin, too; but in addition, the ruin has another one of the same order: the destruction of the spiritual form by the effect of natural forces, that reversal of the typical order, is felt as a return to the 'good mother', as Goethe calls nature. Here the saying that all that is human 'is taken from earth and to earth shall return' rises above its sad nihilism. Between the not-yet and the no-longer lies an affirmation of the spirit whose path, it is true, now no longer ascends to its peak but, satiated by the peak's riches, descends to its home. This is, as it were, the counterpart of that 'fruitful moment' for which those riches which the ruin has in retrospect are still in prospect. That the overwhelming of a work of the human will by the power of nature can have an aesthetic effect at all suggests that nature has a never completely extinguished rightful claim to this work, however much it may be formed by the spirit. In its material, its given state, it has always remained nature, and if now nature becomes once more completely mistress over it, she is merely exercising a right which until now has remained latent but which she never, so to speak, has renounced.

For this reason, the ruin strikes us so often as tragic – but not as sad – because destruction here is not something senselessly coming from the outside but rather the realization of a tendency inherent in the deepest layer of existence of the destroyed. For this reason, too, the aesthetically satisfying impression, which is associated with the tragedy or secret justice of destruction, is so often lacking when we describe a person as a 'ruin'. For even when we mean by this that the psychic layers we designate as natural in the narrower sense – the drives or inhibitions connected with the body, the inert, the accidental, that which points toward death – have become master over the specifically human, rationally valuable ones, we still do not feel that a latent right is being realized through these tendencies. Rather, such a right does not exist at all. We believe – rightly or wrongly – that such derogations, inimical to the spirit, do *not* inhere in the nature of man in its deepest sense: they have a right to everything external that is born with him, but not to man himself. Reflections and complexities in other contexts aside, man as a ruin, therefore, is so often more sad than tragic, lacking that metaphysical calm which attaches to the decay of a material work as by virtue of a profound *a priori*.

When we speak of 'returning home', we mean to characterize the peace whose mood surrounds the ruin. And we must characterize something else: our sense that these two world potencies – the striving upward and the sinking downward – are working serenely together, as we envisage in their working a picture of purely natural existence. Expressing this peace for us, the ruin orders itself into the surrounding landscape without a break, growing together with it like tree and stone – whereas a palace, a villa, even a peasant house, even where they fit perfectly into the mood of their landscape, always stem from another order of things and blend with that of nature only as if in afterthought. Very old buildings in open country, and particularly ruins, often show a peculiar similarity of color to the tones of the soil around them... [no doubt due to] the influences of rain and sunshine, the incursion of vegetation, heat, and cold must have assimilated the building abandoned to them to the color tone of the ground which has been abandoned to the same destinies. They have sunk its once conspicuous contrast into the peaceful unity of belonging...

The aesthetic value of the ruin combines the disharmony, the eternal becoming of the soul struggling against itself, with the formal satisfaction, the firm limitedness of the work of art. For this reason, the metaphysical-aesthetic charm of the ruin disappears when not enough remains of it to let us feel the upward-leading tendency. The stumps of the pillars of the Forum Romanum are simply ugly and nothing else, while a pillar crumbled – say, halfway down – can generate a maximum of charm.

To be sure, we may well be inclined to ascribe this peacefulness to another motif: the character of the ruin as *past*. It is the site of life from which life has departed – but this is nothing merely negative, added to it only by thought, as it is for the countless things which, once immersed in life and accidentally cast on its bank, are by their very nature capable of being again easily caught by its current. In the case of the ruin, the fact that life with its wealth and its changes once dwelled here constitutes an immediately perceived presence. The ruin creates the present form of a past life, not according to the contents or remnants of that life, but according to its past as such...

Thus, purpose and accident, nature and spirit, past and present here resolve the tension of their contrasts – or, rather, preserving this tension, they yet lead to a unity of external image and internal effect. It is as though a segment of existence must collapse before it can become unresisting to all currents and powers coming from all corners of reality. Perhaps this is the reason for our general fascination with decay and decadence, a fascination which goes beyond what is merely negative and degrading. The rich and many-sided culture, the unlimited *impressionability*, and the understanding open to everything, which are characteristic of decadent epochs, do signify this coming together of all contradictory strivings. An equalizing justice connects the uninhibited unity of all things that grow apart and against one another with the decay of those men and works of men which now can only yield, but can no longer create and maintain their own forms out of their own strength.

58

John Piper

1947

The English painter, architect, and critic John Piper distinguished between ruined buildings and those whose decay was 'pleasing'. Pleasing decay was the ruin's preliminary. Buildings in this state still allowed use and inhabitation; ruins did not. His essay, first published in the *Architectural Review* for September 1947, and later republished as a chapter in his book *Buildings and Projects* (1948), used the theme to remind his readers of the beauty of things that get old. Designers, he thought, should consider a built work's *visual* as well as *functional* future. He wrote in reaction and opposition to the then current fascination with all things new, in some ways invoking the alternative posed decades earlier by Alois Riegl (*see* Extract 55) between 'age-value' and 'new-value'. Piper emphasized that decay is a continuing process, not a stationary condition.

That distinction led him to the conflict between proponents of restoration – the English counterparts of Viollet le Duc (*see* Extract 52) – and the advocates of conservation, whom he linked to figures such as Ruskin (*see* Extract 51), William Morris (*see* Extract 53), and the Society for the Preservation of Ancient Buildings (SPAB). In terms that had by then become colloquial, this was the conflict between the 'scrape' and 'anti-scrape' gangs. A third alternative was what he called the 'Picturesque Way', which meant leaving a ruin alone and letting it fall to pieces as a stimulus to reflection on time's passing and nature's claim on what was taken from it, as Georg Simmel (*see* Extract 57) had argued a few decades earlier. Piper was against the excavator's misguided sense of tidiness, the requirement for mowed and leveled ground around ruins, but advocated forcefully for the use of ruins to train the artistic eye, for visual education was then in a sadly neglected state.

'Pleasing Decay' in *Buildings and Prospects*
(London: The Architectural Press, 1948)

Buildings that are beginning to go 'back to nature', crumbling, growing moss and lichen, were so much admired by our grandfathers that we are still self-conscious about them...

John Piper, *Somerset Place, Bath*, graphite, ink, and gouache on paper, 1942. Tate Britain.

At the moment we are naturally over-concerned with what a new building shall look like *new*. Soane made drawings of some proposed buildings as they would look in a state of ruin; indicating that men should make buildings, as God made men, to be beautiful in age as well as in youth. A building 'built to last' has a visual future as well as a functional one, and a good designer will have half an eye on this visual future of his work, remembering that some people will see it as an aged warrior or matron, not just as a brave baby. The admiration of his great-grandchildren will be as important to him as that of his friends.

For the good town-planner decay – *present* decay, as well as possible future decay – should surely be one of the tricks in his box of tricks to be used, as the country gentleman used it in the late eighteenth and early nineteenth centuries, for certain specific purposes. For instance, the planner might find it sensible to retain the tower of a redundant church, and the fabric of a nonconformist chapel as visual points of interest in one new development scheme, a decayed warehouse or a terrace of houses of decayed charm in another. These in fact have a visual point, not only for their own sakes but for the sake of relief and contrast. The specialist must decide how far decay can go, how far it can be conserved, even cultivated, in such cases; always remembering that decay is not a stationary condition but a growing and continuing process that attacks all buildings in time – even the Co-operative Stores built of shiny bricks on the High Street...

Since Morris's day the situation has not changed much. The sensibility which he (through the SPAB, and by other means) tried to awaken has been, to some extent, awakened. It has become more active in its expression, but it has not increased in quantity. Sensibility to visual excellence in old buildings – as opposed to practical, and historical-associational, considerations – is still thinly spread. Certainly, we love old buildings, but we love them for what they stand for rather than for what they look like. And alas, it is usually *after* an old building has been permed, and has had its eyebrows plucked, that we notice that its whole character has been changed. It is after the flood-lighting and the new radiators have been installed in a church that we notice that the old oil lamps and the cracked Tortoise stove has a certain visual charm. Nor is this sentiment only; they had the same visual charm, compared with the more labour-saving, up-to-date system, that an antiquated steam locomotive has on an electrified railway.

There are three existing general plans for dealing with a building in an advanced state of decay:

To leave it alone and let it fall to pieces (the Picturesque way, taken to the extreme.)

To 'restore' it. (The 'Scrape' way.)

To 'conserve' it, by arresting the decay. (The 'Anti-Scrape' way.)

There is a lot after all to be said against all three plans, and not much to be said in favor of any of them. Anyone who adopts any one of the three existing policies stands to be shot at...

The only hope is to open the eyes, and treat every building – every surface, even – on its individual merits. *To regard the present state of the building as, possibly, virtuous in itself*, and to use it as an element of charm, or beauty, or even merely of contrast – if it proves to have virtues – in its present landscape or townscape, and to keep a weather-eye on it in the future development of these. When the eye has become accustomed to it, it accepts, gracefully and naturally, pleasing decay in old buildings. The tendency of nature is to induce every building to come back to her arms, sooner or later; rust, lichen, moss, the cracking and powdering of mortar in joints, of the stone and brick itself – all these are the forms of nature's expression of jealousy at the presence of man's creations. Nature never lets up on her passion to see buildings in her own image...

Pleasing decay is to be found everywhere, but not all decay in buildings *is* pleasing. What Ruskin would have called the 'moral' aspect may over-ride the aesthetic aspect. Here comes the whole question of 'right' building and 'wrong' building, and it is tenable (to take a minor illustration) that a building that has had its stonework laid with the grain the wrong way may 'peel' less attractively than one rightly laid. I say 'may' (when Ruskin, and presumably many other people, would say 'must') because I belong to an age that admires Utrillo as well as Cotman...

Public policy about major ruins shows the recent ascendancy of the archaeologist's influence, and the diminishing influence of the artist. The artists have largely lost interest, having become otherwise preoccupied, and the excavators and preservers have taken over in default. The artist and the architect with an eye must regain interest or all will be lost...

Architects and town-planners have another task to add to their present ones: to re-educate themselves visually, taking note of these characteristics [of sublime beauty]. But just as we have learned (as I have said) to appreciate Utrillo as well as Cotman, there are other characteristics that can, and must, be added to Ruskin's elements of 'picturesqueness' to-day; and had he himself lived to-day he would certainly have added them. The incorporation of Picasso and Matisse, Ernst and Miró into our visual philosophy may mean an uncomfortable stretching of the word 'picturesque' to embrace our beliefs; but it is certain that if the lessons of these painters are properly learned 'pleasing decay' will be found to have a very large place in our present-day visual consciousness. Their works must have a strong bearing on architectural and planning practice in the long run, and the shorter we can make that run the better. They prophesied the beauty as well as the horror of bomb damage, and as visual planners they are at the moment unrivalled. Bomb damage has revealed new beauties in unexpected appositions – a rich source of information for the planner who would retain picturesque elements from the past that can be opposed in size, colour and shape to new buildings and groups of buildings, whether by way of contrast or agreement...

By mere age a city or a building is able to evoke powerful emotions in primitive as well as sophisticated breasts, yet this, the most potent visual weapon possessed by the planner, is generally not treated as a weapon at all. Old buildings are ruthlessly restored by those who cannot distinguish between the *fact* of age and the *effect* of age. The official friends of old buildings are often their worst enemies, in that on the plea of preserving it for posterity they will renovate a venerable building is such a way that the old building loses the one quality which made it venerable – the effect of age. But to prolong the life of an old building by removing the effects of its age is like prolonging the use of a pram by throwing away the baby...

59

Dimitris Pikionis

1957

The new path to the ancient Acropolis in Athens was intended to articulate the classical landscape's remote antiquity in palpably material terms. Reclaimed stones and tiles from recently demolished buildings were laid out as wide stretches of pavement, raised up as benches, and built into a few buildings that aligned the walk. Ruins weren't rebuilt and individual buildings weren't recalled; instead, something more basic was summoned – their world. And they were meant to signify more, the chapters or seasons of natural history, described in Pikionis's *Sentimental Topography* as a play of forces: exhalations, tremors, and rotations. He thought the worn, chipped, discolored, and stained fragments would testify to the transformative power of wind, rain, and sun, making and unmaking what cultures had built.

Bodies, buildings, and landscapes are all of a piece in this narrative, but not only in the static and material, also the active and environmental sense – an interplay of forces that resulted in erosion and sedimentation. 'Rocks, broken boulders, dust born of fruitful soil', shaped and unshaped by forces human and beyond the human give the soil its visible lineaments. But the reassembled fragments are not only retrospective, for they were reworked by a modern architect with modern sensibilities. Threaded between and connecting the shards are slabs of concrete that have been shaped in imitation of the works of some of his favorite modern painters, particularly Paul Klee. If the mind and eye discern differences between then and now, the feet know no real distinction between past and present.

A Sentimental Topography
(London: Architectural Association, 1989)

As we walk upon this earth, our hearts experience anew that rapturous joy we felt as children when we first discovered our ability to move in space – the alternating disruption and restoration of balance which is walking.[4]

We rejoice in the progress of our body across the uneven surface of the earth and our spirit is gladdened by the endless interplay of the three dimensions that we encounter at every step, the shifting and changing that occurs with the

Paths and landscaping at the Acropolis and Filopapou, 1954–57.
Photograph: Antonios Thodis.

mere passage of a cloud high up in the sky. We walk past a rock, or a tree trunk, or a shrub's tufted foliage; we move up and down, following the rise and fall of the ground, tracing its convexities, which are the hills and mountains, and its concavities, which are the valleys.

Then we rejoice in the wide, flat expanse of the plains; we measure the earth by the toil of our bodies.

This deserted country lane is far superior to the thoroughfares of the large modern city, for all its twists and curves and infinite changes of perspective show us the divine hypostasis of singularity when submitted to the harmony of the whole.

We meditate upon the spirit which emanates from each particular land or place.[5]

Here the ground is hard, stony, precipitous, and the soil is brittle and dry. There the ground is level; water surges out of mossy patches. Further on, the breeze, the altitude and the configuration of the ground announce the proximity of the sea. Further on still, the vegetation runs riot, in an extreme culmination of the earth's thrust towards form, towards a perfect attunement of its clothing to the rhythm of the seasons.

Natural forces, geometry of the earth and quality of light and air single out this land as a cradle of civilization. Mysterious exhalations seem to rise from the ground. Here are ancient, venerable places of worship – a precipice that fills one's soul with awe, a cave where mysterious spirits, supernatural powers dwell. In face of these primeval images of the earth, the soul is shot through with a mystical tremor, like the waterfinder when his divining rod comes upon the invisible presence of a subterranean stream...

Here are stone formations shaped by divine forces – rocks, broken boulders, the dust born of the fruitful soil, its particles as uncountable as the stars.

I stoop and pick up a stone. I caress it with my eyes, with my fingers. It is a piece of grey limestone. Fire moulded its divine shape; water sculpted it and endowed it with this fine covering of clay that has alternating patches of white and rust, with a yellow tinge. I turn it around in my hands. I study the harmony of its contours. I delight in the way hollows and protrusions, light and shadows, balance each other on its surface. I rejoice in the way the universal laws are embodied and fulfilled in this stone – the laws, which, according to Goethe, would have remained unknown to us, had not an innate sense of beauty revealed them to the poet and the artist.

In truth, it occurs to me, O stone, that as the incandescent mass of this planet was torn away from the sun and set spinning around like a ring of fire, eventually condensing into our earth, you came to occupy a place within its vast expanse that was in no way accidental. The harmony of the whole, which determined the inclination of our planet's axis, also assigned this particular place to you as your home, as the generator of your supremely spiritual form, within an atmosphere and light that are spiritually attuned to you...[6]

Stone, you compose the lineaments of this landscape. You are the landscape. You are the Temple that is to crown the precipitous rocks of your own Acropolis. For what else does the Temple do but enact the same twofold law, which you serve?

More than anything else, is not the Temple also 'an explanation of the way in which the entirety of things is arranged'? Is its equilibrium not similar to that of the mountains of vegetation, of all living creatures...

As I paced upon this soil, as I journeyed across this kingdom of limestone and clay, I saw the limestone change into a lintel, and the red clay colour the walls of an imaginary shrine. The large round pebbles of the Cladeus River appeared to me as the heads of heroes, and the statues on the pediments as mountains. Zeus' long hair became a sheer precipice, and this mountain of a thousand shapes – which I gradually pieced together as I walked across it, recomposing in my mind the harmony of its contours – took on the form of a Greek statue...

It is in moments like this, O Doric column, that your mystery is revealed to me. Now I understand: the 'tension' that governs your lines is not meant only to serve the laws of statics, extending natural beauty into a form of art;[7] the grooves of your fluted body are not meant only to distribute light equally across your surface, inserting shade into light and light into shade, so that the tones of your stone shaft blend with the tones of the sky above and the rock below. You are, it seems to me, an animate being thirsting for union as you revolve upon your own axis, your grooves like eyes that strive to retain, within their revolving motion, what has come to pass and to contemplate, full of trepidation, what is about to happen – but this is not all. More than any of these things, this hour reveals that this longed-for union would project and condense the culmination of nature's dramatic mystery within an art form corresponding to nature itself.

There is an undecipherable connection between these stories, this bitter grass, these green shadows, these voices that streak the air, the southern breezes, the torn plumes of the clouds, all this dramatic mystery which appears to be composed of irreconcilable opposites; all these are made one in the equation of your grooves.

Is not your own form made of irreconcilable opposites held together in perfect balance? And the coldness of the marble, the austerity of your vertical shaft, your parallel lines – have they not merged with the warmth of the sun, with the unsurpassable sensitivity of the spirit, to make you what you are?...

But in this wintry hour I think of you again, O Doric cyma, of the stern music of your form poised high up on the Acropolis, high above the sheer rocks and the clay soil of the olive grove. I reflect upon the winter light falling on your harmonious incurvatures, upon the cool shadows that nestle among them and constitute your darkness.

There is something awesome about the austerity, the sharpness, the sensitivity of your shape, rising out of a perfect mathematical formulation [8]

This journal is by no means complete but does it really matter? Is it not enough if the perusal of what there is helps to make manifest the principle which I believe nature wishes to teach us: nothing exists on its own; everything is part of a total harmony. All things are interconnected; for they are all affected and changed by each other. We can apprehend one thing only through the intermediary of everything else.

60

ROBERT SMITHSON

1967

Robert Smithson has inspired many modernist perspectives on the world that we wouldn't otherwise have noticed. His 1970 land art *Spiral Jetty* in the shallows of Great Salt Lake in Utah became an object to preserve, as it was submerged in the brackish water, then in times of drought re-emerged, an act of natural preservation. Yet *Spiral Jetty* was difficult to reach and seen by few. Just three years earlier he had taken a trip from New York, later written up as 'A Tour of the Monuments of Passaic, New Jersey', part of a series of excursions throughout New Jersey, published in the December 1967 issue of *Artforum*.[9] This wonderful, multi-faceted essay has some intriguing comments on the idea of 'ruin'; at one point he writes of what he sees as 'ruins in reverse', i.e. new constructions that would take the place of what had been there. Much of what might be seen today as wasteland or derelict objects may be ruins transformed by how they are presented – by work created out of the rubble of a slate quarry or, in Smithson's case, by photographs. His 'Instamatic (or what the rationalists call a camera)' is used to capture a series of 'monuments' in the New Jersey landscape, each of which – pipelines, a children's sand box – is now glossed with a new designation of the monumental.

The early response to ruins in the 18th century had been to recreate them in the imagination, peopling them with associations. Part of this for Smithson is celebration, part irony, as his deliberate *factoid* writing lists the irredeemable facts of existence in New Jersey – the number of the bus he took out of the city, the place where he alighted, a map of his encounters, the book he was taking with him to consult, Brian Aldiss's *Earthworks*.

What he found and recorded in words and with his Instamatic camera was, as Ann Reynolds noted in her commentary in *Robert Smithson, Learning from New Jersey and Elsewhere*,[10] a 'carefully constructed experience' of something anybody might see and yet would almost probably neglect. The experience was 'preserved' in his text, where it opened up a world of largely unnoticed and unimportant ordinariness. It is a key document, an early moment of '*terrain vague*', or even 'ruin porn' *avant la lettre*, as he explored quarries, abandoned airstrips and derelict industrial sites. His endeavors recall, more absurdly and parodically, Le Corbusier's celebration in the 1930s of American grain elevators as monuments.

61

LOUIS I. KAHN

1969

For the architect Louis Kahn, ruins were neither the end of architecture nor its beginning, but their meeting point in the present historical moment. Throughout his life he studied ancient works of architecture, some unknown and anonymous, built within vernacular traditions in the United States and Europe, and others commonly thought to be canonical, in Egypt (Giza), Greece (Athens), and Italy (Rome – particularly the Pantheon and Baths of Caracalla). Mostly they had fallen to ruin, a fate his sketches acknowledged. Yet no tears fell on the pages of his pastel drawings, for the loss of architectural detail, as well as evidences of use and inhabitation, revealed something much more important than *the solution to needs*, assumed to be architecture's primary purpose only by those who misunderstand the art. Ruins reveal architectural *order*, a big word for him. Ruins served Kahn as an indictment of practices that attended primarily to circumstantial contingencies and passing concerns. More positively, they disclosed the principles that governed the work's genesis, how it came to be what it is – in essence.

Kahn was not the only modern architect to see the ruin as a manifestation of architecture's basic reality. Two decades earlier, the great French architect Auguste Perret posed a similar contrast between the appearance and reality of architectural order: 'The Palace of Versailles is badly built; the vault above the Hall of Mirrors is made of a thick layer of rubble, attached to an inferior framework, and in the course of time, what will remain of the palace will not be a ruin, but an anonymous heap of debris. This is not architecture; *architecture is what leaves beautiful ruins*.' Beauty here is less aesthetic than intellectual, a mental or spiritual grasp of a work's irreducible substance. For these two moderns, the elements of construction that survive the centuries show a face unsoiled by cosmetic representations – hardly pristine but inaugural just the same.

LOUIS I. KAHN

Interviews with Heinrich Klotz, 1969–70, in *Louis I. Kahn in Conversation* (New Haven: Yale University Press, 2015)

HK: Did you want to do anything else, before you became an architect?

LIK: I would say that it happened quite circumstantially. There is no denying that I would have been either a painter, sculptor, musician, or architect, because of my love for that which yet is not. If I had to describe the very core of the decision, it would [have] to do most basically with that which is in question, that which is not yet. You see, it refutes need. It only deals with desires.

HK: By needs, do you mean everyday desires for money, shelter, and all these other…

LIK: Need stands for what is already present, and it becomes a kind of measurement of the already present. Desire becomes a sense of the yet not made. That is the main difference between need and desire.

HK: Doesn't the architect ever build just for needs?

LIK: No. Never build for needs! As an [outcome of] art, a space is made [with] a touch of eternity. I think a space evokes its use. It transcends need. If it doesn't

Louis I. Kahn, *View of the Acropolis from the Olympeion*, pastel on paper, 1951. Architectural Archives, University of Pennsylvania.

do that then it has failed. One might say that architecture is directed by function more than painting is. A painting is made to be sensed for its motivation beyond seeing, as space is made to inspire use. It's psychological. There is something about a building which is different from a painting. When a building is being built, there is an impatience to bring it into being. Not a blade of grass can grow near this activity. Look at the building after it has been built. Each part that was built with so much activity and joy and willingness to proceed tries to say when you're using the building: *Let me tell you about how I was made.* Nobody is listening because the building is now satisfying need. The desire in its making is not evident. As time passes, when it is a ruin, the spirit of its making comes back. It welcomes the foliage that entwines and conceals. Everyone who passes can hear the story it wants to tell about its making. It is no longer in servitude; the spirit is back.

62

Carlo Scarpa

1978

Carlo Scarpa's attitude toward ruins is more apparent in his buildings than in his few writings, but 'A Thousand Cypresses' – one of his very few authored essays (1978) – and an interview, also of 1978, show his unique approach to the problem of intervening in a dilapidated site and the role ruins play in design thinking.

Paradoxical though their double function may seem, ruins both constrained and liberated Scarpa's architectural invention. Problems had to be solved if the remnant were to be inhabited again, but solved creatively. At Castelvecchio in Verona, he wanted to preserve the 'originality and character' of every room, but not the 'wooden beams'. Restoration wasn't the aim, for what had been, if made complete again, wouldn't serve current purposes – a castle isn't a museum. Nor was conservation

Carlo Scarpa, *cortile* of the Fondazione Querini Stampalia, Venice, 1961–63.
Photograph: John Dixon Hunt.

Carlo Scarpa, Castelvecchio, Verona, 1958–75. Photograph: John Dixon Hunt.

intended, especially not safeguarding and saving all that remained, for much of it was low in quality. 'At Castelvecchio everything was fake.' This was true for the many entrances and exits, as well as small non-structural beams inserted centuries ago, that were nothing more than 'dummies'. Some fragments, such as the equestrian statue, had to be kept of course, because of their beauty and cultural importance, or, in the case of the statue, its magnificence.

Another space Scapa transformed was the small *cortile* of the Fondazione Querini Stampalia, where he reinvented aspects of older, now lost, Venetian courtyards and gardens: a well-head, a miniature Venetian Lion, a channel of water. Fake, yes, but a telling gesture to lost gardens in the city.

For Scarpa, work with ruins required not only a non-sentimental assessment of quality, but also an insight into the hidden or obscured identity of the work, for that was what the renovation sought to make legible again. In the case of Castelvecchio, the equestrian statue of Cangrande had to be hoisted up in the air so it could be seen from many vantages, and inclined at an angle, to make it stand out from the body of the building. The same interpretative/transformative work was required of the ruin's 'Gothic' character, destroying its inappropriately symmetrical form, in order to restate its 'vertical values'. No work of this kind was possible, he observed, without historical understanding, which the ruin itself partly sustained.

63

ALDO ROSSI

1981

The excerpt from the concluding paragraphs of Aldo Rossi's *Scientific Autobiography* included here, like his image *Architecture Assassinated*, dedicated to Manfredo Tafuri, describes a fractured, splintered, and ruined architecture. What has (been) broken? First of all, emblems of Rossi's personal background, memories of the Lombardian landscape with which he identified, for which he longed, like a lost love. Also falling to pieces are the results of his typological analysis and historical study. Unlike the emblems of the Lombardian 'locus', the remnants of type study were non-territorial, but analytical and 'scientific'. Elements were, in this sense, rather like tools, carried from site to site, project to project. Lastly, the ruins in the picture include examples of Rossi's own built work: in the foreground is a section of his Gallaratese Housing project in Milan with its knees broken.

Seen together, the elements that comprise this pile-up show that ruination accomplishes its undoing across several registers: personal biography/memory, historiography, and contemporary practice. All together, they show the ways architecture suffers 'time with a tooth': every beginning, optimistic as any constructive act must surely be, is also the secret promise of an ending. But the reverse is no less true: each of these forms has been repeated, and will be in future, as if time didn't really matter, didn't really pass. The *Scientific Autobiography* elaborates this back-and-forth movement. Though ruins suggest how architecture's broken bones might be reset, projects in the post-war period would never make convincing promises about what cities, landscapes, and our lives within them would be; each – including those of Rossi himself – could never be more than a remote possibility or melancholic hope, rooted in the debris of modern cities.

Scientific Autobiography
(Cambridge, MA: MIT Press, 1981)

I love the beginning and end of things; but perhaps above all I love things which are broken and then reassembled, as in archaeological and surgical operations. Throughout my life I have often been hospitalized for fractures and

Aldo Rossi, *Architecture Assassinated*, on the cover of Manfredo Tafuri's *Architecture and Utopia*, 1974. Aldo Rossi Foundation, Milan.

other injuries to my bones, and this has given me some sense and knowledge of the engineering of the body, which would otherwise have been inconceivable to me.

Perhaps the only defect of the end, as well as the beginning, is the fact that it is partly intermediate. This is true because it can in some ways be foreseen. And of course the most foreseeable end is death.

I relate all this to my childhood impression of the prophet Elijah, to the memory of an image and an event. In large books full of Biblical stories, I used to look at the figures that issued from the dense, black text with their burning colors – yellows, blues, greens. A fiery chariot rose toward a sky that was crossed by a rainbow, and a great old man stood erect in it. As always, a very simple caption was printed under the illustration: 'The prophet Elijah did not die. He was carried off by a fiery chariot.' I have never seen such a precise representation and definition – almost never do events of this kind occur in fairy tales. The entire Christian religion is founded on death, deposition, and resurrection, and this is a most human iconography to represent man and god. In the disappearance of the prophet Elijah, I sensed something threatening to common sense, a challenge, an act of immense arrogance. But all this came close to satisfying my inclination for an act that was absolute and extremely beautiful. Perhaps I would later find part of this in Drieu La Rochelle, but the meaning was different.

I now believe that the beginning and end of things have been most important for me, and they have acquired much clarity: there is a close relationship between my initial search to reestablish the discipline of architecture and my final result of dissolving or forgetting it. It seems to me that modern architecture, as it originally presented itself, was a set of vague notions dominated by a secondhand sociology, a political deception, and a suspect aestheticism. The beautiful illusion of the Modern Movement, so reasoned and moderate, was shattered under the violent yet definitive collapse caused by the bombings of the Second World War. And I sought what was left not as though it were a lost civilization, but rather by pondering a tragic photograph of postwar Berlin where the Brandenburg Gate was still standing in a landscape of ruins. This was perhaps the victory of the avant-garde; there are no longer any remains of the Frankfurt housing or of modern Dutch building intermixed with an amiable landscape from the time of Umberto I. Only among the ruins of these places did the avant-garde win and lose: in the tangible surrealist landscape and the layers of rubble, which are certainly a gesture, although a destructive one. Not the architecture but the city of man was struck; and what was left certainly did not belong to architecture. It was rather a symbol, a sign, at times a tiresome memory.

64

ISSUES OF CONSERVATION/ PRESERVATION

1998 AND 2002

In all great projects that invite restoration, it is evident that each must respond carefully to a specific site, a specific challenge, and a specific goal: you cannot 'do' a High Line in any other city than New York, nor does Peter Latz's Duisburg-Nord Waterpark, his Parco Dora, in Turin, nor his extraordinary reclamation of Hiriya Mountain in Tel Aviv allow easy imitations (*see* Extract 66). All such conservations or preservations (the terms used respectively in UK and USA) demand their own specific judgments. These ideas were raised by one of the remarkable historians of derelict houses and landscape, John Harris.

He was, early on, a persistent and resourceful enquirer into ruined mansions, derelict interiors and, especially, lost or decayed gardens. He read widely in early texts and current writing and wrote about his discoveries years later in a style that reflected his curiosity, his tenacity, his enthusiasm, and the occasionally mischievous acts of trespass. He also worried to what extent exact balance was needed, especially in the conservation of gardens, for any act of preservation involves both contemporary perspective and an acute historical sense of what had been there.

In *No Voice from the Hall* (1998), he wrote about his first discovery of Painshill (*see* Chapter 34) in Surrey, where he later became a member of its accomplished restoration committee. The Désert de Retz (*see* Chapter 44) was another site into which Harris stumbled, or trespassed, in 1952, an 'enchanted... and ornamental landscape garden' laid out by Monsieur de Monville between 1774 and 1779. He 'could hardly believe that the Broken Column House and the Maison Chinoise might have survived'. But they did. In *Echoing Voices* (2002) he described the forlorn estate, finding on his first encounter the remains of the astonishing Chinese Pavilion, made of teak imported from China, and then on a subsequent visit lamenting its disappearance.

Harris followed up his explorations by reading books such as Osvald Sirén's *China and the Gardens of Europe of the Eighteenth Century*[11] (1949), where both Painshill and Retz were discussed, and subsequently found in the Paris Musée des Arts Décoratifs

George-Louis La Rouge's *Jardins anglo-chinois la mode* of 1765 (*see* Extract 35), in which Retz was illustrated.

JOHN HARRIS
No Voice from the Hall: Early Memories of a Country House Snooper
(London: John Murray, 1998)

[At Painshill] I had no Ordnance Survey map to guide me. The path then descended, below an eminence on which stood a ruined temple – of the 'peripteral' sort, as I was later to learn. It had lost all its side columns, and the capitals of the portico were just hanging from the Doric entablature, a single wooden post used as a prop preventing the pediment from collapsing. This was the Temple of Bacchus, designed by Robert Adam in 1761, and the ornamental landscape gardens into which I had intruded, its history then unknown to me, was Charles Hamilton's Painshill. I glimpsed below the path the silvery glitter of the river Mole; descending to it, I marveled at a huge cast-iron water-wheel next to a weather-boarded pump house – all overgrown and rusted.

In fact I was following the windings of the river that formed the southern boundary of the gardens. I recall a brick triumphal arch (this was the Mausoleum), and where the path narrowed I found myself on the edge of a lake clogged with weed. I walked around it to a Gothic ruin spied on the further bank, and the path opened to a clearing with a view of a large timber bridge of six arches... This was my opportunity to cross the rickety bridge onto the island. Here I experienced my very first grotto... I glimpse a Gothic temple on the crest of a prominence and, crossing to it, rested under its tottering open, umbrella-like rotunda...

JOHN HARRIS
Echoing Voices: More Memories of a Country House Snooper
(London: John Murray, 2002)

Mature reflection has led me to view that M. de Monville's garden buildings and ornaments were overcrowded, that the Désert de Retz lacked the expansive layout and properly designed landscape setting of, for example, Painshill... this was typical of many French 'Picturesque' gardens. At the time [of his visit], however, the Désert seemed to many the *ne plus ultra* of an abandoned garden.

In its heyday the Grotto Entrance of the Désert must have been spectacular. Just two blocks survived of this vast rusticated, almost megalithic stone portal, taken from Piranesi's *Carceri*. The wooden door was still there, but the grotto behind it was only a pile of stones and tufa. It is difficult now to remember exactly what the Désert was like when I first saw it. Today M. de Monville's garden is as well documented as any in France – although vigorous dispute still rages as to whether Hubert Robert contributed to its making. I contest this; the garden bears all the hallmarks of Racine de Monville as its amateur designer. As its present owner and saviour M. Choppin de Janvry has shown, however, de Monville did have an *exécutant* in François Barbier, a garden architect.

In 1953 all demarcations had been obliterated by brambles, and nearly all the buildings were covered with creepers and surface ivy. The first to catch my eye from the entrance, to my left, was the Pyramid (called by Le Rouge *La Glacière* [icehouse]), looking like nothing more than a pile of ivied stones. The apprehensive silence of trespass lay heavy upon me: I was distracted from the Ruined Gothic Church beyond by a glimpse of the Broken Column House through the tracery outline of a vast linden tree. I almost burst with glee. André Breton and his Surrealists were fascinated by this edifice, which functioned as a proper house, furnished in a simplified Louis Seize style; they saw the *bizarrerie* in it...

The door to the Column House was broken down, the vestibule derelict. Fallen plaster, splintered wood battens, lumps of stonework, dusty brick formed piles to be climbed over to get to the spiral stair, which at first glance appeared to defy ascent, not so much from its precarious condition as because of the rubbish blocking the way and the nursery of cats that scattered at my approach. Much of the upstairs décor had survived, however. The reception *salons* were on the third floor, for the view across the gardens through oval windows, and here, as Sirèn had discovered, the pretty Louis Seize chimney-pieces were still intact... And then, framed by an oval window, I spied the roof of the Maison Chinoise. I shivered with anticipation and went scurrying down the stair, afraid I might be apprehended by the '*agressif*' farmer Passy before I had had a proper look a this most famous of all European Chinese houses... There it stood, in terrible and terminal decay, yet somehow electrifying...

Pushing upon a varnished door, I realized why Sirèn had published no photographs of the interior. All was darkness: the windowed shutters had been nailed up. I don't know whether he ever ventured upstairs. I did. The door leading off the stairs opened with a hefty push to reveal a well-it room paneled in acajou wood, recognizably a library. A photograph taken about 1900 survives, clearly showing the skillful and graceful harmonization of Chinese and Louis Seize elements. A pantry still retained its beautiful beaten-copper sink, and in the ground-floor bedroom there were scraps of an orange-patterned silk in the walls. But something I saw, and Sirèn did not, was particularly exciting: half a dozen or more rectangular panels stacked against the wall, painted and varnished with green and brownish chinoiserie subjects. No doubt when the Maison Chinoise vanished they disappeared into the maw of an *antiquaire*.

Then came the heart-stopping moment. Still in the upper salon, I heard crunching footsteps and barking dogs... I furtively peered from a window, to see an elderly, rough-looking man with a gun under his arm, accompanied by two largish dogs... I knew I must wait, I knew, so curled up in a corner, and until dusk approached amused myself with daydreams in which I took down de Monville's books from the shelves, imagined him discussing with M. Barbier his design for the Chinese House. He lived in the Broken Column House, I thought, and used the ground-floor bedroom of the Maison Chinoise for amorous pleasures. It all seemed right and proper...

65

CINEMATIC RUINS

1979, 1987, AND 2010

In the decades since the Second World War, ruins have fascinated film-makers as much as they did earlier writers and artists. The destruction they typically document is not so much the result of natural forces but of human misdeeds and hubris: bombed cities, toxic landscapes, and urban decay, evidence of the 'decline and fall' of modern nations and empires, following the pattern, or sharing the fate of earlier powers, as descried by Gibbon in the 18th century and Scipio in the second. Three representative examples are illustrated in the still images we include here: the ruins of a scientific lab from Andrei Tarkovsky's *Stalker*; the ruins of the old train station from Wim Wenders's *Wings of Desire*; and an abandoned carwash from Robert Graef and Julien Temple's *Requiem for Detroit*.

In each case, the scenes and narratives combine expected sentiments of melancholy and loss with unexpected (and maybe improbable) expressions of hope and optimism. Irony plays its part, too, especially in the images of Detroit's abandoned streets and shops. A ruined car wash is a poignant emblem of the fall of the Motor City (also Motown) whose rise coincided with the spectacular growth of the automobile industry, later 're-tooled' to supply vehicles of war. Abandoned factories and workshops play the same role in *Stalker*. Their demise and destruction of which resulted in this case too from their own successes. A science professor and writer follow the Stalker through a toxic landscape, called the 'Zone', whose typical elements include muddied streams, overgrown vegetation, and feral animals – most vividly, a curious, scared, and homeless dog.

Two of these films were based in part on recent novels, *Stalker* on *Roadside Picnic* by Boris and Arkady Strugatsky, and *Wings of Desire* on Peter Handke's *Repetition*. But for viewers their power is less literary than visual. Static views present single scenes that closely resemble ruin paintings from earlier centuries. Though sequence is important in each of these narratives, the pace is very slow, as if the primary intention was to allow present moments to drag their past toward what's to come, despite its incompleteness.

Broadly speaking, *Wings of Desire* explains the emptiness and desires of an angel, whose in-between role (eternally mediating between gods and men) has kept him too

Andrei Tarkovsky, *Stalker*, 1979: en route to the Room of Fulfilled Desires.

distant from the immediacy and concreteness of earth-bound experience, emblems of which include Marion, the circus acrobat he desires, and those incidents of everyday life listed by the Dying Man in the excerpt below: the child's eyes, the swim in the waterfall, the first drops of rain, the sun, and of course, the city's sidewalks and streets, in various states of deterioration or ruin. Lines from one of Handke's poems are repeated several times in the film: 'When the child was a child,' as if memory could overcome the discontinuities that trouble human life. Along similar lines, an elderly man named Homer who survived the destruction addresses the paradox of identity-through-change with a rather solemn invocation: 'Tell, Muse, of the story-teller, the childlike ancient one, who ends up at the edge of the world, and let Everyman be recognized in him.' Demonstrating how recognition may be possible in a landscape of ruins is also the task of the American actor Peter Falk, cast as the fictional character that gave him his fame (Columbo), who happens to be visiting the city to star in a movie about the Nazi period. Both famous and familiar, which is to say transcending and condemned to time, the actor can sense the presence of the emissary from above because he, too, was once angelic, though now with us is fallen.

WIM WENDERS AND PETER HANDKE
Wings of Desire (*Der Himmel über Berlin*), 1987

Driver: Are there still borders? More than ever! Every street has its borderline. Between each plot, there's a strip of no-man's-land disguised as a hedge or a ditch. Whoever dares, will fall into booby traps or be hit by laser rays. The trout are really torpedoes. Every home owner, or even every tenant nails his name plate on the door, like a coat of arms and studies the morning paper as if he were a world leader. Germany has crumbled into as many small states as there are individuals. And these small states are mobile. Everyone carries his own state with him and demands a toll when another wants to enter. A fly caught in amber, or a leather bottle. So much for the border. But one can only enter each state with a password. The German soul of today can only be conquered and governed by one who arrives at each small state with the password. Fortunately, no one is currently in a position to do this. So... everyone migrates and waves his one-man-state flag in all earthly directions. Their children already shake their rattles and drag their filth around them in circles.

The Dying Man: The Far East. The Great North. The Wild West. The Great Bear Lake. Tristan da Cunha. The Mississippi Delta. Stromboli. The old houses of Charlottenburg. Albert Camus. The morning light. The child's eyes. The swim in the waterfall. The spots of the first drops of rain. The sun. The bread and wine. Hopping. Easter. The veins of leaves. The blowing grass. The color of stones. The pebbles on the stream's bed. The white tablecloth outdoors.

Wim Wenders, *Wings of Desire*, 1987: ruins of the old train station.

Robert Graef and Julien Temple, *Requiem for Detroit*, 2010: demolition in the city center.

The dream of the house in the house. The dear one asleep in the next room. The peaceful Sundays. The horizon. The light from the room in the garden. The night flight. Riding a bicycle with no hands. The beautiful stranger. My father. My mother. My wife. My child.

66

DROSSCAPE AND AFTER: 1, DUISBURG-NORD

1991

These final chapters discuss what, in the present day, we might actually *do* with ruins, by way of preservation, conservation, adaptive reuse, appropriation or inhabitation. Many of the projects discussed here are examples of adapted reuse rather than of formal, material-based preservation that relies on using original materials and precise historical sources

Beyond drawing and photographing ruins, exploring what they would originally have looked like, as Lauro (*see* Extract 17) did in the Renaissance, or free-associating with memories about what they might have looked like, there are other options, all the more so these days, when many are interested in preserving the past while at the same time making something new. Victor Hugo (*see* Extract 49) lamented the early 19th-century determination to forget old structures and fill France with new examples. Viollet le Duc (*see* Extract 52) thought they should be completely restored to a state that may not have existed. Today, while destruction and total replacement are still a possibility, some ingenious designs have seen new infusions into existing ruins.

Drosscape is a word coined by Alan Berger in his book *Drosscapes: Wasting Land in Urban America* (2006).[12] 'Dross' is derived from Edmund Spenser's sonnet where he affirmed that 'all world's glory is but dross unclean'. Dross is not exactly ruin, but it is often something that dismays or disfigures what may once have been an original 'glory'. Berger looked at several American examples of dysfunctional and unclean dross that had vanquished an original golden landscape with contamination and urban sprawl. Berger promised a book in which he would address how to rethink these sites.

But in many ways, and not just in the United States, drosscapes had already been rethought, reworked, and something of the good and the gold re-burnished. Ruins do not need to be wholly erased, as Victor Hugo feared would happen, for they can be refurbished. By the late 20th century everywhere was reckoning with derelict factories, unused rail lines and harbors, and huge waste dumps of refuse; but all of those have attracted landscape architects to resurrect the gold, even as they show how the

Peter Latz, Gardens in old bunkers at Duisburg Nord, Germany.
Photograph: John Dixon Hunt.

surviving dross has found a new life. 'Dark satanic mills', in William Blake's words, have yielded truly modern parklands.

Examples of how ruins can, as it were, both stay in place and achieve a new life within them were inspired, above all, by the work of Peter Latz & Partners. Books by him and about his work in Germany (the Saarbrücken Harbor project and the former steel works in Duisburg-Nord), in Italy (Parco Dora in Turin), and the Hiriya Mountain in Tel Aviv have established his vision as central to how we may revive derelict structures and yet be reminded of the significance of these ruins. A rather different recuperation of an old factory took place on the site of the Vitali iron foundry in Turin, at the Parco Dora, where an austere parkland emerged to provide a new housing complex, itself reusing housing built for the 2006 Winter Olympics. The tall steel pillars that supported a roof have survived, climbed by shrubs that will make a canopy (what Latz calls a 'technical canopy'). Flowerbeds, benches, and a water garden have been installed in the concrete foundations of the factory, and a concrete lid has been raised to create a 'futurist' effect.

The designer has also won a competition to response to a huge reformulation of Hiriya Mountain in Tel Aviv: once a monstrous garbage dump, emitting methane, polluted water and drawing masses of vultures and seabirds that were a real hazard for nearby Ben Gurion Airport. Again, the instinct of the design was to keep the mountain and make it into a place of recreation and pleasure.

PETER LATZ
Rust Red. Landscape Park Duisburg-Nord
(Munich: Hirmer, 2016)

The challenge for our work was to consider industrial wasteland as landscape or even parkland and refrain from sweeping the industrial remains under a carpet of lawns as in an English landscape garden. At the time, the typology of green space had not extended as far as brownfields. Consequently, there was neither a hard-and-fast model for the transformation of industrial wasteland nor a repertoire of professional methods.

We organized our work according to ecological criteria
- Energy balance,
- Secure a wide range of species,
- Treat or remove contamination,
- Restore natural water cycles.

In addition to the usual criteria such as cost saving, low maintenance and accessibility...

The rusty ruins of iron smelting were former symbols of mass production on the one hand and destruction of the environment on the other. They could be retained and their infrastructure serve a new purpose, even if these new uses would have nothing to do with the former function. Question such as, 'Which elements are suitable for a park and therefore worthwhile keeping?' or 'which elements are unsuitable and should be demolished as soon as possible?' no longer arose.

For myself and my staff the question in hand was the exact opposite. 'What uses could be, or must be invented or order to keep the existing structure? And which interventions are necessary in order to obtain a metamorphosis of objects from industrial functionality to elements in a public park?' We asked ourselves 'what skills are required to maintain a repertoire of yet unknown technical elements and a wide range of vegetation? How hazardous is the existing contamination, will we be able to dispose of it or clear it up on site? Is it possible to develop a park on the site at all and will it be accepted by the public?' We were faced with a chaotic flood of questions, which seemed to echo the site itself. The quest for a design method that would help to deliver a successful scheme, to overcome the chaos, was just pointing to 'all available methods...'

67

9/11

2001

Ruins have occurred by accident and deliberation. Weather, war, time, terrorism, neglect, poor maintenance, a building's loss of purpose – even, after the Dissolution of the Monasteries, abbeys in Great Britain were pillaged to provide stone for neighbouring mansions. Yet the attacks in the United States of 9/11 wreaked destruction on lives, property, institutions, and basic human tolerance. Perhaps the most famous, because of its being captured on film and broadcast widely, was the attack on the twin towers in lower Manhattan, the site of the World Trade Center.

An initial response was to rebuild, but the sense that this destruction itself had somehow to be memorialized for generations who did not witness the appalling event led to a competition to seek designs for how the site might be re-envisaged. We needed a sense of both *that* place and its role in a much larger meditation.

The competition was won by Michael Arad, with his remarkable gift for capturing both emptiness and consolation – the noise of waters pouring into the two square pools, representing the footprints of the original skyscrapers; he was later joined by the landscape architect Peter Walker to establish a place of great power, associative memories and quiet, and potentially unfolding calm – a combination of a grove, quietness, engraved names, representation, hints of what had been there.

Michael Arad, *Reflecting Absence (9/11 Memorial)*, New York, 2013. Courtesy Peter Walker.

68

DAVID CHIPPERFIELD

2009

Rebuilding the ruins of Berlin started as soon as the Second World War ended. Countless anonymous survivors slowly and sadly started the work, soon to be followed by professionals commissioned by successive governments. In the early years, all efforts were focused on housing needs, later on urban infrastructure and then public institutions. The models that followed arose from a number of competitions and building exhibitions (led by IBA or *Internationale Bauaustellung*, first in 1957, then between 1979 and 1987), to which many non-Germans made significant contributions. Attending to pressing needs didn't prevent passionate debate about what to remove completely, what to preserve, and what to transform. Among the recent examples of ruins being transformed, the Neues Museum project, resulting from the collaboration of the English architect David Chipperfield and the architect-preservationist Julian Harrap, also English, is perhaps the most well-known and interesting case.

The Neues Museum ('new' because it was built after the nearby 'old' museum, Karl Friedrich Schinkel's Altes Museum) was designed by Friedrich August Stüler and built between 1841 and 1859. The destruction by Allied bombing was extended by neglect in the subsequent decades, as the partial roofs, broken walls, and abandoned spaces suffered the effects of wind, rain, and snow.

A common and intelligent goal of architectural additions and alterations is to achieve a new wholeness or remade completeness for the building. In his occasional essays, interviews, and project descriptions, Chipperfield often stresses the importance of 'coherence' in architecture, that design intends works that are self-same and unified. But that aim is particularly hard to achieve when a ruin is the point of departure, for what has been lost will never be recovered, yet what is new should not conceal or erase the memorable qualities of the old. The text we've selected, from an interview conducted shortly after the project was finished, acknowledges the ruin's power, something the design sought to celebrate. Traces of the original building were preserved, but also evidence of the war-time damage, especially on the building's surfaces. Joints or passages between the original, damaged fabric and renewed elements, spaces, and surfaces function rather like chapter divisions in a story, or intermezzi in musical or theatrical composition: breaks that mediate distinct phases or periods.

DAVID CHIPPERFIELD

A conversation between Wolfgang Wolters and David Chipperfield, Treppenhalle, Neues Museum, 17 September 2009, in *Neues Museum Berlin*, and eds. Rik Nys and Martin Reichert (Cologne: Walther König, 2009)

WW: The Neues Museum is part of the Museum Island complex of buildings and collections – a UNESCO World Heritage Site. UNESCO insists on two conditions – authenticity and integrity. Your answer to this specific situation was the reestablishment of form and figure. Where do we find authenticity and integrity?

DC: When we began the project, we were not that well informed about the arguments of repair, restoration or reconstruction, which was not a bad thing. Our first response was an intuitive one. The building had such power, and was so impressive, and we were aware that whatever we did should celebrate this. If you build a house next to the sea you want to enjoy the sea. If you build a house in a big field you want to borrow from your situation. And the context here was not a field or the sea, but a quality of space that was quite Piranesian and almost a geological condition. It seemed to me that the ruin had established its own

David Chipperfield, Neues Museum, Berlin, 2009.
Photograph © Ute Zscharnt for David Chipperfield Architects.

authenticity. That authenticity was one created by accident and therefore it contained many other stories inside of it – the main story being the intentions of the original architect. So I think that in terms of authenticity and integrity there were two original motivations. The first was that we should try not to lose, through the repair of the building, the 'undressed' condition, which imbued it with a power that a traditional restoration of the building would have lost. Secondly, the remaining fragments were in danger of becoming scenographic and somehow totemic if they were not put back into some meaningful context, because the alternative would be a strange collage of broken and unbroken pieces. Therefore, I think that this desire to try and give back a sense of place to the fragment and establish the meaning of the original building was very important in the concept. Those were our intuitive responses, which we started to look at in the terms of the traditions of repair, restoration and reconstruction and we found that we were aligned with the theoretical positions.

69

Drosscape and After: 2, The High Line

2009

James Corner would have encountered Peter Latz at the University of Pennsylvania, where they both taught, and his design from Field Operations for the High Line in Manhattan offers yet another, different, celebration of 'parks in the 21st century'. In the same fashion as Latz's work, it honors an old and derelict structure (that would have been impossible, financially or technically, to remove). So, at the same time, it provides a very modern rethinking of how such drosscapes could be envisaged, while keeping a distinct and vital aspect of early New York and the area of the former Meatpacking District.

James Corner and his associates published a large and extremely detailed and colorful account of the concept, the making and the use of the High Line.[13] It included, as brackets to its collection of photographs and design drawings, two conversations, on 'Forethoughts' and 'Afterthoughts', printed in three columns across the page, that read like the minutes of their discussions. The former considered the ways forward with a difficult and challenging project; the latter reviewed what had been achieved. It is somewhat rare to encounter such a frank and freewheeling debate on a project before and after it was achieved. The participants were James Corner and Lisa Swikin from Field Operations, and three architects from Diller Scofield + Renfro.

Forethoughts raised issues of what the work should look like – an elevated street, but with any shops and cafes? More than just preservation, but what exactly? Something different from the Parisian 'Promenade Plantée' that they visited and found too neat and manicured? Central to the whole endeavor was how people could know or visit the derelict railway line; old photographs were invoked, and when the team actually saw it, they were blown over by the excitements it promised. There was strong enthusiasm from the newly formed Friends of the High Line, to whom the book is dedicated, and from the key role played by Amanda Burden as commissioner of city planning. The site became a major topic in university design studios, yet that pedagogical tool would translate into a much wider public appreciation of how cities might be envisaged and renewed.

Afterthoughts reflected on the ten years of designing and building: the surprises – that it has been achieved at all – and its successes – that it was compelling as well as feasible. They were amazed by the 'sheer diversity of visitors', by its uses at different times of day and night, its welcome to private activities and its celebration of public space, and by the 'magical disorientations and freedom of the city' over which it passed. Corner argued that there had been 'a certain psychological condition prompted by the High Line. The new life and optimism spawned from dereliction and neglect may very well provide a stimulating setting for new forms of interaction. It's this liberating sense of displacement that allows people to see themselves, one another, and the city in new ways.'

The High Line is now both a 'ruin' and a new event. Corner remembered that 'when we started, we asked the question: what will grow here? We meant this in two ways: first in terms of natural ecosystems – soils, plants, birds, butterflies, and entire habitats – and second in terms of communities – programs, activities, economies, and buildings. In retrospect, it was smart that we left the question open, because we never could have answered it properly. Most of what has grown on and around the High Line has been out of our control. The High Line was a catalyst for open and dynamic things to happen. It continues to be a stimulant in a larger and still-evolving urban ecology.'

The High Line, New York, 2009. Photograph: John Dixon Hunt.

The High Line, New York, 2009. Photograph: John Dixon Hunt.

This was achieved in part by the extraordinary work of the Dutch planting designer Piet Oudolf, who discusses his work mid-way through the volume. And all of the High Line was designed with 'a certain level of spontaneity and unexpectedness', since pubic behavior cannot be anticipated. We also suspect that Corner's recollection of abandoned railways in Great Britain in the 1960s and their takeover by wild flowers and plants, as well as by walkers and joggers, sustained this central aspect of the High Line. And it is something far more authentic in its recollection of old within the new than the formalisms of the Paris promenade. Yet the designers were also sure that only a deep understanding of a particular city's needs would allow them to succeed, and furthermore that the High Line could not be replicated in other urban areas.

Notes

Ancient and Medieval

1 We are here indebted to the dissertation work of Anna Johnson Lyman (*see* Further Reading).
2 Authors' translation using original texts and some other versions, with some omissions from the original.

The Long 18th Century

1 Quoted in Ralph M. Williams, *Poet, Painter and Parson: The Life of John Dyer* (New York: Bookman Associated, 1956).
2 Authors' translation using original texts and some other versions, with some omissions from the original.
3 Peter Aram, 'Studley Park: A Poem', in Thomas Gent, *The Ancient and Modern History of the Loyal Town of Rippon* (York: 1733), p.24.
4 Authors' translation using original texts and some other versions, with some omissions.
5 Rose Macaulay, *Pleasure of Ruins* (London: Thames & Hudson, 1953).
6 Joseph Heely, *Letters on the Beauties of Hagley, Envil and the Leasowes*, vol.1, Letter VIII, pp 172–76. Hirschfeld quotes from the German edition but uses no quotation marks and cuts slightly more than one-fifth of the text.

The 19th Century

1 William Wordsworth, *The Illustrated Wordsworth's Guide to the Lakes*, ed. Peter Bicknell (New York: St Martin's Press, 1984).
2 Cavendish was the family name of Dukes of Devonshire, who owned the Abbey.
3 See *Charles Marville: Photographer of Paris*, ed. Sarah Kennel (Washington, DC: National Gallery of Art, 2013).
4 Hugo has punctuated the lines from Virgil's *Aeneid*, 'Fuit Ilium, et ingens gloria Teucrorum' (Ilium has passed, and the great glory of the Teucrians) (II, 324) to give the word *Gloria* an ironic twist.
5 An artificial mound composed of fragments of ancient pottery, located next to the Tiber River, near the Porta San Paolo in Rome.
6 Authors' translation using original texts and some other versions, with some omissions.
7 Dorchester: Dorset Natural History and Archaeological Society, 1966.

Modern and Contemporary

1 Authors' translation using original texts and some other versions, with some omissions.
2 Authors' translation.
3 Authors' translation using original texts and some other versions, with some omissions.
4 In an attempt to analyze the human act of walking, Rodin remarked admiringly: 'Man is a walking cathedral' (*Les cathedrales de France*).

5   The geometry of a place or land is a product of its composition. By composition I mean the nature of the materials that go into its making, and also the nature of the diverse forces that have worked or are still working upon it. The nature of matter has to do with chemistry, which is ruled, like all things, by number. But the operation of external forces (such as fire, water or earthquakes), though it may appear wanton and uncontrolled to human eyes, is really as strictly calculated by nature as the proliferation of the minutest living creatures in the universe.

6   The profound sense of wonder aroused by the sight of the perfect accord between the air and light of a land and the geometry of its soil compels us to accept the existence of a harmonious unity linking all three elements. How else could one explain the incomparable harmony between the pure, spiritual, perfectly modelled shape of the mountains of Attica, and the fine, mellow air and brilliant light in which they stand? Indeed, I do not think it would be presumptuous to say that this harmony is no accident but the rigorous consequence of the inherent harmony, which informs the whole principle of creation: on the contrary, it would be fully in accord with our innate sense of cosmic harmony. We may therefore accept as an axiomatic truth that the geometry of the ground and the air and light of a country are entirely consonant elements.

7   The sensitivity of nature penetrates into the work of art through the sensitivity of the spirit. What appears to be the rectilinear geometry of architecture is in reality the geometry of curves. The theoretical definition of the tensions and equations in these curves, and their translation into matter, can only be achieved by the finest artistic sensibility.

8   The austerity of the Greek column is of a different nature to the theocratic austerity of the Egyptian column. In the latter, it amounts to a subjection to divine attributes, whereas in the Greek column, it emerges as the product of a spirit that is austere, but also human and free.

9   The Holt/Smithson Foundation does not allow extracts from his works to be reproduced: the full text is available in *Robert Smithson. The Collected Writings*, ed. Jack Flam (Berkeley: University of California Press, 1990), pp. 68–74.

10 Ann Reynolds, *Robert Smithson, Learning from New Jersey and Elsewhere* (Cambridge, MA: MIT Press, 2003).

11 Osvald Sirén, *China and the Gardens of Europe of the Eighteenth Century* (Washington, DC: Dumbarton Oaks Reprints, 1990).

12 Alan Berger, *Drosscapes: Wasting Land in Urban America* (New York: Princeton Architectural Press, 2006).

13 James Corner Field Operations, Diller Scofidio + Renfro, *The High Line* (London: Phaidon Press, 2016).

Further Reading

Ahn, Susan and Regine Keler, 'False Nature' in Christophe Girot, Dora Imhof, eds, *Thinking the Contemporary Landscape* (New York: Princeton Architectural Press, 2017)
Barkan, Leonard, *Unearthing the Past. Archaeology and Aesthetics in the Making of Renaissance Culture* (New Haven: Yale University Press, 1999)
Brilliant, Richard and Dale Kinney, eds, *Reuse Value. Spolia and Appropriation in Art and Architecture from Constantine to Sherrie Levine* (Farnham, Surrey: Ashgate, 2011)
Cairns, Stephen and Jane M. Jacobs, *Buildings Must Die. A Perverse View of Architecture* (Cambridge, MA: MIT Press, 2014)
Coffin, David R., *Pirro Ligorio: The Renaissance Artist, Architect, and Antiquarian, with a Checklist of Drawings* (University Park: Pennsylvania State University Press, 2004)
Coffin, David R., *The Villa d'Este at Tivoli* (Princeton: Princeton University Press, 1960)
Corner, James, *The High Line* (London: Phaidon Press, 2016)
Cronon, William, 'The Trouble with Wilderness; or, Getting Back to the Wrong Nature', in William Cronon, ed., *Uncommon Ground: Rethinking the Human Place in Nature* (New York: W. W. Norton & Co., 1995)
Gubser, Michael, *Time's Visible Surface. Alois Riegl and the Discourse on History and Temporality in Fin-de-Siècle Vienna* (Detroit: Wayne State University Press, 2006)
Halbwachs, J. Maurice, *On Collective Memory*, with an introduction by L. A. Coser (Chicago and London: University of Chicago Press, 1992)
Harbison, Robert, *Ruins and Fragments. Tales of Loss and Rediscovery* (London: Reaktion, 2015)
Herman, Arthur, *The Idea of Decline in Western History* (New York: The Free Press, 1997)
Hill, Jonathan, *The Architecture of Ruins. Designs of the Past, Present and Future* (London: Routledge, 2019)
Hui, Andrew, *The Poetics of Ruins in Renaissance Literature, Verbal Arts: Studies in Poetics* (New York: Fordham University Press, 2017)
Janowitz, Anne, *England's Ruins: Poetic Purpose and the National Landscape* (Oxford: Basil Blackwell, 1990)
Johnson Lyman, Anna, *Reading the Pays: Ruins and Historical Writing in England 800-1400* (Philadelphia: University of Pennsylvania Press, 2020)
Latz, Peter, *Rust Red. Landscape Park Duisburg-Nord* (Munich: Hirner Verlag, 2016)
Lowenthal, David, *The Past is a Foreign Country* (Cambridge: Cambridge University Press, 1985)
Macaulay, Rose, *Pleasure of Ruins* (London: Thames & Hudson, 1953)
Marot, Sebastién, *Sub-urbanism and the Art of Memory* (London: Architectural Association, 2003)
Mortier, Roland, *La poétique des ruins en France* (Geneva: Librairie Droz, 1974)
Piggott, Stuart, *Ancient Britons and the Antiquarian 'Imagaination'* (London: Thames & Hudson, 1989)
Piggott, Stuart, *Ruins in a Landscape: Essays in Antiquarianism* (Edinburgh: Edinburgh University Press, 1976)

Pinto, John A., *Speaking Ruins. Piranesi, Architects, and Antiquity in Eighteenth-Century Rome* (Ann Arbor: University of Michigan Press, 2012)

Randall, Margaret, *Ruins*, foreword by V.B. Price (Albuquerque: University of New Mexico Press, 2011)

Réda, Jacques, *The Ruins of Paris*, trans Mark Treharne trans (London: Reaktion, 1996, original French edition 1977)

Richardson, Margaret, ed., *Visions of Ruin. Architectural Fantasies & Designs for Garden Follies* (London: Sir John Soane Museum, 1999)

Rogger, Andre, *Landscapes of Taste. The Art of Humphry Repton's Red Books* (London: Routledge, 2007)

Shaw, Samuel, 'Weighing Down the Landscape: The Quarry as a Site of Rural Modernity' in Kristin Bluemel, Michael McCluskey, eds *Rural Modernity in Britain: A Critical Intervention* (Edinburgh: Edinburgh University Press 2018)

Simmen, Jeannot, *Ruinen-Faszination* (Dortmund: Harenberg, 1980)

Stewart, Susan, *The Ruins Lesson. Meaning and Material in Western Culture* (Chicago: University of Chicago Press, 2022)

Weilacher, Udo, *Syntax of Landscape* (Berlin: Birkhäuser, 2008)

Weiss, Allen S., 'The Limits of Metaphor: Ideology and Representation in the Zen Garden', *Social Analysis: The International Journal of Social and Cultural Practice*, vol.54, no.2, (Summer 2010):116-129

Williams, Rosalind, *Notes on the Underground: An Essay on Technology, Society and the Imagination* (Cambridge, MA: MIT Press 2008)

Woodward, Christopher, *In Ruins* (New York, Pantheon Books, 2001)

Acknowledgments

Acknowledgments are due to Peter Walker, Peter Latz, James Corner, André Rogger, John Harris, and Emily T. Cooperman for help with some modern images and texts. And to the libraries of the University of Pennsylvania for their inestimable advice and collections. We are grateful for a grant from the School of Design for pre-publication costs.

IMAGE CREDITS

Numbers refer to pages. Every effort has been made to seek permission to reproduce the images in this book. Any omissions are entirely unintentional, and details should be addressed to the publishers.

10 Creative Commons-Share Alike 3.0; 11 Courtesy of Museum of Fine Arts, Warsaw; 12 Courtesy of University of Pennsylvania Libraries; 15 Wikicommons, GNU Free Document License; 16 Photograph John Dixon Hunt; 20, 25 Photograph David Leatherbarrow; 27 Courtesy of the Fisher Fine Arts Library, University of Pennsylvania; 36 Courtesy of San Domenico, Siena (WikiCommons); 40 Courtesy of the British Museum; 48 Courtesy of Biblioteca Nazionale Marciana, Venice; 55 Courtesy of University of Pennsylvania Libraries; 56 Courtesy of University of Pennsylvania Libraries; 65 Courtesy of Bibliotecca Communale, Ferrara; 69 University of Pennsylvania; 72 Courtesy of the Fisher Fine Arts Library, University of Pennsylvania; 79 Courtesy of National Gallery of Art, Washington, D.C.; 83, 87 Courtesy of the Fisher Fine Arts Library, University of Pennsylvania; 90 Courtesy of the Fisher Fine Arts Library, University of Pennsylvania; 101 Courtesy of British Library; 104 Courtesy of British Library, Lansdowne MS 914; 104 Courtesy of British Library, Lansdowne MS 914; 111, 112 Photograph John Dixon Hunt; 115 University of Pennsylvania; 119 Courtesy of the Fisher Fine Arts Library, University of Pennsylvania; 119 Courtesy of the Fisher Fine Arts Library, University of Pennsylvania; 122 Photograph John Dixon Hunt; 124 Wikicommons; 127 Wikimedia Commons, WGA 1989; 131 Courtesy of the Fisher Fine Arts Library, University of Pennsylvania; 134 Wikicommons; 141 Courtesy of the Fisher Fine Arts Library, University of Pennsylvania; 145 Courtesy of Städel Museum, Frankfurt; 149 Courtesy of the Fisher Fine Arts Library, University of Pennsylvania; 154 Wikicommons; 158 Courtesy of Cornell University Library; 164, 165 Courtesy of the Fisher Fine Arts Library, University of Pennsylvania; 168 The J. Paul Getty Museum, Los Angeles; 177 Photograph John Dixon Hunt; 181, 182 © Sir John Soane's Museum, London; 186 University of Pennsylvania; 210, 211, 213 Courtesy of the Fisher Fine Arts Library, University of Pennsylvania; 216 Dorset Natural History and Archaeological Society, 1966; 220 Courtesy of Alte Nationalgalerie; 229 Courtesy of Fondation Le Corbusier, ARS/AGADP; 233 Photograph WikiCommons; 238 Courtesy of Tate Gallery; 242 Photograph Antonios Thodis; 247 Courtesy of the Architectural Archives, University of Pennsylvania; 249, 250 Photograph John Dixon Hunt; 253 Courtesy of the Aldo Rossi Foundation, Milan; 264 Photograph John Dixon Hunt; 267 Courtesy Peter Walker; 269 Photograph © Ute Zscharnt for David Chipperfield Architects; 272, 273 Photograph John Dixon Hunt.

INDEX

Illustrations are listed in italics at the end of each entry.

Adam, Robert 256
Acropolis, Athens 25, 227-30, 244-47 *25, 229, 242, 245*
Aislabie, John 122-3
Alberti, Leon Battista 58, 64, 90
Anglo-Saxon writings 33-5, 37-8, *10*
antiquarianism 103
Arad, Michael 266
Ariosto, *Orlando Furisoso* 74-6, *75*
Athens 24-5, 227-30, 241, 244, *229, 242, 245*
Beaumont, Georges *186*
Bellay, Joahim du, *Les Antiquitez de Rome*, 70, 169, *13*
Bellotto, Bernardo *154*
Berger, Alan 263
Bernini, Gianlorenzo 92-4, 205, *93*
Besozzo, Leonardo da 60
Biondo, Flavio 13, 58-63
Birgo, Giovan Pietro 40
Blake, William 264
Blenheim, ruins of Woodstock 101-2, *101*
Blesius, Pseudo, *Adoration of the Magi 11*
Bramante, Donato 64
Britten, Benjamin, re Tennyson 14
Browne, 'Capability', 162
Buck, Samuel, 103-5, *104*
Burke, Edmund 126, 162
Burnet, Thomas 96-7, *97*
Byron, Lord 14, 196-8
Carthage 20-4
Castiglione, Baldassare 64
Chateaubriand, Francoise-René de 191-5
Chipperfield, David 268-70, *269*
China, Chinese 111, 136, 141-2, 255-8
Christ, birth and adoration, ruined settings and 10, 37-8, 47, 51
Clough, Arthur Hugh 205
Cock, Hieronymous *79*
conservation / preservation issues 255-8, 263-73

Corner, James (Field Operations) 271-3, *272, 273*
Cotton, Charles 96, 98-100
Cunningham, John 129-32
Defoe, Daniel 106-7
Derbyshire, Chatsworth « Devil's Arse » 98-100, *99*
Désert de Retz 142, 176-8, 255, 256-8, *177*
Detroit, *Requiem for Detroit* 15, 259, *262*
Diderot, Denis 126-8
Dissolution of the Monasteries (UK) 13, 142, 266
Doré, Gustave *159*
Druids 187, *189*
Duisburg Nord 255, 263-5, *264*
Dyer, John 113-7, *115*, 169
Egypt 71-2, 73, 93, 193, 199, 241
Ehreberg Castle, Austria *223*
Erlach, Fischer von 118
Fountains Abbey, Yorkshire 122-3, *122, 139*
Fréart de Chantelon, Paul 93-4
Friedrich, Caspar David 221-2, *220*
Furness Abbey 187, 189, *190*
Movies 269-62
Gerald of Wales 10, 39
Gilpin, William 14, 107, 133, 136-40, 163, *134, 137, 138*
Giorgio, Francesco di 37, *36*
Goethe, J. W. von 143-7, *145*
Grand Tour 13, 14, 106
Graef, Robert *262*
Greece, Greek fragments 21, 24, 71, 73, 150, 155, 165, 179-80, 193, 201, 241, 246, 288
Hadrian 70
Herculaneum 9
Hagley Park 11
Hardy, Thomas 14, 199, 215-7, *216*
Harris, John 255-8
High Line, New York 271-3, *272, 273*

Hirschfeld, C.C.L., 148-52, *149*
Hugo, Victor 14, 200-4, 263, *201*
Hypneromachia Poliphili 10, 54-6, *3, 55, 56*
James, Henry 9, 191
Janvry, Choppin de 255, 356-8
Jerusalem 10, 42-6, 160, *43*
Johnson, Samuel 124
Jones, Inigo 10, 90-91, 106, *90*
Kahn, Louis I. 241-3, *242*
Kenilworth, 169, 171-3
Kent, William 111-2, 136, *112*
Kirkstall Abbey 187
Knight, Richard Payne 162-6
Laborde, Alexandre de 176-8
Langley, Batty 129, 133, *131*
Latz, Peter 255, 263-5, 271, *264*
Lauro, Giacomo 87, 263, *87*
Le Corbusier 227-30, 248, *229*
Le Duc, Viollet 200, 209-11, 237, 263, *210, 211*
Le Rouge, Georges Louis 141-2, *141*
Leonardo da Vinci 14, 37
Ligorio, Pirro 13, 70, 112, *69, 83*
Louis XIV 92, 93, *93*
Macaulay, Rose 129
Malmesbury, William of 39-41
Marville, Charles 200, *202*
Miller, Sanderson 13, *15*
Misenum 30-2
Morris, William 14, 212-4, 237, 238-39, *213*
Netley Abbey *109*
New York 248, 255, 266-7
Nicholson, Marjorie Hope 96
Oudolf, Piet *273*
Ovid 69
Painshill, Surrey 255-6
Palladio, Andrea 65, 91, 119, 143
Paris, Promenade Plantée 271
Pausanias 9, 24-5, 47-53
Periodical verses on ruins 169-75, *170*
Peruzzi, Baldassare 64, 180, *65*
Petrarch 10, 47-53
Pierrefonds, castle *210, 211*
Pikionis, Dimitris 244-7
Piper, John 14, 237-40, *238*
Piranesi, Francesco 27
Piranesi, G. B. 14, 118-21, 143, 256, *119*

Pliny, the Younger 9, 26-35
Plot, Robert 13, 14
Plutarch 23
Pocono Mountains, Pennsylvania 15
Polybius 20-3, *20*
Pompeii 9-10, 26-35, 56, 277, *10*
Pope, Alexander 108-10
preservation *see* conservation
Price, Uvedale 162-6, *164, 165*
Raphael (Sanzio) 13, 54, 64-9
Repton, Humphry 14, 162, 167-8, *167, 168*
Riegl, Alois 221-6, 237
Robert, Hubert 14, 126-8, 257, *127*
Roche Abbey 151-2
Rome 10, 13, 33, 47-53, 57, 58-63, 64, 65, 67, 69, 71-3, 77-8, 80, 83, 87, 111, 113-7, 118-20, 136, 143-7, 197, 205, 231, 241 *48, 60, 111*
Rossi, Aldo 252-4, *258*
Rousham, Oxon 111-2, *112*
Royal Society 14
Ruskin, John 14, 189, 196, 206-8, 239-40, *207*
Saint-Pierre, Bernadin de 153-5
Scarpa, Carlo 249-51, *249, 250*
Scipio Aemilianuis 9, 20-4, *20*
Scott, Sir Gilbert 212
Shelley, Percy Bysshe 199
Shenstone, William 124-5, *124*
Serlio, Sebastian 13, 71-3, *72*
Simmel, Georg 231-236, 237
Sirèn, Osvald 255
slate mine, disused, *16*
Smithson, Robert 248
Soane, John 118, 179-83, 238, *181, 182*
Society of Antiquarians 103
Spenser, Edmund, *The Faerie Queene* 13, 77, 82-6, 90
Steward, Susan 153
Stonehenge 12-3, 139, *90*
Stukeley, William *107*
Tafuri, Manfredo 252
Temple, Julian 263
Theoderich 42-6
Tarkovsky, Andrei 14, 259, *260*
Tennyson, Alfred, *The Princess* 14
Tivoli, Villa d'Este 13, 69-70, *69*
Troy 9, 21, 23, 133

INDEX

Tourism in UK 106–8
Vanbrugh, John 101–2, 133
Venice 73, 118, 120, 144, 196, 231, *48*
Venturini, G. F 70
Vesuvius, Mount 27–30, *10*
Volney, C.F. 156–61, 191, *158*
Vitruvius 68, 120
Walker, Peter 266, *267*
Walpole, Horace 91
Webster, John 88–9
Wenders, Wim 14, 259–62, *261*
Whately, Thomas 133–5, 148
Wordsworth, William 186, 187–90
   Guide to the Lakes 14, 197, 190
Yorke, Philip 123